Vol 1 From Horses and Carts to Tractors and Trailers

TONY ATKINS

crecy.co.uk

Dedicated to the late Fred Batsford, who started as a GW van-boy at South Lambeth, and to the late Gordon Mustoe who gave me all his research on GWR Agents.

First published in 2018 by Crécy Publishing

All rights reserved. No part of this book may be reproduced or transmitted in any form or by any means electronic or mechanical, including photocopying, recording or by any information storage without permission from the Publisher in writing. All enquiries should be directed to the Publisher.

© 2018 Tony Atkins

A CIP record for this book is available from the British Library

Printed in Malta by Melita Press

ISBN 978 1 909328 79 2

Crécy Publishing Limited
1a Ringway Trading Estate,
Shadowmoss Road, Manchester M22 5LH

www.crecy.co.uk

Note: Illustrations are credited where known. If no annotation is shown this is because there was nothing quoted on the rear of the print. We apologise to any photographer should this result in a missing or incorrect interpretation.

Publisher's Note: It is with great sadness that we have to record the author of this work, Tony Atkins, died in September 2018 following a short illness. He had worked diligently to complete both the volumes in this series before his passing and these, together with his numerous other Great Western books, will stand as testimony to a stalwart of research into the history of the old company.

Front cover top: **Taken in 1925 horse lorry No 2116 (with old-pattern naves) is being towed by fleet No 390 (on side of radiator), XP2166, of September 1923 that has a low roof over the driver. A brakeman sits in the dickey seat; the head of the tractor driver is below the feet of the brakeman. On the radiator header tank are painted BAW 17-1-10/UW 1-7-2-10/FAW 10-1- 0, indicating how the total unladen weight of 1 ton-7cwts-2 quarters-10lbs was divided between the rear (17cwts-2qtrs) and front axles (10cwts-1qtr).**

Front cover lower: **A pair of horse wagon (to Diagram D12) with two chain horses in front outside the main gates of the Mint stables at Paddington in 1909. Chains are attached to front of shafts and it will be noted the tailboard has been used for loading. Among the boxes on the wagon are those of Messrs. 'S J Wright & Co Ltd/Ham & Bacon Curers/Taunton' and 'Sulis Water'. GWR/D J Hyde collection.**

Rear cover from top:
Fleet 801 AEC YC 45hp 3½ ton ex-army lorry of 16/6/21 fitted with hoop sticks and tilt. Flexible wagon tarpaulin No 118 on which GW 'Luggage in Advance' poster has been stuck. *GWR/P J Kelley collection*

Six-ton Scammell mechanical horse C2737 on tranship traffic between London termini. Posed photograph with tractor and trailer detached in Warwick Avenue, Maida Vale, in 1937. *GWR/D J Hyde collection*

S20 Foden steam three-way tipping lorry of 1929, photographed on 6/10/31. *GWR/P J Kelley collection*

A pair-horse lorry and 4-hoop tilt to Diagram D11, with a single chain horse ahead. Photographed outside gates of Paddington Mint stables. *GWR/D J Hyde collection*

Three-ton one-horse lorry fleet 3822 with shafts disconnected from splinter bar and laying on the vehicle. *GWR/D J Hyde collection*

Underneath rear images:
Engineering drawing of one-horse lorry, dating from 1920. The drawings indicates options for a small driver tilt (Birmingham) and dickey seat (Paddington). *GWR/D J Hyde collection*

Contents Volume One

Preface		4
Chapter 1	**INTRODUCTION**	6
Chapter 2	**HORSE-DRAWN VEHICLES**	18
Chapter 3	**HORSES & STABLING**	64
Chapter 4	**'MECHANICALLY-PROPELLED' GOODS VEHICLES BEFORE 1920: PARCELS TRAFFIC**	85
Chapter 5	**COLLECTION & DELIVERY MOTOR VEHICLES AFTER WW1**	111
Chapter 6	**DEMOUNTABLE BODIES: TRACTORS & TRAILERS; THE MECHANICAL HORSE**	146
Index		174

INCLUDED IN VOLUME TWO:

7. Repairs, Garaging and Management of Motor Vehicles
8. Livery and Vehicle Numbering
9. Cartage Agents
10. C&C Concentration Schemes: Country Lorry Services; Railhead Distribution; Zonal Collection and Delivery
11. Cattle Markets, Horse Fairs and Agricultural Shows
12. Special Cartage Facilities
13. Containers
14. Economics and Costs of Cartage

Appendices
Fleet list
Motor number plates
Steam wagons
RAC formula for horse power
Legal traffic regulations
Accidents involving GWR vehicles

Preface

THE emphasis of this book is on the chronological development of GW goods cartage. It is the last in a series of books dealing with GWR goods services which has encompassed goods depots, GW docks, the working of goods trains and much else. How horse and cart was superseded by motor vehicle is traced and how, after World War 1 (WW1), competition from unregulated private road hauliers took traffic from rail. Initially the railway could not compete on equal terms owing to the 19th century regulations covering Common Carriers. With changes in the law, the GW Road Transport Department fought back, not only replying to competition using the same methods as private road hauliers to compete on the streets, but also becoming involved in novel 'throughout-road' services and special contract work.

A number of admirable books, listed in the bibliography, have been published on railway-owned road vehicles, but there's more yet to be told. Access to GWR New Work Orders, vehicle Diagram Indexes, fleet lists, and contemporary operating documents has enabled the history of GWR cartage to be explored even deeper than before. Why certain developments took place in the prevailing context of the time is explained, such as the reluctance of the broad gauge GW to become involved in collection and delivery (C&D), and hence the need to rely on cartage agents.

Freight, the lifeblood of the railway, represented here at Paddington goods and a large and heavy crate being mantled on to a waiting GWR lorry under the watchful eye of the owner perhaps. *Author's collection*

PREFACE

Also, for the first time, carriers employed as agents by the GW at different stations and the dates during which they operated are listed. The relative costs of cartage by the railway and by agent are investigated.

It has been possible to delve deeper and complement already-published information thanks to the kindness and generosity of many people. First and foremost is David Hyde without whose generosity in letting me use his cornucopia of photographs and documents, and his general advice and guidance, this book would not have been possible. David has asked me to record his thanks to his evening class students and audiences whose memories have contributed over the years to produce a wider picture of the GWR: in this connection, those to be thanked are David Colcombe, Keith Ettle, Paul Gilson and the late Trevor Saunders. Equally I am extremely indebted to Philip Kelley for letting me go through his collection of photographs and documents, again without which this book would not have been possible. I am also very grateful to all those who have helped with photographs, in particular to Elaine Arthurs and her team of volunteers at STEAM Swindon, and to the GW Trust at Didcot for sight of the horse-drawn vehicle Diagram Index. I have tried not to use illustrations already published, except where necessary to highlight a particular point; to help the reader I cross-reference photographs and engineering drawings in other sources when appropriate. The late Gordon Mustoe sent me his research notes on GWR Cartage Agents in general, and the firm of Thomas Bantock based at Wolverhampton in particular, and I gladly acknowledge that very important source of information. Some of the information on distribution of cartage vehicles by Goods District is down to John Copsey. Chris Turner has provided information on the pioneering Zonal Scheme that was the last reorganisation of the GWR C&D service, and was copied by all regions of British Railways after nationalisation.

As goods cartage is the principal topic, GWR buses are not discussed except mostly in relation to the period before WW1 when there were only a few goods road motors that had to be maintained by the bus repair system, and which was a period when motor staff were moved and promoted across both passenger and goods sides. At that time, buses, vans and lorries were given sequential running numbers as they joined the fleet and that requires interpretation. The motor vehicle Fleet List, from the first two buses on the Lizard to the 1930s, compiled by the late John Cummings, and kindly made available by Philip Kelley, is reproduced. It should be recognised that GW buses conveyed parcels and packages of goods up to 1cwt in the early days, and played an important role in C&D. We note that up to the 1930s and beyond, in Parliamentary Acts and other documents, the term 'car' was employed for any type of 'mechanically-propelled' vehicle such as motor buses, motor lorries and even steam wagons. Because the book has little to say about rail vehicles (already covered in detail in our other books), we spell 'wagon' for road vehicles rather than the alternative 'waggon'. We also note that the word lorry — nowadays meaning a vehicle driven by an internal combustion engine — originally applied to horse-drawn goods drays.

Research and sources of information relate to GWR public and private documents: MacDermot's History of the Great Western Railway; the Railway Magazine; the Railway Gazette; and the Great Western Railway Journal. In the text, references to books listed in the bibliography are mostly via the name of the author without the title of the book. Where dates are given for introduction of horse-drawn, and motor, vehicles it may sometimes refer to when authorisation was given in GW documents for construction or purchase of the vehicles; or it may mean when completed at the Road Wagon shop in the Carriage Works at Swindon; or delivery of motor chassis from the makers — it is not always clear from the records. Similarly, for scrapping dates and for approval, completion and opening of buildings and works.

Anglicised spelling of Welsh place names is used throughout as it was by the GW. Mistakes are down to me and I should be grateful to hear about any.

Tony Atkins

CHAPTER ONE

INTRODUCTION

IN October 1837, before the first section of the new GWR London-Bristol broad gauge line was opened for traffic, A J Drewe, a carrier who realised the possibilities of the new form of transport, sought an agreement with the company for the rail conveyance of all his goods between London and Maidenhead, whence it was proposed that the goods should go forward to all parts of the West of England (by his horse vans on the roads and lighters on the canals). Until there was an extensive rail network covering the whole country, carriers used the railways (rather than the other way around) to speed up parts of their own long-established routes. Goods traffic by rail built up and after the broad gauge GWR opened throughout in 1841, the revenue was passengers and mail £275,025; merchandise (including minerals and livestock) £46,775; parcels £15,208. By 1850, goods traffic receipts on the GWR had risen to about a third of those from parcels and passengers (£99,850 and £295,100) and a new post of Goods Manager was created to look after this growing side of business. As related in the 1935 GWR Centenary number of *The Times*, the person appointed was Mr. Drewe. By 1855 goods receipts had risen to just over half of those for parcels and passengers (£436,394 and £848,880). In 1855 the GW took over the two Shrewsbury railways north of Wolverhampton, and MacDermot says that goods management for the expanded GWR was divided between three independent officers 'with co-ordinate authority': A J Drewe in the south; J S Forbes in the west based at Gloucester; and W L Newcombe in the north. Newcombe soon became Chief Goods Manager of the GW and, when he left in 1857 to become General Manager of the Midland Rly, he was

C & G Ayres were established in 1825 in Reading and became agents as soon as the GW arrived. A 1-horse, 4-wheel van is lettered 'GWR/Parcels Delivery/C & G Ayres Ltd/ (indecipherable)'. *C & G Ayres*

INTRODUCTION

An Ayres removals container on one of their flatbed diesel lorries showing the 'GWR' agency sign over the doorway of the firm's office in Friar St, Reading.
C & G Ayres

succeeded by James Grierson. Forbes, of course, became General Manager and later Chairman of the London, Chatham & Dover Rly. Goods and passenger receipts on the GW balanced out in 1867 at just over £1 million each and thereafter, until nationalisation, income from goods traffic always exceeded that from passenger.

The carriage of light goods by passenger train had become common in the early days of the broad gauge GW and an agreement was entered into in the 1840s with the London Parcels Company (later owned by Carter, Paterson & Co) for the delivery of parcels to all parts of London at a uniform scale of charges; Pickfords were appointed agents to the GWR in 1843. Nevertheless, immediately after the line between London and Bristol had been opened throughout in 1841, the GW seemed content for traders and the public living elsewhere to pick up or drop off goods that had come by rail, or for customers to make arrangements with local carriers to do so on their behalf. As the goods side of the railway began to increase in importance, independent carriers (soon to be called 'goods agents') were engaged by the GW to cart parcels and goods, especially in larger towns such as Reading where C & G Ayres did all the work. Outside these urban areas however there still was little interest in arrangements for collection and delivery ('C&D' — later called 'smalls' traffic).

Attitudes were different in the northern areas of the expanded GWR under Newcombe's goods managership. After the opening in 1854 of the Birmingham, Wolverhampton & Dudley Rly — a broad gauge extension northwards of the GWR — a large goods depot was established at Hockley and here, for the first time, cartage began to be performed by the GW itself. So, when in 1863 the West Midland amalgamated into a 'greater GWR', there was a stud of railway-owned horses and cartage vehicles based in Birmingham, when there was none owned at Paddington. The 'old' GW eventually realised what could be achieved by performing its own cartage in areas where there was sufficient regular work and by the 1870s decided itself to become involved in cartage with its own equipment at various stations. This took time to build up and it was only after the original Mint stables at Paddington were opened in 1883 that the London stud of horses became larger than that in Birmingham, at which time the headquarters for horse traffic was moved to London. After that time contractors were gradually phased out. For example, from 1889 consignments from Paddington for the London fruit and vegetable markets were delivered by the GW's own teams instead of by carriers as formerly.

In order to better serve the general community as the 19th century progressed, railways had penetrated off the main lines into the hinterlands of the country. Although such rural lines were expensive to construct and operate, the policy could be justified so long as there was sufficient traffic and so long as the railway enjoyed a virtual monopoly of inland transport. By the end of that century there were few places of any size on the GW system at which horse-drawn C&D services were not provided, either directly by the railway or through local cartage agents. The examples illustrated from the 1907 *GWR Towns & Villages* book prove this point: much detail was included for each location, and even delivery to factory and colliery sidings is listed.

In the largest towns served by different railway companies, there was overlap in cartage provision which, it could be argued, did not make sense. All the individual railway companies were rivals and competed for business. In very large towns, there were enormous staffs of railway employees called 'canvassing agents' whose job was to tout for business for their particular railway to the exclusion of all rival railways who could take the goods between the same towns. A *Railway Magazine* article of 1903

Private, and for use of the Company's Servants only.

GREAT WESTERN RAILWAY.

Towns, Villages, Outlying Works, Etc.,

Adjacent to and served by the Great Western Railway.

Showing the Stations to which Goods and Parcels should be sent, unless otherwise consigned by the Senders, or unless standing orders exist to the contrary. . . . . .

NOTE.—For Instructions respecting Traffic for London and Suburbs, reference must be made to the "Book of Instructions relating to London Goods Traffic," and to the Circular Instructions relating to Parcels Traffic.

1907.

Printers: Sir Joseph Causton and Sons, Limited, London.

GREAT WESTERN RAILWAY.

Paddington Station,
July, 1907.

This book is intended to be a guide for the Company's Staff when dispatching

GOODS AND PARCELS

for places served by the Company's Stations, in the absence of specific orders from Senders; and especially to indicate those places which, although having Stations on other Companies' Lines, can be conveniently served by G.W.R. Stations, for instance,

DARLASTON—with a Station on the L. & N.W. Railway—is within the G.W.R. Company's Wednesbury free cartage area,
and
FISHPONDS—with a Station on the Midland Railway—is within the G.W.R. Company's Lawrence Hill free cartage area.

Station Masters and Station Agents are expected to make use of the information supplied, in order to secure Traffic to this Company's Route throughout; and they must see that the Staff under their control understand the instructions given.

The book is not to be put into the hands of the public; but information may be given to Senders to enable them to correctly consign traffic.

It is not the intention to alter existing arrangements, which have been made for the convenience of the public in regard to traffic passing regularly to any G.W.R. Station; and, should it be found that the instructions contained herein do not agree with such arrangements, the Sender must be consulted before any alteration is made; and the case must be reported to Manager.

Nothing contained in this book is intended to imply any alteration in the particulars given in the Handbook of Stations, which must be referred to whenever necessary. The details given are in respect of ordinary traffic, and subject to the existence of the proper accommodation for dealing with heavy weights, furniture vans, horses, carriages, etc., at the Stations named in the third column.

JAMES C. INGLIS,
General Manager.

Station.

INSTRUCTIONS.

Where not otherwise stated the particulars given in this book refer to both GOODS AND PARCELS. Where "Siding" is shewn as the mode of conveyance from Station, it is to be understood as referring to Goods traffic only.

COLLECTION AND DELIVERY.

The remarks in the column, headed "Mode of Conveyance from Station," indicate what arrangements exist for the Collection and Delivery of traffic to and from the place named.

The sign * indicates that the place is within the Company's free cartage boundary, and that traffic charged at C. and D. rates is collected and delivered free to and from the Station named in the third column. When any particular class of traffic is specified, the sign refers only to such traffic.

Examples:—

G.W.R. Carts	means that both Goods and Parcels (unless otherwise specified) are collected and delivered, but NOT FREE.
*G.W.R. Carts	means that both Goods and Parcels are collected and delivered FREE.
*G.W.R. Carts—Goods	means that only "Goods" traffic is collected and delivered, and that the service is performed FREE.
G.W.R. Carts—*Goods	means that both Goods and Parcels are collected and delivered, but that Goods traffic only is collected and delivered FREE.

The same distinctions apply where the collection and delivery is shewn as being performed by Agents or Porters.

When a place is not wholly within the boundary, the word "Partly" has been added, except when more definite information has been possible; if further information be required it should be obtained from the Goods Agent or Station Master.

ROAD CARRIERS, ETC.

It must be clearly understood in giving information in this respect, that the Company has no control over outside carriers, and does not in any way hold itself responsible for them.

G.W.R. MOTOR OMNIBUSES AND MOTOR LORRIES.

As a rule Motor Omnibuses convey parcels and small packages of General Merchandise up to 5 cwts. in weight, provided the weight of each package does not exceed 1 cwt.; Motor Lorries convey general merchandise. Full particulars should be obtained from the time tables, handbills, and standing instructions.

The following illustrations are explanatory of cases where alternative instructions are given, and it should be noted that where more Stations than one are shewn in the third column against any place, the Station to which traffic should be sent depends upon the respective distances and services from the forwarding Station, the charges and the nature of the traffic.

Avebury	.. Wiltshire	{ Marlborough .. 6½ miles	..	Carrier G.W.R. Motor Omnibus
		{ Calne .. 7 ,,	..	G.W.R. Motor Omnibus

Avebury is situated between Marlborough and Calne, and is served by the G.W.R. Company's Motor Omnibus from both Stations; also by Carrier from Marlborough, so that traffic arising in the London direction should be sent to Marlborough, and traffic arising in the Bristol direction should be sent to Calne.

2. Badger .. Salop { Albrighton .. 4 miles
                    { Wolverhampton 10 ,, .. Carrier.

In this case, the Company does not undertake delivery, and there is no regular conveyance from the nearer Station. In the absence of instructions to the contrary, traffic should be sent to Albrighton.

3. Abbots Leigh .. Somerset { Pill .. 2 miles .. Carrier.
                            { Bristol .. 3½ ,, G.W.R. Carts.

Traffic for Abbots Leigh requiring delivery by the Company should be sent to Bristol, but other traffic should be sent to Pill.

4. Acocks Green .. Worcester { Goods—Tyseley 1 mile .. *G.W.R. Carts.
                              Parcels—Acocks
                              { Green & South } 1 ,, .. *G.W.R. Carts.
                              Yardley

Goods traffic for Acocks Green should be sent to Tyseley, from which the G.W.R. Carts deliver free, and Parcels traffic should be sent to Acocks Green and South Yardley, from which G.W.R. Carts deliver free.

COLLIERIES, WORKS, ETC., CONNECTED WITH G.W. LINE BY SIDING.

In cases in which the necessary information is given in the Handbook of Stations, the particulars are not shewn in this book; except in such cases as that below, where, in addition to full truck loads being dealt with by Siding, traffic charged at C. & D. rates is delivered free by the Company's Agent.

Abercarn Tin Works .. Monmouth .. Abercarn .. ¼ mile .. Siding and *G.W.R. Agent.

Communications calling attention to new arrangements, &c., necessitating alterations in this book should be addressed to the Chief Goods Manager, by whom it has been compiled.

INTRODUCTION

argued that the consequence of canvassers fighting against each other was both (a) to force down the rates charged by railways in general; and (b) to introduce concessions to traders. All of that sort of thing resulted in increasing railway operating costs and reducing profitability. The article went on to discuss the role of the many railway company Receiving Offices in the main streets of large towns. In London, in particular, there might have been half-a-dozen such depots belonging to rival companies practically next door to one another. The offices were expensive to provide and it was argued that the entire operation could have been worked by one or two receiving offices shared by the rival railway companies. The same sort of thing could be said about all the C&D horse vans of the competing railway companies in large towns; they usually were collecting and delivering goods in small lots and they often blocked narrow streets causing congestion. The article said that all the goods together might well have filled one single vehicle.

At the turn of the 19th/20th centuries there was a move for railways to dispense with agents and perform all cartage work by themselves with their own vehicles. While there may have been economic sense for an individual railway to dispense with its own particular cartage agents, the broader picture showed that 'unco-ordinated scrambling' for miscellaneous traffic was far costlier than some system of collaboration between railways by which more efficient loading could be achieved for both cartage and railway vehicle. Similar things were being mooted about the cost and inefficiency of duplication of goods depots in large towns. About the time of WW1, A W Gattie (whose *New Transport Co*

The Receiving Office at 26 Charing Cross Road WC1 in September 1924 which closed in 1928, business transferring to the nearby office at 7/8 Charing Cross Road. The traffic receipts for 1926 were £20,035 and was the highest figure for all the London receiving offices. The staff comprised the agent; two clerks; two checkers; one porter; one carter; and one van-guard. *GWR/A G Atkins collection*

The operation of horse-drawn cartage vehicles is evoked in an article in the February 1937 *GW Magazine*, at a time when road motors were massively replacing the horse. R J Blackmore describes the scores of obsolete and redundant vehicles standing in the yard outside the Road Wagon shop at Swindon Carriage Works waiting to be broken up. He reminisces about "……. the sound of rolling wheels on hard roads, of wheels that grind in the grip of brakes on some familiar hill…. The high vibrant note of the express delivery van bowling along merrily to the rhythm of an exhilarating tattoo struck by the shoes of a spirited grey [that] merges with the deliberate rumble of the heavy wagon and the steady, patient clip-clop of sturdier hooves……. all accompanied by a faint persistent jangle of harness……."

Very early in the 20th century trials began with so-called 'mechanically-propelled cars' for cartage (steam, or petrol, or electric 'self-propelled' lorries) which might extend C&D areas to some 10 miles' radius. The first non-horse-drawn vehicle on the Great Western was a goods collection and delivery steam wagon tried out at Hockley in Birmingham in 1902 — a year before the first motor bus service on the Lizard in 1903 — and the first motor goods lorry between Paddington, Billingsgate and the GW depots in the London Docks ran in 1905. The GW built up a wide experience of petrol-engined vehicles before WW1 through the fleet of buses run by its *Road Motor Car Department* ('car' continued to be used for many years by government and the GW for any mechanically-propelled vehicle. As late as 1940 a New Work Order was issued to install a new 'car wash' adjacent to the Cardiff Newtown goods depot to clean goods lorries and vans).

The cartage fleet in 1913 comprised 67 road motors for parcels and goods; 3,507 horse-drawn wagons and carts; and 51 'miscellaneous' specialist horse-drawn vehicles, such as floats for conveying plate-glass and for pianos, lorries for conveying boats and timber carriages. In addition, in 1913 there were 99 passenger buses and 26 horse buses. The total number of horses for all types of road vehicles in 1913 was 3,223.

By 1914 there were 70 GW motor vehicles for parcels and cartage (still very small in number compared with the number of horses owned by the GW at that time, leave alone all the horses of cartage agents). The motor vehicles did their job more quickly than horses but were, perhaps, not fully reliable at that time. This changed after WW1 because the needs of the army resulted in improvements in design, manufacture and reliability. After the war there were thousands of ex-army surplus vehicles on the market and many made their way into the GW cartage fleet.

Given that cheap ex-army motor vehicles were available, and that demobilised servicemen had been taught to drive in the war, both already-established road haulage contractors expanded their businesses after WW1, and also many new road haulage firms sprang up. New bus companies also came into being using cheap ex-army chassis and they began to undercut railway bus and train services. Unregulated private hauliers and bus companies, using similar motor vehicles to the GW, extended the effective radius of road goods haulage from a pre-war 12 miles to about 30-50 miles, yet railway companies were permitted only to collect and cart goods that were going to be taken forward by rail, or to cart and

had invented a number of mechanical-handling appliances) was pointing out the benefits of one central goods depot for the whole of London!

In horse-drawn days, the area over which C&D was performed was determined by the physical capacity of the horse. The usual limit for GW cartage was about a mile-and-a-half, extending to 3 miles in large towns, depending upon the terrain and loads. In London, with the GW's 36 Receiving Offices, an area of 80 square miles was covered, the longest journeys being the 10-12 miles between Paddington and Poplar Docks and the Victoria & Albert Docks. The use of GW horse transport from the London Docks instead of a rail journey was because the GW did not have running powers over the North London Railway; nor did the GW want to pay for NLR haulage unless it was unavoidable, such as when traffic was in full truck loads or was exceptional in some way and had to travel by rail.

deliver goods that had arrived by rail. They were prevented from performing 'road-only' cartage work. Road motor transport began to reach those remote villages and hamlets that had been inaccessible by rail even with all the Victorian rural branch lines. In consequence, private hauliers began to take a lot of medium-distance goods traffic from railways all over the country. Competition for goods traffic by road hauliers became increasingly serious for the railways. Many businesses, keen to minimise costs, re-evaluated their rail-road transport arrangements, and this often led to longer-term switches to road transport away from rail.

The railways argued that the position was unfair as the private road hauliers were unregulated. They did not (unlike the railways) have to publish their rates for conveyance; and they could thus 'cherry pick' their traffic. It was very easy to set up a road haulage firm immediately after WW1: there were no legislative barriers prior to 1933; little skill or training was necessary; and even after the supply of cheap war-surplus lorries had dried up, new vehicles could be obtained on hire-purchase. Furthermore, it was argued that road motor carriers remained in business because the cost of maintaining the roads for their use was paid out of public funds (the railways paid rates to every parish they had tracks passing through). The chief losses to railways was traffic that paid the highest rates, with the result that charges on lower-rated and heavy traffics had to be increased; the Railways Act of 1921 was designed to ensure a definite net revenue, so that any losses by the railways in consequence of unfair road competition were borne by traders and public. Furthermore, it was unfair that railways, as ratepayers, had to contribute to the costs of constructing and maintaining roads, but were not allowed the same unrestricted use of them as their competitors. It was the 1921 Act that created the Big Four railway companies (viz: an enlarged GWR, LMS, LNER and SR) at the so-called Grouping of 1922/3.

Only by provision of door-to-door transit everywhere could railways offer services comparable to those provided by independent road hauliers. Hence collection and delivery services became ever more important in the operation of the railway as a whole. To this end, the management of all cartage affairs on the GW was reorganised in 1922 into one new 'Road Transport Department' (previously, horse-drawn vehicles were under separate control from motor vehicles). At the time of the re-organisation, there were 66 buses, 257 goods and parcels motor vehicles and 18 horse omnibuses. The motor cartage element of the fleet grew so rapidly that in 1926 there were 650 goods and parcels vehicles.

The *Horse Department* and the *Road Motor* (later *Road Transport* and later still *Road Motor Engineer's*) *Department* were

Fleet 801 AEC YC 45hp 3½ ton ex-army lorry of 16/6/21 fitted with hoop sticks and tilt. Flexible wagon tarpaulin No 118 on which GW 'Luggage in Advance' poster has been stuck. Canvas awning over driver. Photographed in Westbourne Park garage yard (Alfred Road). 'load not to exceed 3-10-0' on bottom plank at left and formal ownership indicated by 'a e bolter (secY) gwr paddington' below fleet number and horn. This vehicle later became fleet 709, and fleet 801 became a Buckingham-bodied Burford 30cwt bus, XU6907. *GWR/P J Kelley collection*

'operating' departments working in conjunction with the Goods Department to provide the requisite numbers of vehicles for collection and delivery (C&D) of goods traffic. They purchased horses and motor chassis, while horse-drawn vehicles and the bodies of road motors were constructed in the Road Wagon shop at Swindon (part of the Carriage Works, managed overall by the Chief Mechanical Engineer) upon request through New Work Order (NWO) numbers from the road vehicle headquarters at Slough, that supplied appropriate drawings (drawings created at Slough received additional and different numbers at Swindon). All mechanical and all mains electrical work at stables, garages and repair shops was done by the CME's department upon request from the road department. Similarly, construction and maintenance of stables, cartage buildings and garages was performed by the Chief (Civil) Engineer's organisation. In all cases estimated costs would have been authorised previously by the GW Board and assigned to be paid from various accounts. Road vehicles were also used in small numbers by the different engineering, signal and telegraph, and stores departments, and were dealt with similarly.

At the Grouping of 1922/3, the GW inherited the bus services of the Cambrian Rlys (empowered by their Act of 1904) and of the Alexandra (Newport & South Wales) Dock & Rly (empowered by its Act of 1906). While the 'new' GW did not make use of the Alexandra Dock powers, it expanded both the ex-Cambrian services in mid-Wales and its own pre-Grouping bus services. The other Big Four railways also inherited various bus powers within the territories of some of their constituent companies, but the

Worcester (Shrub Hill) goods depot photographed shortly after it was extended in 1929. Here, at the new loading/unloading dock protected by a long verandah, most of the cartage vehicles are horse-drawn. The motor lorry is fleet 1443, YX5011, a new Thornycroft type 'A1'. *GWR/P J Kelley collection*

legal powers of the new amalgamated companies to run motor bus and motor cartage services were unclear. In fact, the 'old' GW had no specific powers to run road motor vehicles at all! [Because the GW retained its name at the Grouping, it is easy to forget that the new company was a brand-new legal entity separate from its previous existence.] The Big Four petitioned the Government to have the same unrestricted use of roads as their competitors and to clarify the status of *all* road services, both passenger and goods. The result was the *Road Transport Act* of 1928. As far as goods traffic was concerned, the 1928 Act not only confirmed that railways could collect and deliver goods by road motors as well as by horses, but also empowered railway companies to carry out road haulage businesses quite separate from rail activities. With these new powers, the GWR significantly developed its cartage business outside the traditional limits of railway operations.

The increased distances covered by motor transport eventually overlapped the areas covered by local railway stations to which traffic had formerly been sent by rail for local delivery by horse-drawn lorry or van. To improve the service in long-distance 'smalls' traffic, rail 'tranship' working was re-organised and 'concentration schemes' were introduced in which motor vehicles were used for parts of the journey from the sending town to the receiving town. Distribution of goods became concentrated at fewer places, each of which covered an area wider than before. Originally, small consignments were consolidated into wagon-loads via the many pick-up trucks that ran across the system between 58 authorised tranship stations and about 102 small junction stations. As a result of analysis of traffic, and the realisation that every transhipment of goods from one railway wagon to another *en route* resulted in a delay of 24 hours, the number of tranship stations for rail wagons was reduced to nine, viz: Paddington, Bristol, Plymouth, Newport, Cardiff, Llanelly, Hockley (Birmingham), Wolverhampton and Chester — a number of which had been modernised at considerable expense. Motor vehicles delivered to local stations, in a few cases, replicated the job of the station truck (see *GWR Goods Services*).

In 1930, of all stations where goods and parcels traffic was dealt with, cartage facilities were available at 735 stations, at 465 of which the company's own equipment was employed as opposed to those of Agents. From the beginning of the 20th century, there had been a move away from employing Agents; when the 'Country Lorry' and other specialised cartage services were introduced at centres in the 1920s, the Great Western's own vehicles were utilised.

Country Lorries offered many services among which was the collection of milk from farms to take to the station for onwards delivery by rail. Here an almost new Associated Daimler (AD) 4/5-tonner, fleet 1910, GU9318, based at Shrivenham, collects churns from a nearby farm in 1929. This was the time when lorries began to have pneumatic tyres (some of the AD vehicles retained solid rubber tyres). *GWR/D J Hyde collection*

INTRODUCTION

A former Duple-bodied Guy OND bus of 11/6/29, employed on the Paddington-Victoria Station continental transfer service, now converted to a goods lorry. Photographed on 23/8/33. Registration UU975, the bus fleet number of 1651 is retained. Normal control. Large front tyres retained from when a 25-seater saloon (see Kelley, p220). '*BODY G.174*' on extreme left of white-painted rave. *GWR/P J Kelley collection*

After the 1928 Act, some of the 'station-to-station' traffic normally dealt with in the mileage yards by consignees now began to be delivered by the GWR road fleet. A whole separate activity of 'special contracts' blossomed, sometimes involving both road and rail, sometimes road only. Traffic concerned the conveyance of bricks, tiles, sand, gravel, cables, pipes (which included the actual laying of pipelines) and so on. Special contracts became commonplace in the late 1930s in connection with the construction of many aerodromes across GW territory. Ordinary C&D vehicles were not suitable for much of this new work so heavy-duty special cartage equipment was bought.

As far as passengers were concerned, the 1928 Act laid down that railway companies could run bus services, but on condition that they must not take a controlling interest in outside bus companies. In July 1928, GW bus services were decentralised, with operation, timetables and so on now being controlled by Divisions rather than from headquarters at Paddington. Given the increasing competition on the bus front, the railways, instead of going head to head with already-existing private bus firms, formed partnerships with them under the aegis of the National Omnibus & Transport Co. New regional companies took over and, with pooled fleets made up of vehicles from both sides, operated all passenger road services formerly run by the respective companies (and introduced many new routes), co-ordinating road and rail transport operations. New, larger, joint bus companies were set up in which the GW contributed capital and nominated numbers of directors to work bus services to the mutual advantage of both railway and previous bus operator. Where there was a local monopoly of rail services the agreements were bilateral (*Western National, Western Welsh*); but where inter-penetrating lines were common, two railway companies with minority shareholdings were involved as, for example, *Devon General* and *Thames Valley Traction* (both GWR/SR), *Crosville* and *Midland Red* (both GWR/LMS). [Crosville had taken over the newly-formed *Western Transport Co* based in Wrexham with which the GW was in partnership; the Divisional Superintendent at Chester represented the GW on the joint committee.] *Bristol Tramways* operated bus services in Central Wales through its subsidiary *Corris Railway Road Services*, and it was at the time of the national bus reorganisation in 1930 that the Bristol Company passed ownership of the narrow-gauge Corris Rly to the GWR. There was no associated bus company operating within the area east of Slough where GW buses had run, and those services were taken over by *London General Country Services Ltd.* During the period of transition the GW passed over their existing buses to the new companies, and many brand-new buses already ordered by the GW were delivered directly to the new companies — for example, in 1929/30, Maudslay ML3B chassis bodied by Vickers, and Duple-bodied Thornycroft A2-type vehicles, all to Western National. [While many bus bodies had been built in the Road Wagon shop at Swindon, others were made by outside coachbuilders, such as Messrs Bartle, Buckingham, Duple, Strachan, Vickers.] At the end of 1933, the last GW chocolate and cream bus was handed over to the *Southern National* company at Weymouth, after which the bus side of the GWR *Road Transport Department* became defunct, leaving it responsible only for vehicles for goods services and special operations. Even so, notes in the 1932 *Road Transport Department* report and in the January 1939 *GW Magazine* indicate that co-ordination between rail and bus services continued since (a) express parcels traffic with through-booking facilities was extended into country districts using buses from railway stations; and (b) bus companies used railway cartage in towns for delivery of road-borne long-distance parcels. For various reasons some buses were not passed over to the new joint companies, and their chassis were converted to goods lorries.

Six-ton Scammell mechanical horse C2737 on tranship traffic between London termini. Posed photograph with tractor and trailer detached in Warwick Avenue, Maida Vale, in 1937. The shirtbutton on the front of the Scammell is a brown-encircled brown GWR on a cream disc on the brown livery; on the planks of the trailer it is a cream-encircled cream GWR and on the upper side is a brown-encircled brown GWR. Mudguard of trailer bashed a bit. The changed fleet number of the trailer is a result of a complete renumbering scheme during 1935-7 of all vehicles and trailers to indicate carrying capacity. *GWR/D J Hyde collection*

After the Grouping, inter-railway competition was on a far smaller scale and, as explained in the first volume of *GW Goods Services*, many of the old GW offices which canvassed for traffic in 'foreign company' territories were closed, and all railway companies tried to get as much traffic as possible to rail from road. Some telegraph code words illustrate this: for example, *Seku* was the code word for 'Endeavour to secure this traffic to rail at best possible rate, not going below.... Advise me the results of your efforts', whilst *Dope* represented 'Wire me rate. Road transport competition involved. Their charge is ......'

In April 1933 the Minister of Transport sanctioned inter-company pooling arrangements and in large towns where more than one of the Big Four railway companies had interests, they collaborated and 'joint cartage fleets' came into existence. Joint supervision and/or united working by the GWR with the LMS was in operation at 36 different stations by the end of 1932 (including the new Railhead Distribution Centre set up that year in Birmingham, Chapter 10). Places involved included Avonmouth, Bilston, Cardiff, Cheltenham, Cork and Southern Ireland, Dowlais, Droitwich, Hereford, Manchester, Newport, Oxford, Stoke Works, Swansea, and Worcester. In Bath there were joint GW-LMS receiving offices. An outcome of the pooling schemes was an arrangement for the inter-availability of traders' season tickets between the railway companies. There was also co-ordination of railway cartage work in London, particularly through-traffic passing between the depots of the Big Four. Collectively, 30 six-ton articulated lorries with 120 (later 163) trailers worked to a timetable between selected depots. In 1935, it was estimated that thirty tractors moved over 1000 tons of goods per day on this inter-London depot transfer service. Similar cross-town transfer cartage occurred in other large cities served by more than one of the Big Four. In Birmingham, for example, traffic arriving at Hockley for destinations within the LMS delivery area would be carted (by horse in this case) across to their Lawley Street depot, and vice versa.

The GW always endeavoured to keep its road vehicles as busy as possible and this is reflected in entries in the telegraph code. For example, *Backmo* meant 'Road motors left at time shown below with the following consignments. Arrange return load, and wire when leaving and particulars of load'. When loading was heavy and beyond the capability of all the local vehicles, road motors would be sent in to assist from other locations within the Goods District (there were spare divisional vehicles and drivers), or from further afield for seasonal traffic such as Cornish broccoli.

By 1932, road freight accounted for about 25% of the total national medium- and long-distance tonnage. Carriage of minerals by road was over 9 million tons which was about 19% of the total; merchandise was over 18 million tons or 30% of the total. The 1933 *Road Traffic Act* (Appendix 5) regulated the activities of private haulage firms and staunched the rate at which traffic left the railways to go by road. Even so, by 1939 road transport had further expanded to convey about one third of the total national tonnage of transported goods. Paradoxically, rail-borne business increased nationally between the wars because *total* national goods traffic increased, and the tonnage of goods train traffic and the number of parcels carted by the GW and its agents increased enormously. For example, over 54 million tons of goods train traffic was carted by the GW in 1930 compared with 4 million tons

INTRODUCTION

Above: Six-ton Scammell drop-frame trailer fitted with body for carrying exhibition and show work photographed on 27/10/37. Fleet T-1004, coded Dyak W (not in 1939 telegraph code book). *GWR/P J Kelley collection*

Above: This GW Thornycroft 'Nippy', fleet A2770, FGT474, suffered blast damage in an air raid at Bristol on 24/11/40. It is photographed in the Road Wagon shop at Swindon awaiting repair. To conform to blackout regulations, the mudguards are edged in white and the nearside headlight has a mask. *GWR/D J Hyde collection*

This canteen was designed to be sent anywhere on the system during emergencies in World War 2 (WW2). It was built on a 6-ton Scammell drop-frame trailer and was hauled by a 4-wheel Thornycroft tractor fleet, B8819, FYU134, just seen on the left. The prefix 'B' seems at variance with the 1935 renumbering scheme (B supposedly for vans). In this posed picture, staff are seen queuing at Paddington in October 1941. *GWR/P J Kelley collection*

The Railways ask for a Square Deal.

Much is being said about the poor financial position of the Railway Industry.

The real position can be stated in a few short sentences.

1. In fixing rates and conditions for carrying merchandise the Railways are bound by statutory controls and regulations which have lasted a hundred years and grown more rigid with age.

2. No other form of goods transport is subject to such restrictions or anything comparable with them.

3. Moreover, no other form of transport has or can have such basic duties and responsibilities to the State as those which the Railways must bear at all times, and more especially in times of national emergency.

4. It will be impossible for the Railways adequately to discharge those national services and duties unless they are allowed now to put their house in order, and to run their business on business lines.

5. The Railways have no desire whatsoever to interfere with other transport services or with any other business.

6. They merely want the chance to put themselves right so that they may be able to meet fair competition in a fair way. The main transport services should all start equal.

7. The time-honoured shackles which fetter the Railways alone, and well-nigh strangle their goods traffic, must go.

8. And they must go before it is too late.

9. A short Act of Parliament must be passed this Session to meet a crying national need.

Left and above: *The Railways ask for a Square Deal* banner hung at the Arrivals side of Paddington station in 1938. An SR Express parcels van at the left has a poster also saying that the railways ask for a square deal. *Author's collection*

in 1923; again, over 22 million parcels were dealt with in 1930 compared with 16 million in 1923. In London as a whole, about 3,300 tons of goods traffic and some 34,000 parcels were collected or delivered daily in 1931, while in Birmingham the GWR carted over 3,000 tons of goods and 5,700 parcels daily. This increase in total cartage activity coincided with a progressive move away from the employment of horse-drawn cartage vehicles to motor vehicles for C&D work.

The use of trailers drawn behind 4-wheeled road vehicles or tractors increased in the 1920s, but a significant development in the early 1930s was the Scammell coupling that permitted easily-hitched/unhitched articulated 2-wheel trailers to be employed. These so-called 'mechanical horses' replicated all the advantages of traditional horse-drawn vehicles, and became a significant proportion of the road motor fleet. Of the 1700 horses owned by the GWR in 1937, 500 were employed in London, mainly at Paddington Goods working side by side with mechanical horses. In contrast, South Lambeth had been an all-motor depot since 1930. In 1939 the make-up of the fleet was 2,450 motor lorries of various capacities ranging from 1 to 12 tons; 23 jointly-owned motor lorries operated by the GWR; 2,164 trailers; 12 jointly-owned trailers; 4 Foden steam wagons; 2,827 horse-drawn vehicles; and 1,045 'miscellaneous'. There were 1,584 horses for road vehicles on the GW in 1939.

Following on from the 1930s 'Concentration Schemes' came the post-WW2 'Zonal schemes' aimed to result in next-day delivery at *all* stations on the GWR. These schemes had their effect on the railway itself, as fewer wagon tranship centres were required for goods during the rail part of a journey. In 1947 the figures for the road motor fleet just before nationalisation were 2,682 parcels and goods motors; 2,357 horse-drawn wagons and carts; 1,849 'miscellaneous' vehicles; and 1,126 horses.

Despite the cartage freedom given to railways by the 1928 Act, competition was still not on a level playing field since the railways were still bound by the 19th century Common Carrier rules which required them to (a) accept all goods offered for conveyance by rail; (b) classify merchandise based on value; and (c) fix and publish standard charges (based on the classification). Once again, railways appealed to the government for a level playing field through the 'Square Deal' campaign of 1938.

The Transport Advisory Council ruled in May 1939 that the railways' Victorian obligations should be repealed so that they were in the same position as private road hauliers and, if it were not possible to obtain an economic price for a service, the railways could abandon it. But war put that on hold, and subsequently both the railways and the private long-distance road haulage firms were nationalised to become British Railways and British Road Services. (Short haul road operators and vehicles carrying the owning firm's goods were not affected.)

H Elliott, in the *British Railways (Western Region) London Lecture and Debating Society* in November 1948, said that "With the passing of the *Transport Act* 1947 the age-old competition and antagonism between the railways and long-distance road carriers has come to an end [and] the two forms of transport will 'jointly and severally' set up their part of the integrated transport system demanded by the Act, not competing but vying with each other in a complementary manner to give the public and industry

INTRODUCTION

Even though South Lambeth became all-motor in 1930, and other depots followed, at nationalisation in 1948 the GW depots in Birmingham, Bristol, Cardiff and Paddington each had over 100 working horses engaged on cartage, and other places had a few dozen. This shows the roadway between the Inwards and Outwards sheds at Cardiff Newtown in August 1948. The goods lift to the subway that connected the two, and gave access to warehouses and cellars, is to the right of the centre stanchion supporting the roof. To its left is a 'GW & LMS' joint vehicle bearing a Weights cigarettes advert on the tilt. At the far back is a Ford GW 'Express Cartage' van. The nearer horse lorries are in brown and cream but labelled 'GW AND LMS RAILWAYS'. The big crate over the rear wheels of the one with a horse in the shafts is lettered 'Perkins Diesel. Use slings. No Grabs'. The 3-ton mechanical horse (CLM774) with a single headlight unusually has no shirtbuttons to the front. On the back of the motor lorry at the left is a cardboard box marked 'Hoover Cleaner' and others for Bibby Best Soap. In the foreground the newly-painted Bedford-Scammell articulated lorry fleet D8945 is attached to a Dyak AF trailer containing a load of pipes. *GWR/D J Hyde collection*

of Great Britain the best possible service for the transport of goods." The Act however lacked clarity about the overlap between rail and road C&D, and in the discussion to the paper it was argued that from a practical operating point of view the Railway Goods Agent should be in complete control of everything at his station including road transport vehicles. In the event, railways retained their C&D cartage fleets and the *Transport Act* 1953 denationalised most of British Road Services, so the private haulier became a competitor again rather than a partner.

It is not an exaggeration to say that, with the rapid growth of motor transport, no aspect of the Great Western Railway's activity underwent so great a change as their cartage service after WW1. The road services' side of the GW had become extremely large and it is worth remembering that, at nationalisation, the railways were the owners and operators of the largest fleets of motor vehicles in the UK, ranging from the small 5-cwt van to the 12-ton lorry.

CHAPTER TWO

HORSE-DRAWN VEHICLES

The policy of the original Bristol-London broad gauge GWR was to rely on agents and contractors to provide a cartage service with their own vehicles and horses. Typical of the vehicles being employed for C&D in London are shown by what the contractor J T Younghusband & Son hired to the GW in 1876 at a rent of £10/month for 20 months: 32 pair-horse vans, 32 general work vans, 2 fish vans and one cloth van. Every vehicle had to have "Great Western Railway Co (Owners)/F G Saunders Secty" painted on each side in a conspicuous manner.

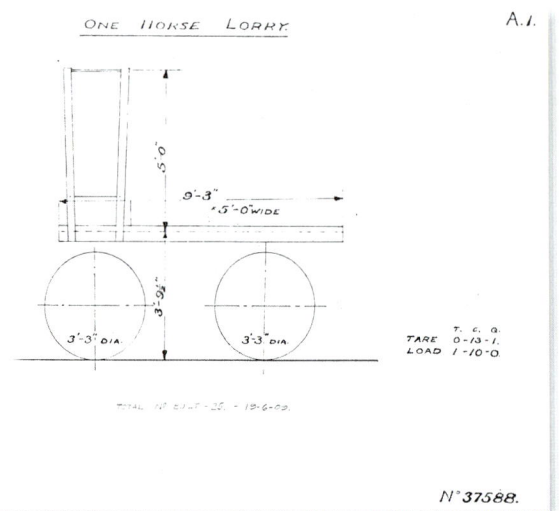

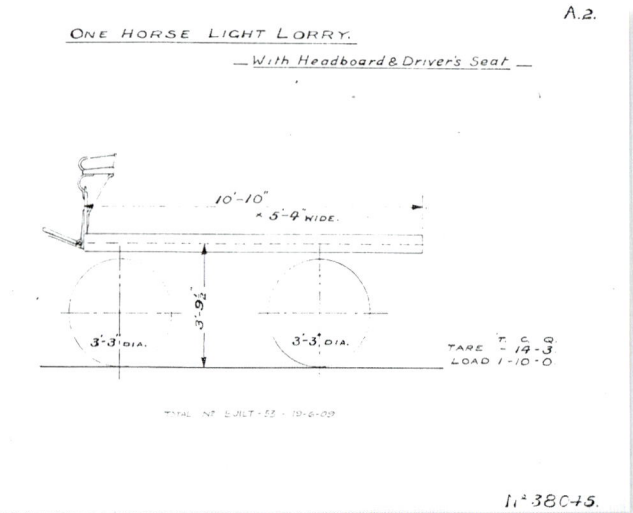

HORSE-DRAWN VEHICLES

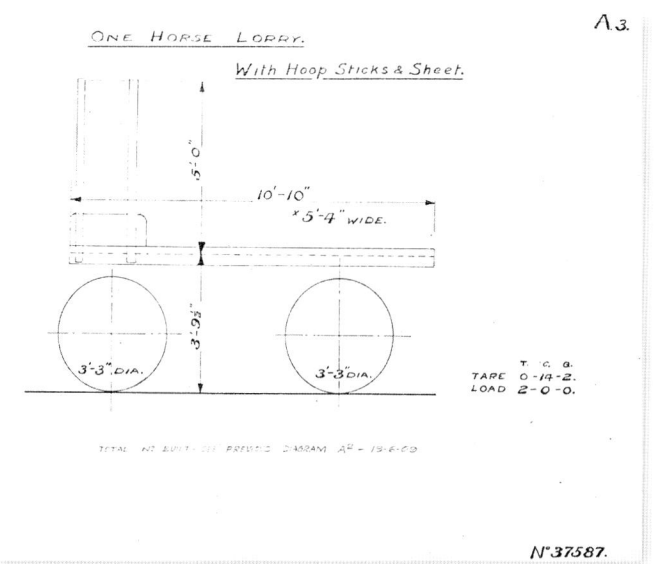

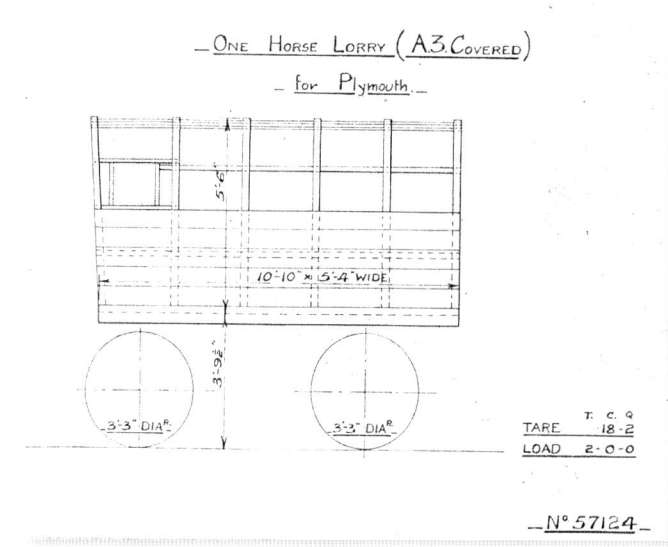

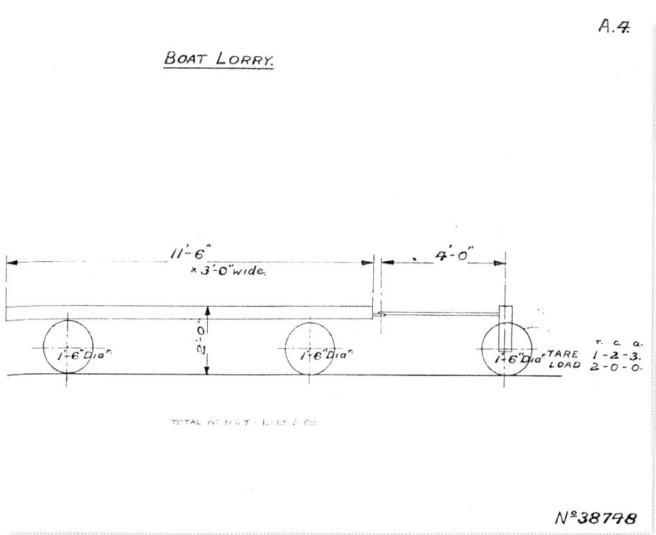

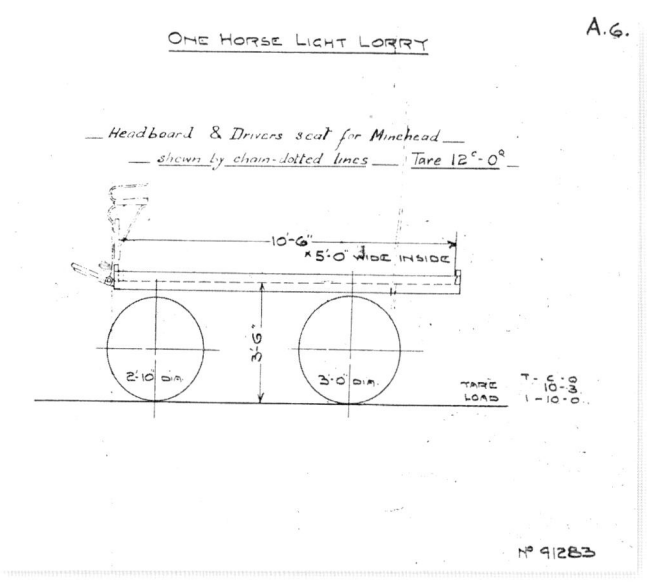

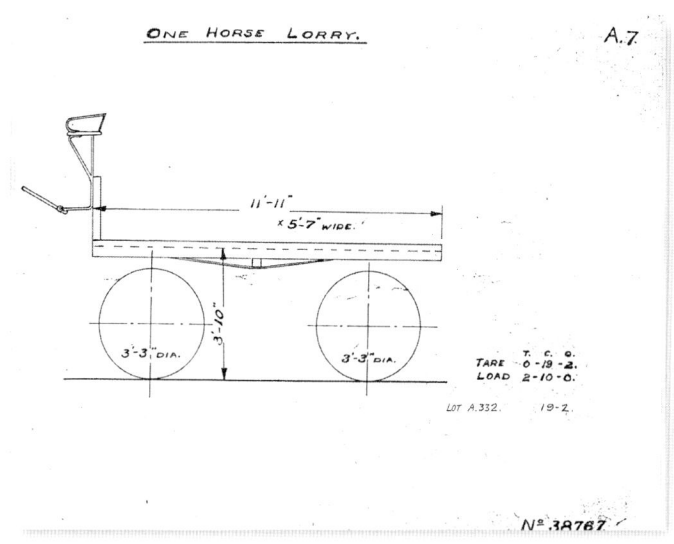

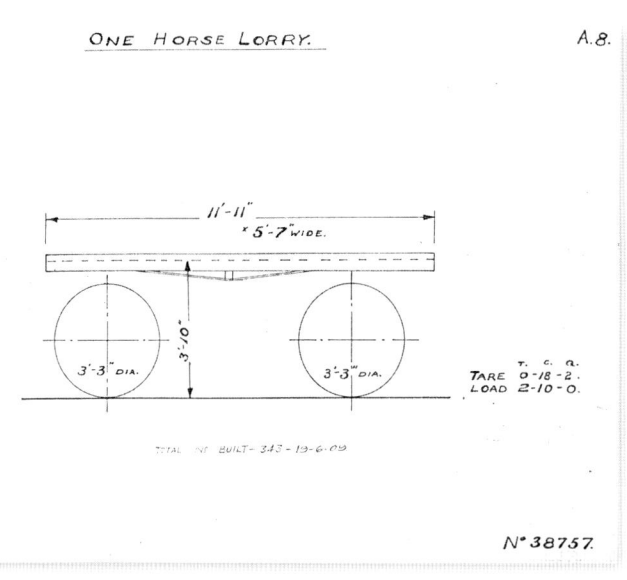

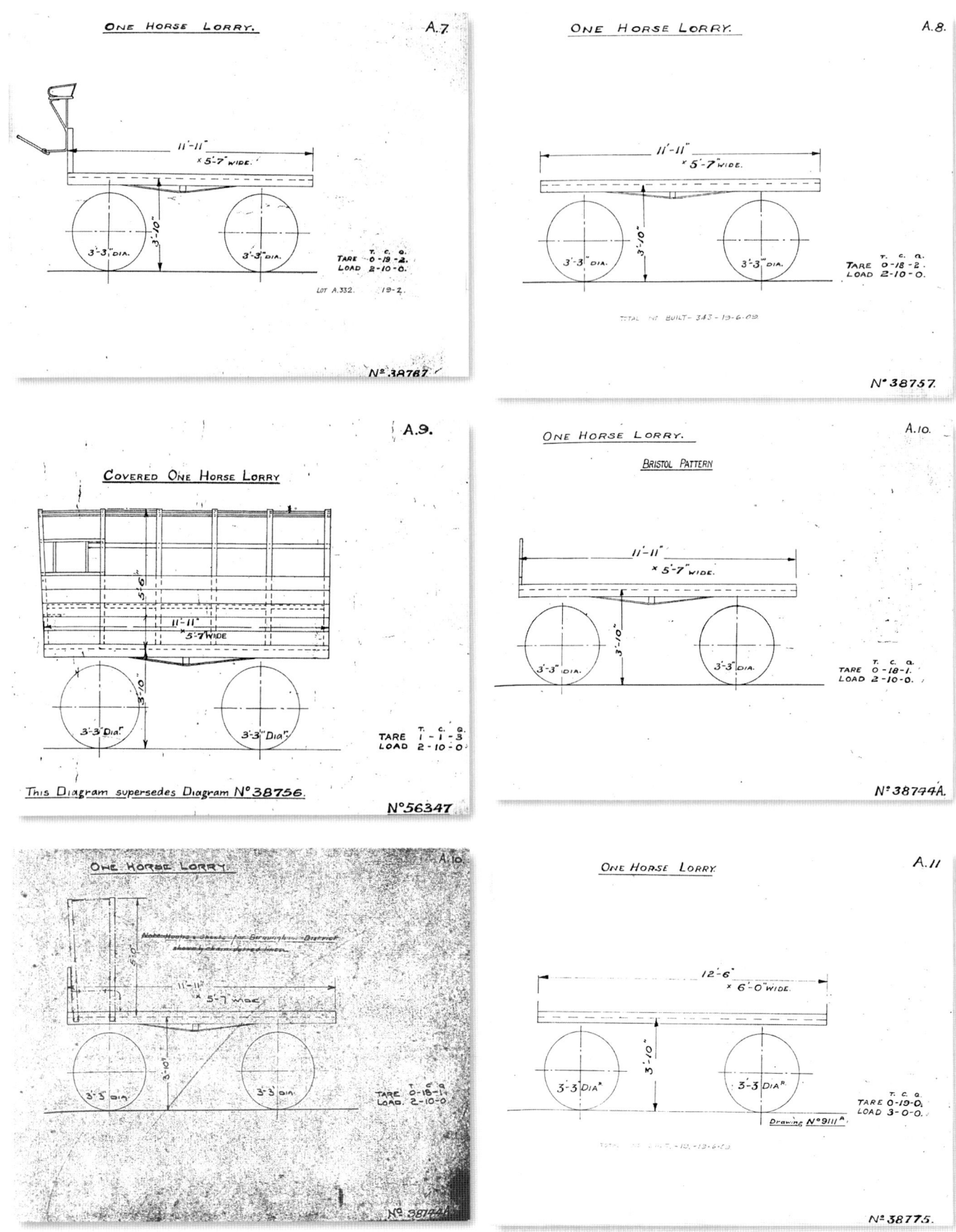

HORSE-DRAWN VEHICLES

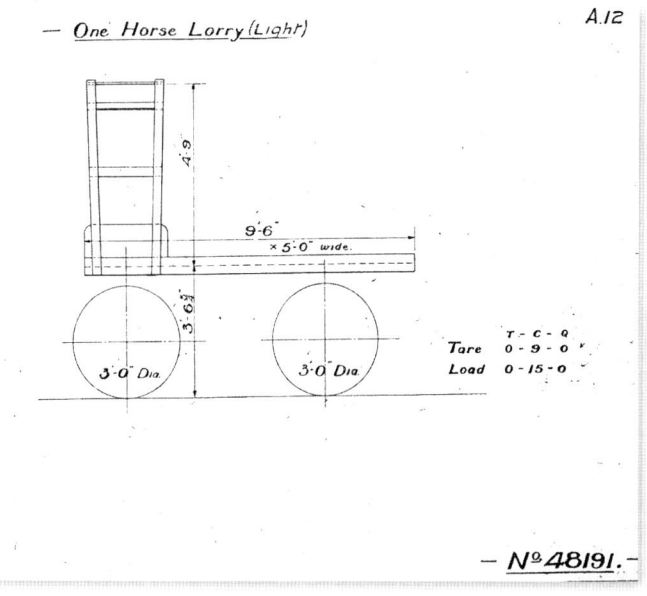

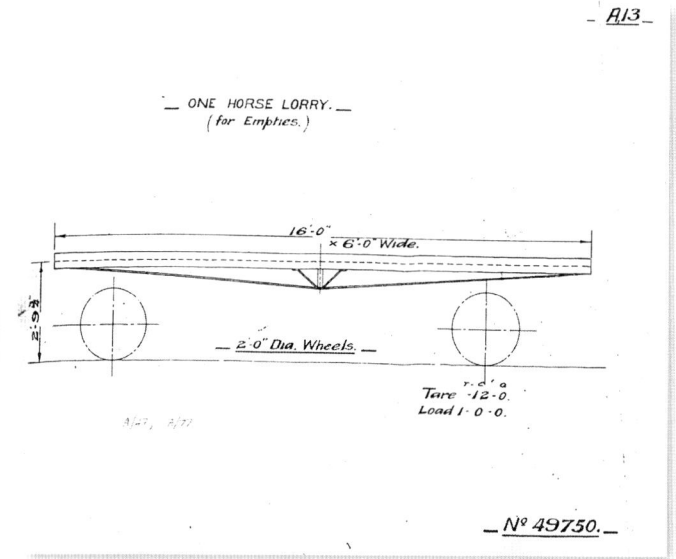

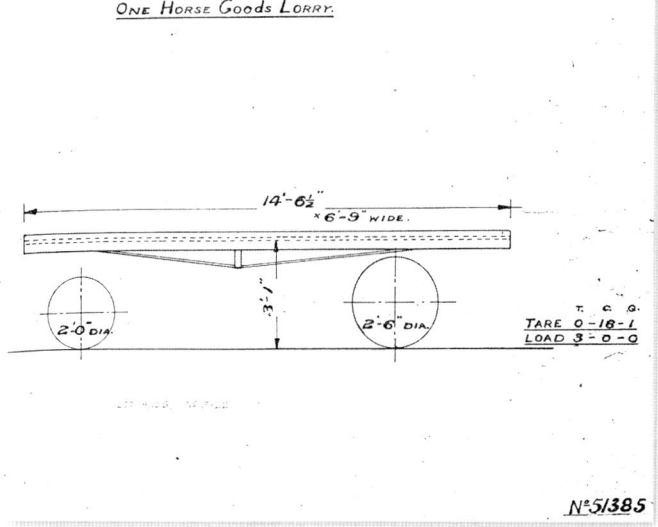

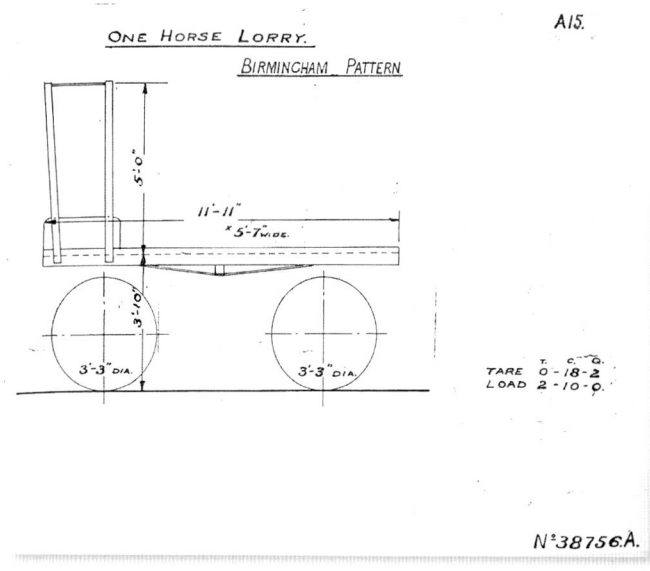

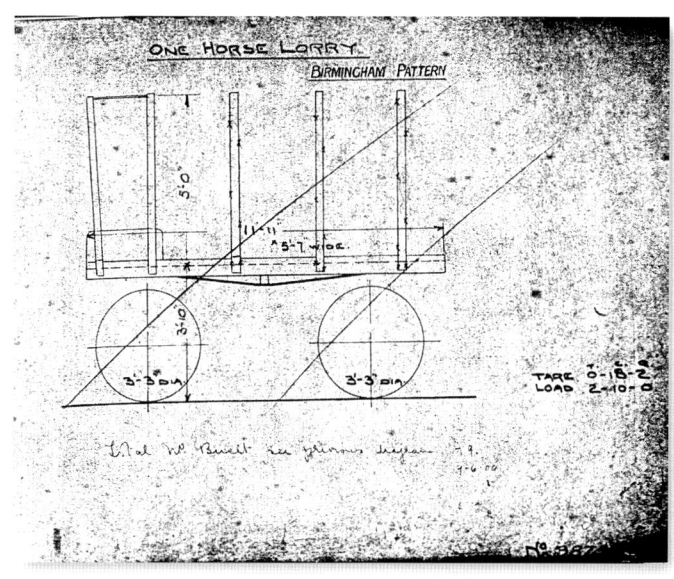

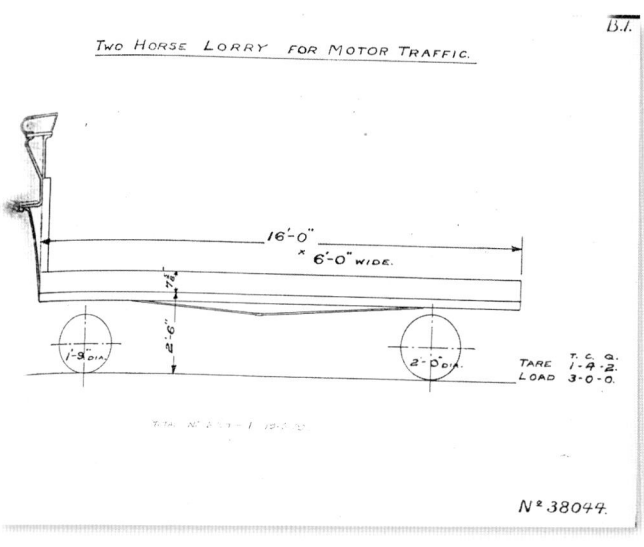

GWR GOODS CARTAGE VOLUME 1

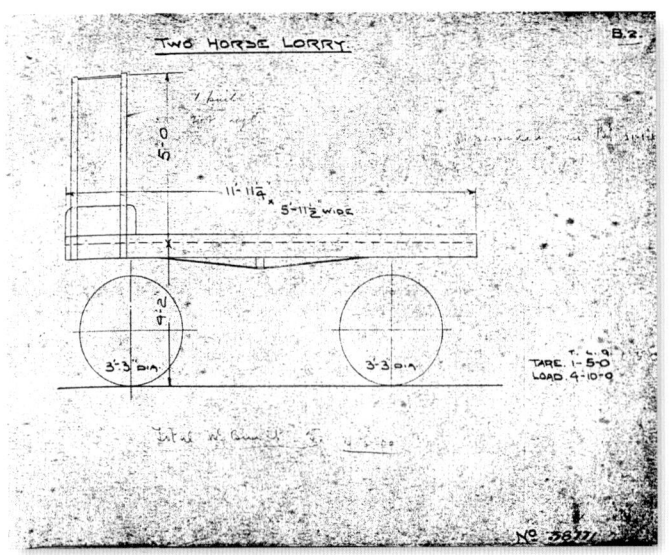

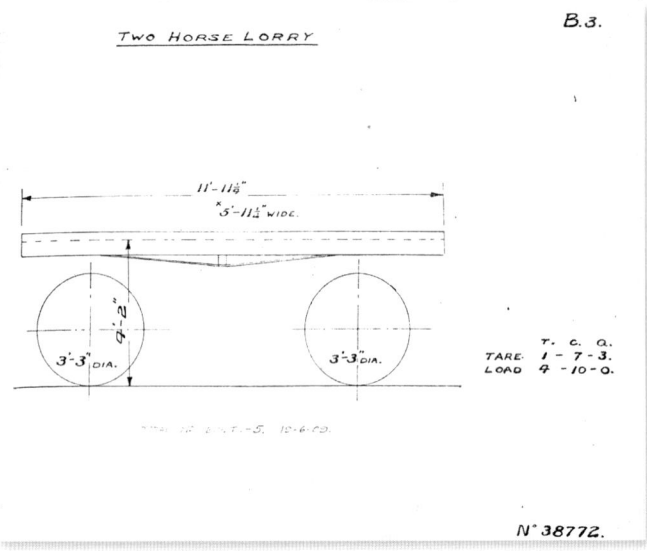

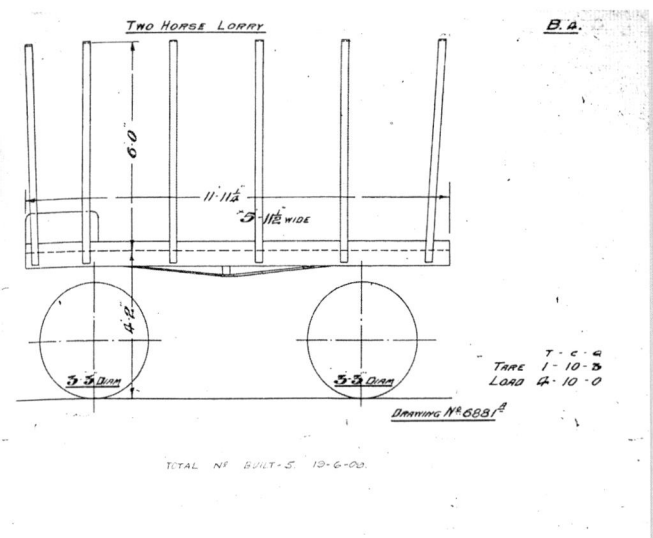

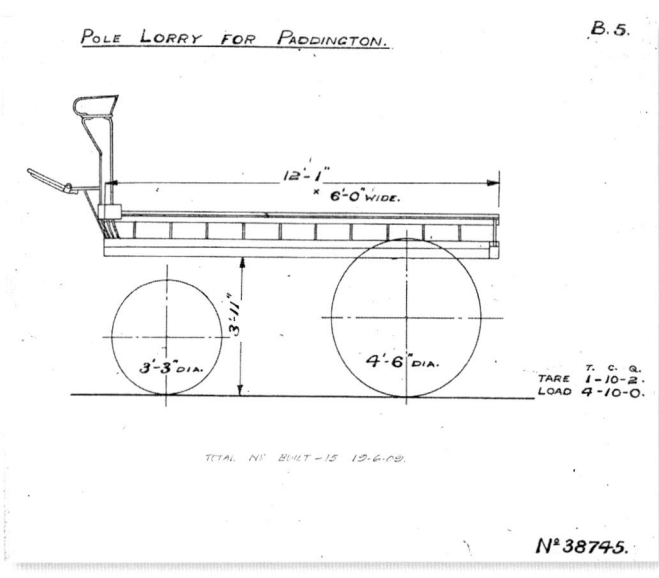

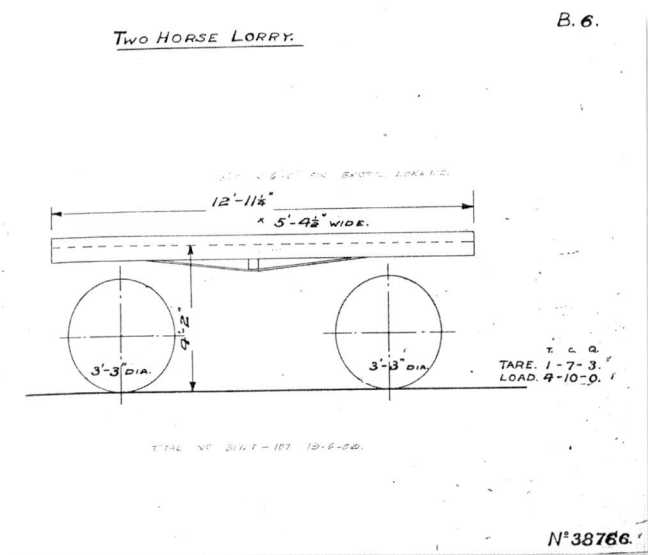

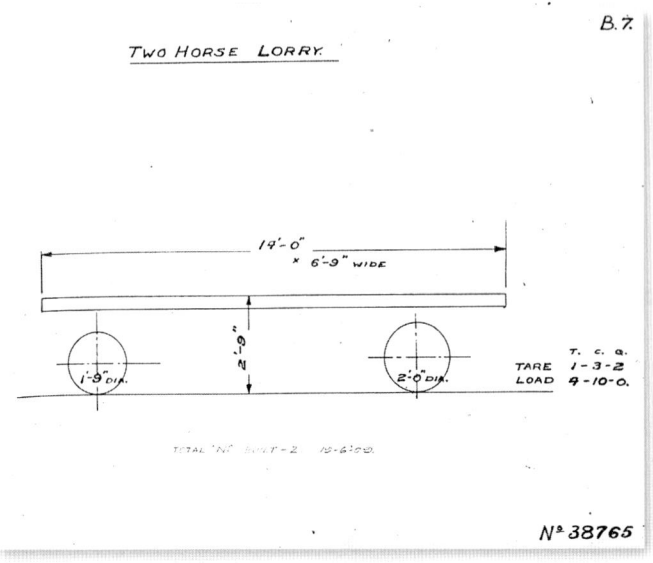

HORSE-DRAWN VEHICLES

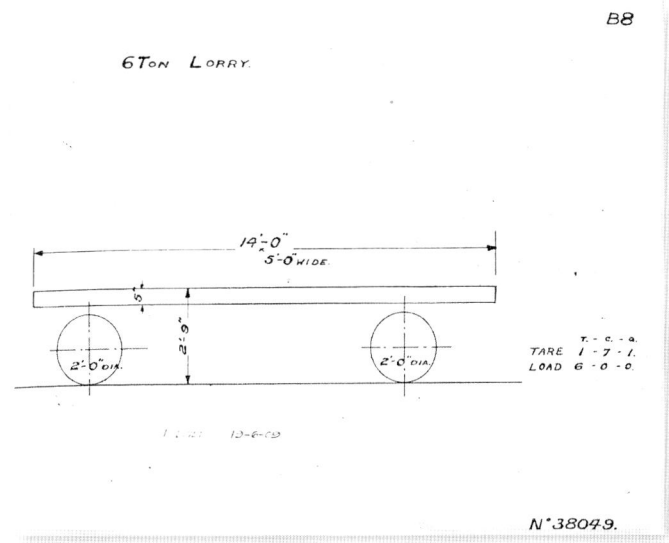

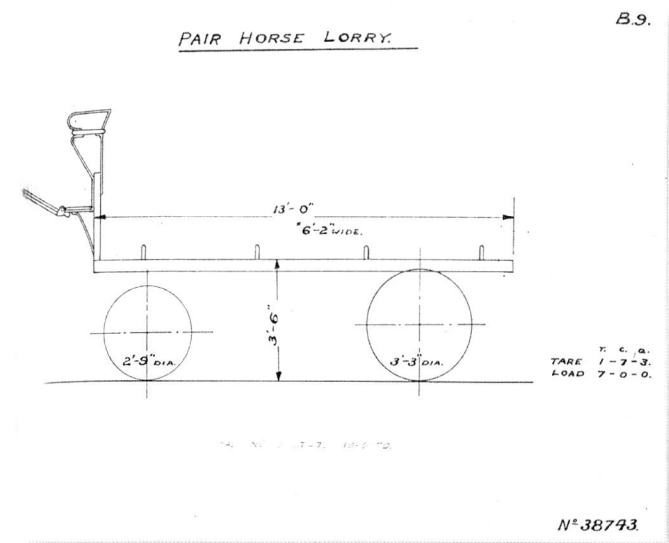

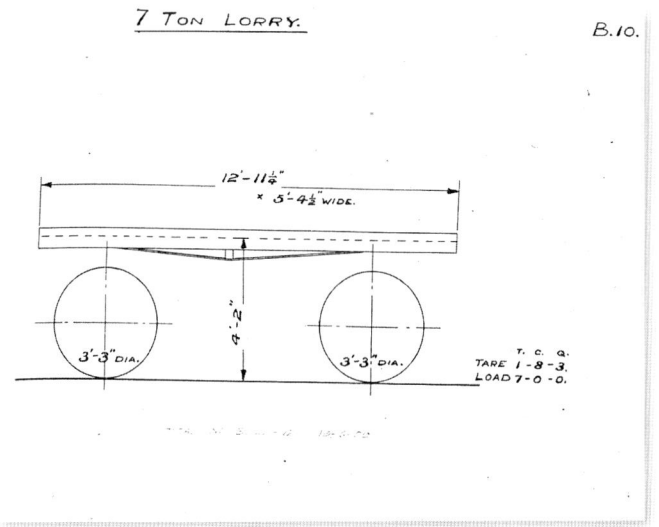

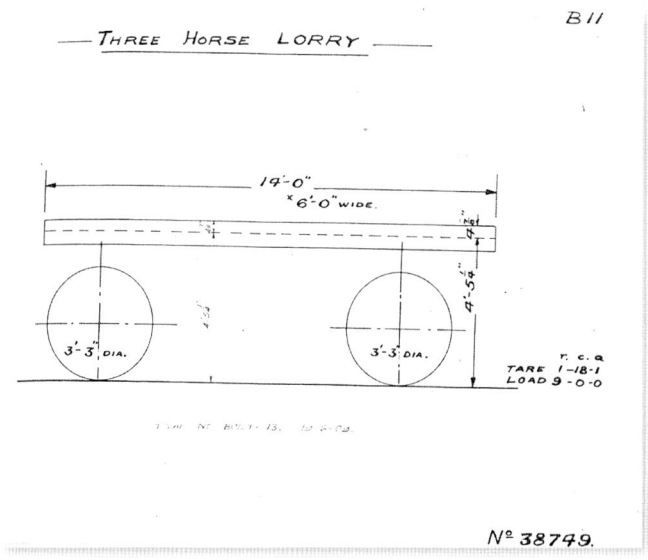

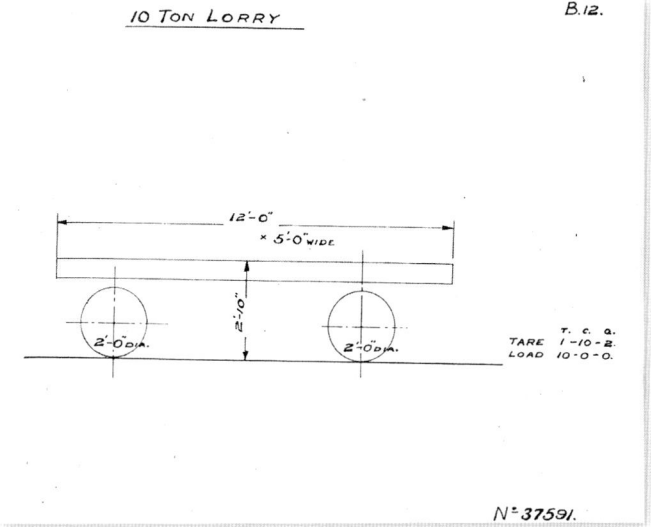

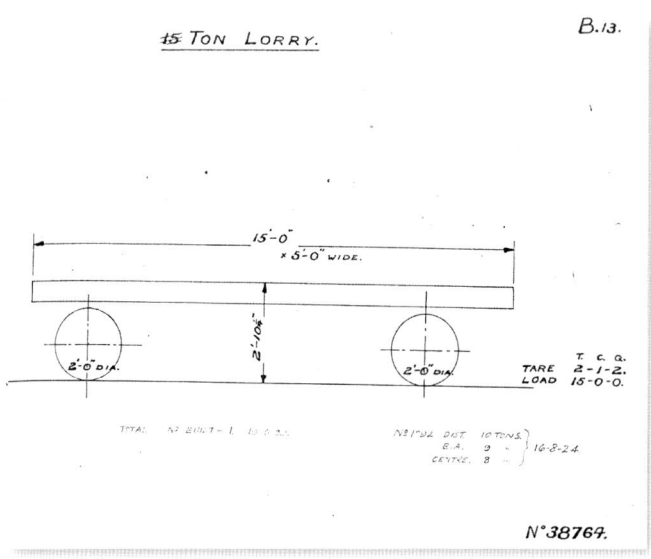

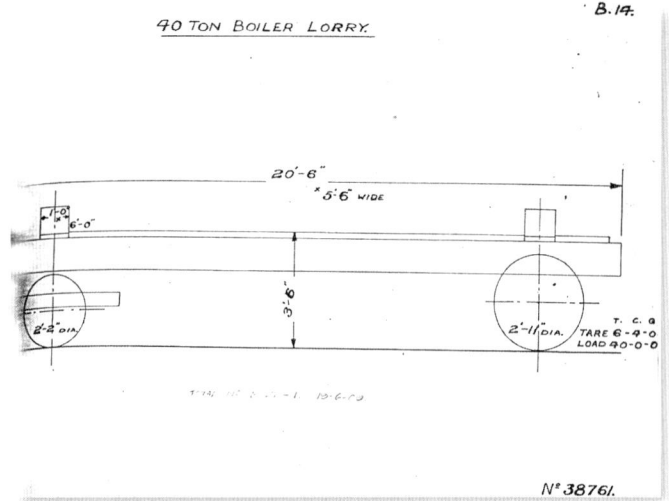

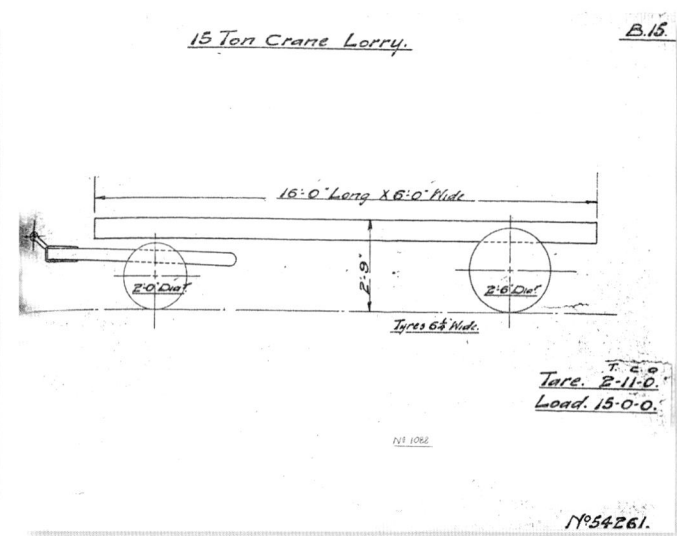

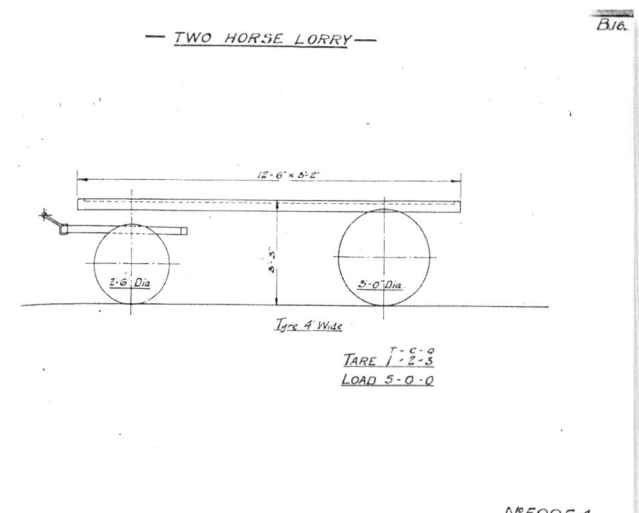

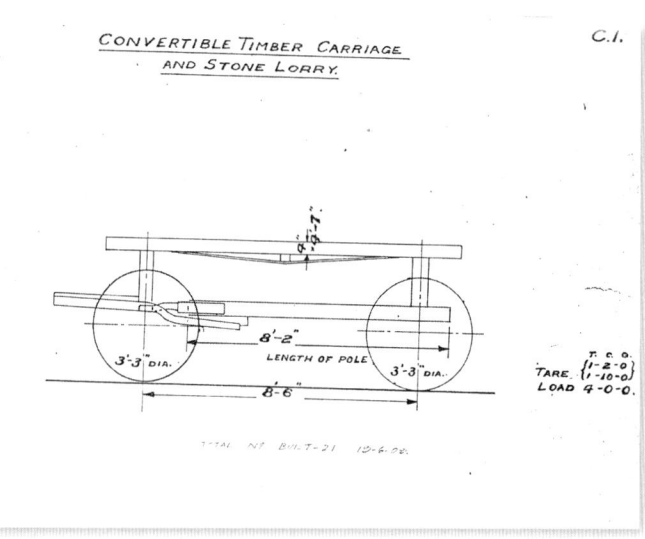

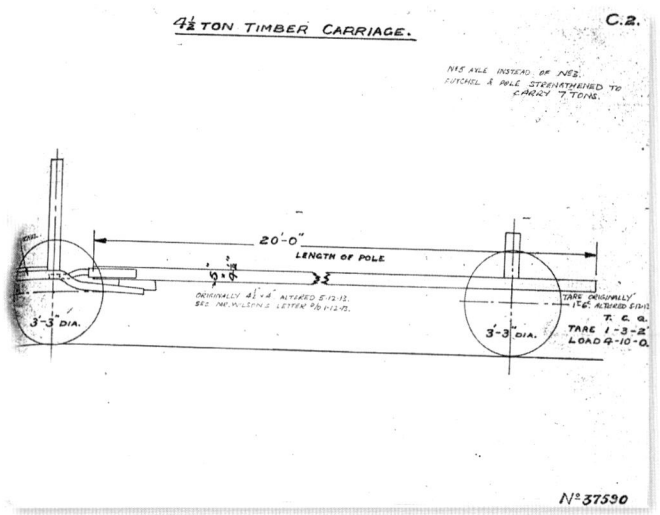

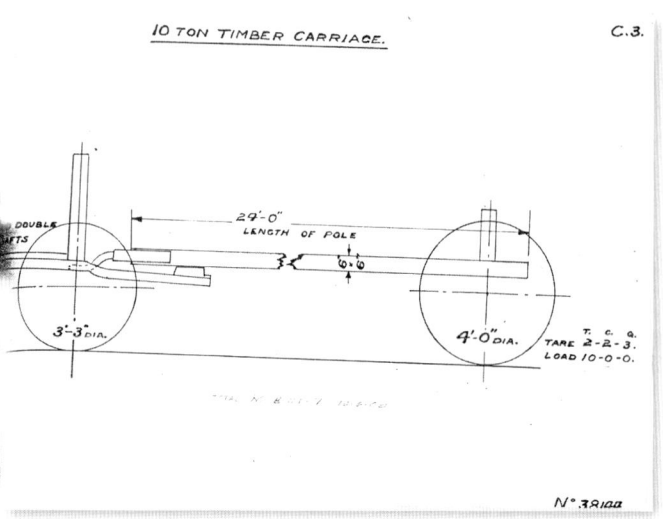

HORSE-DRAWN VEHICLES

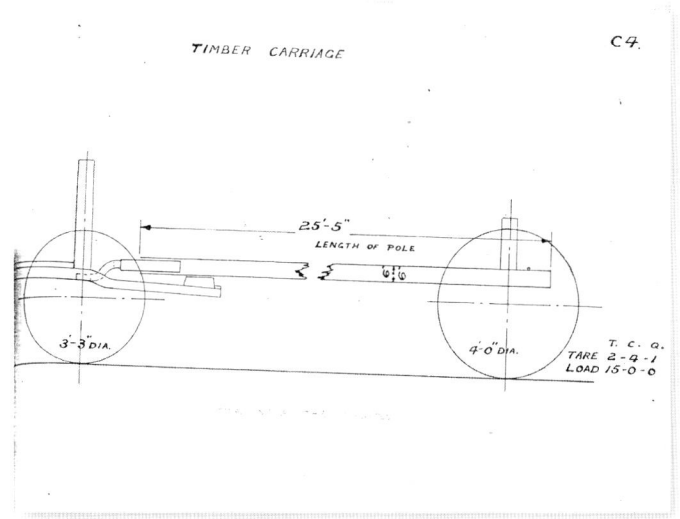

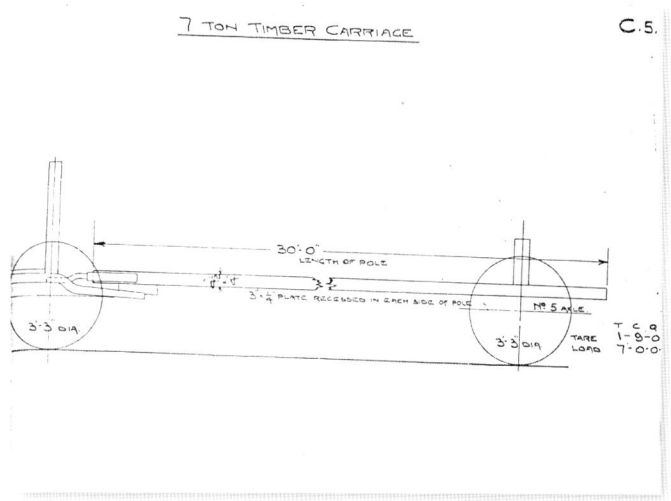

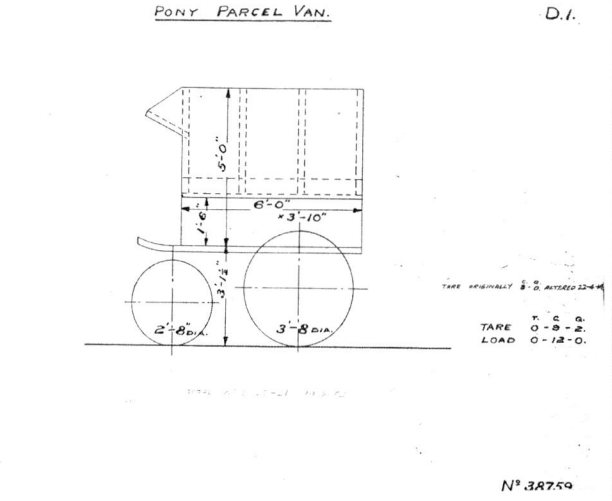

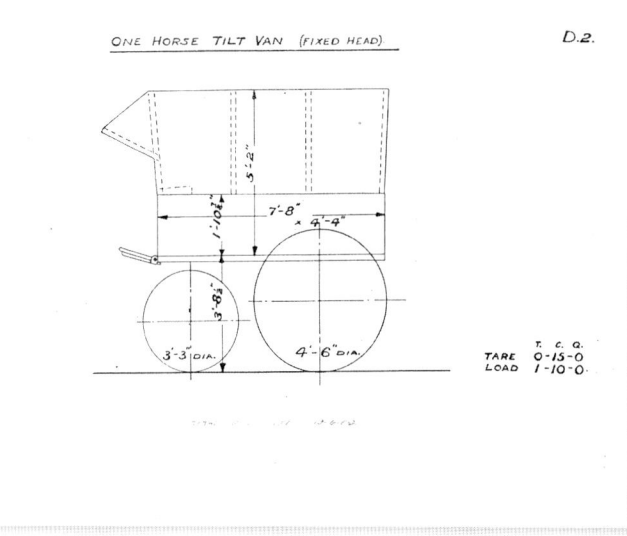

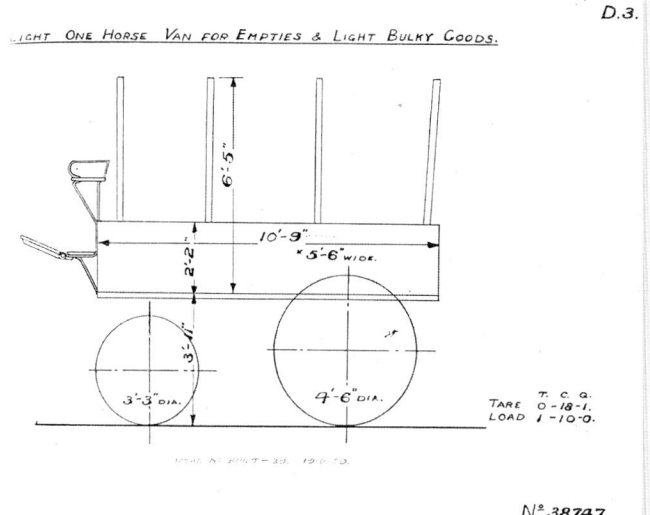

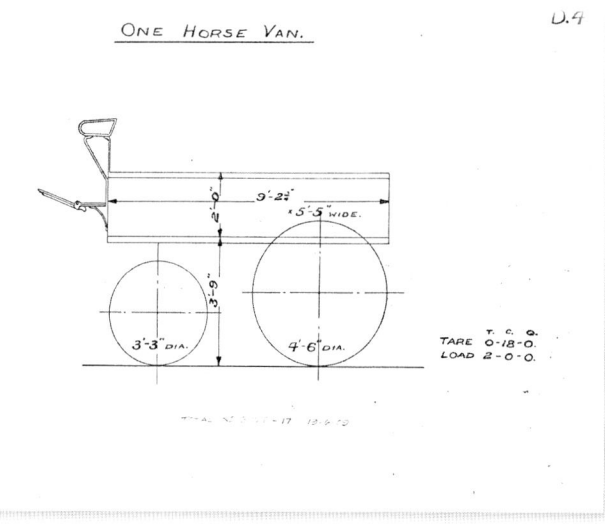

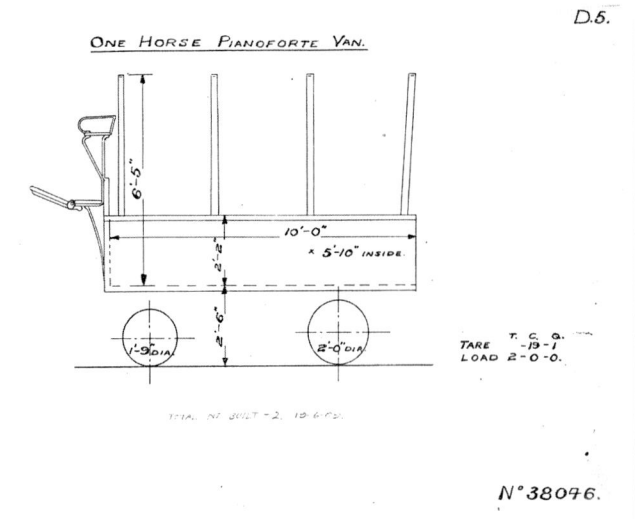
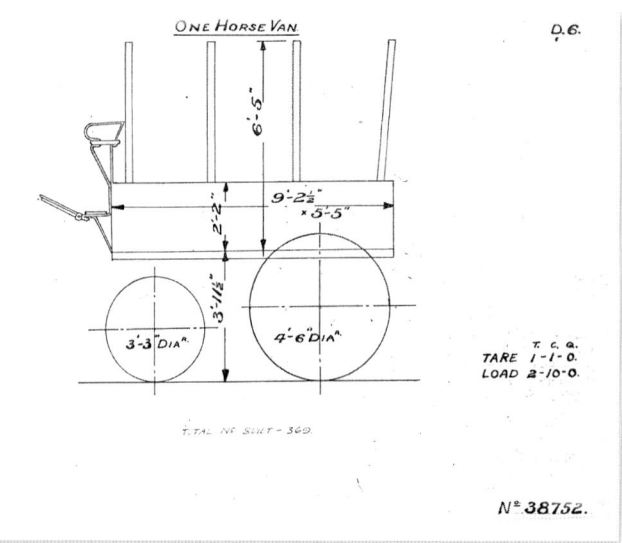
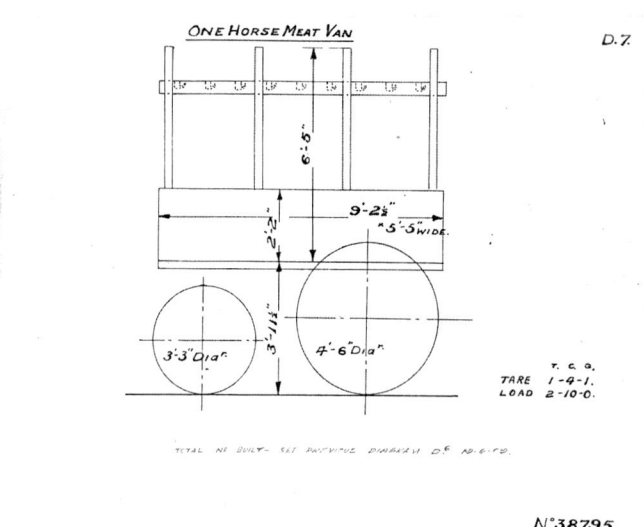
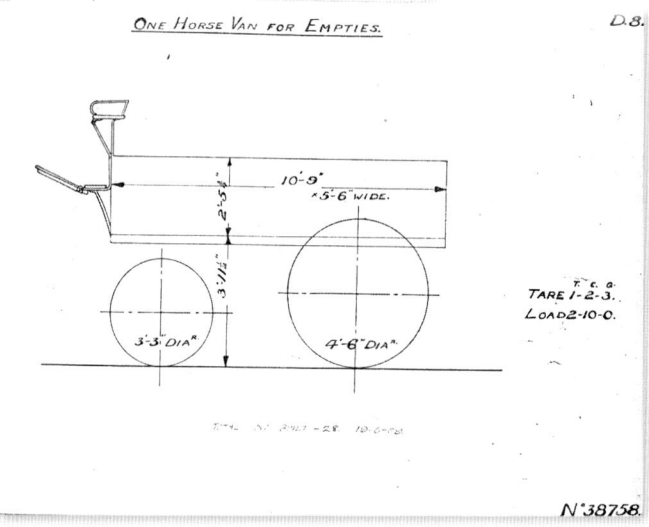
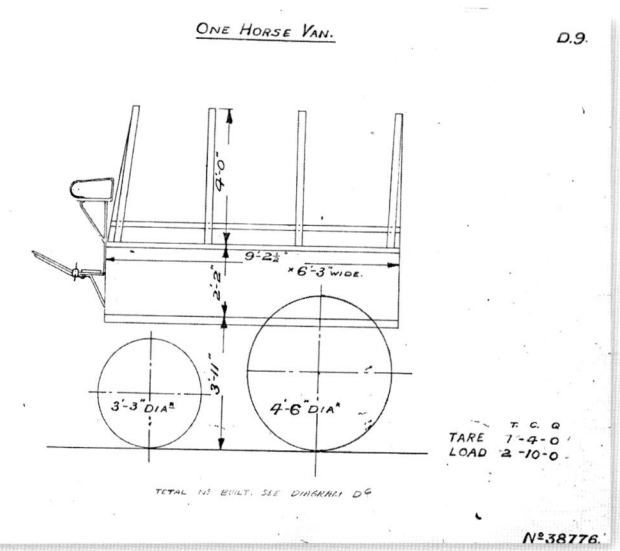
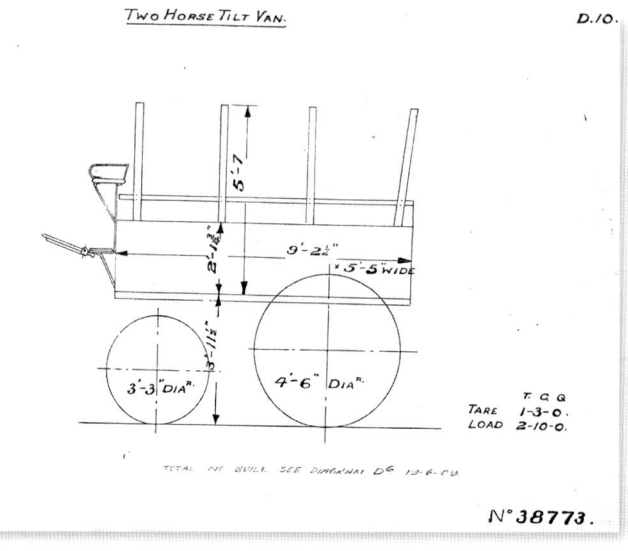

HORSE-DRAWN VEHICLES

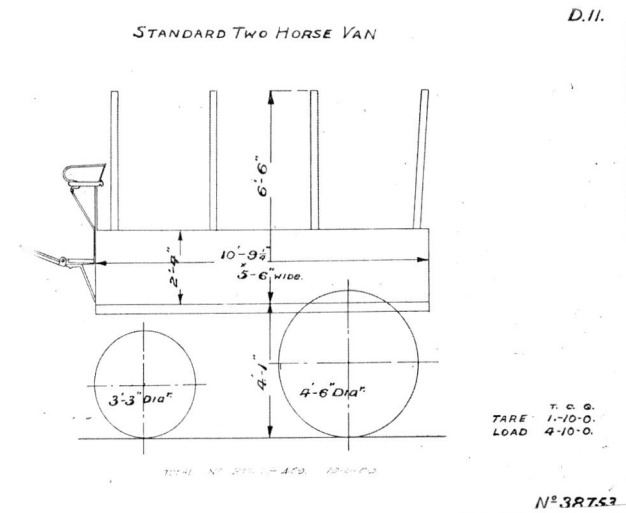

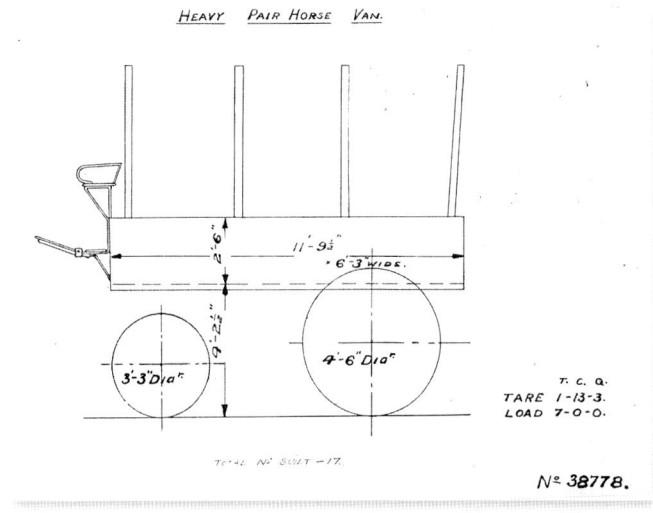

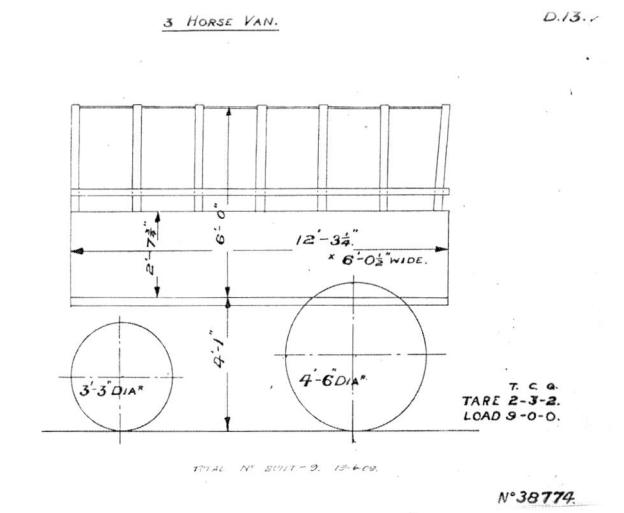

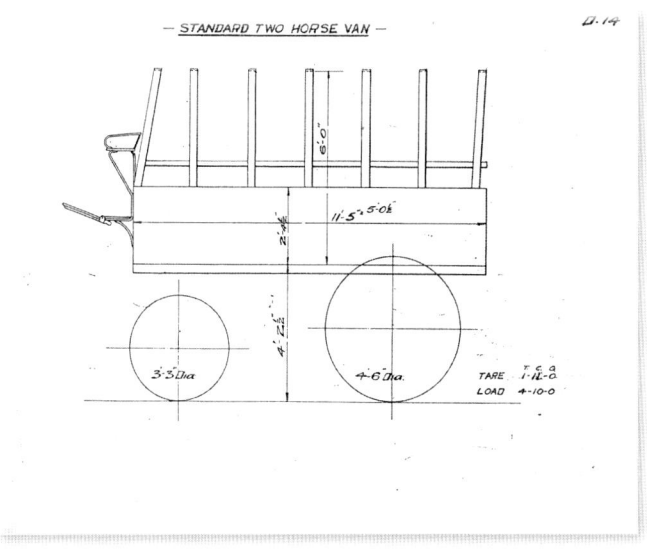

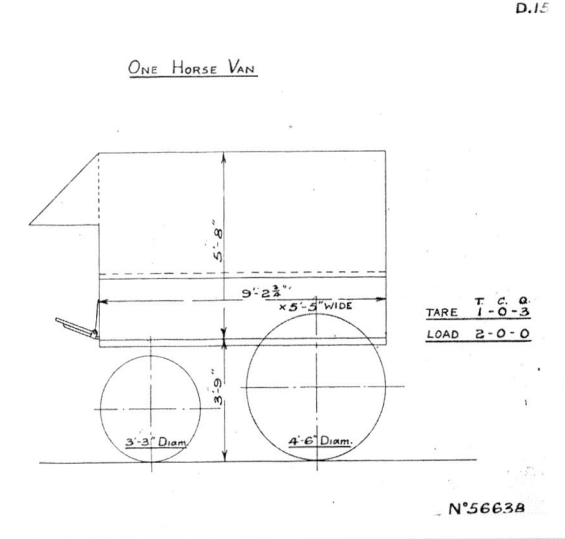

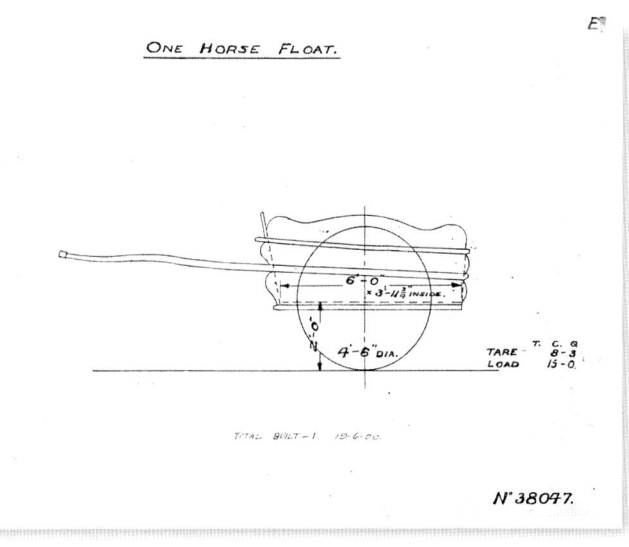

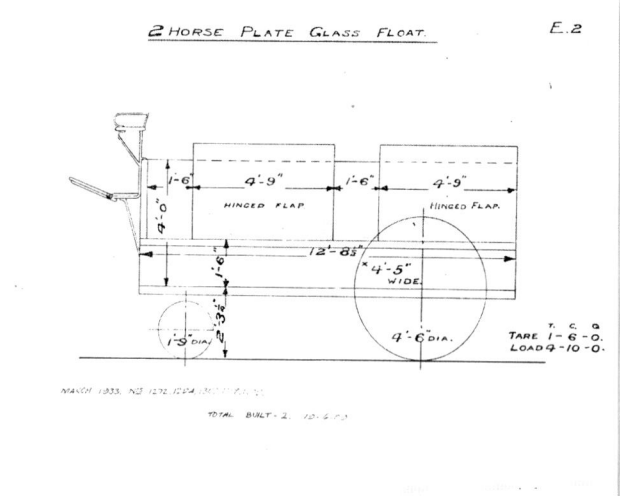

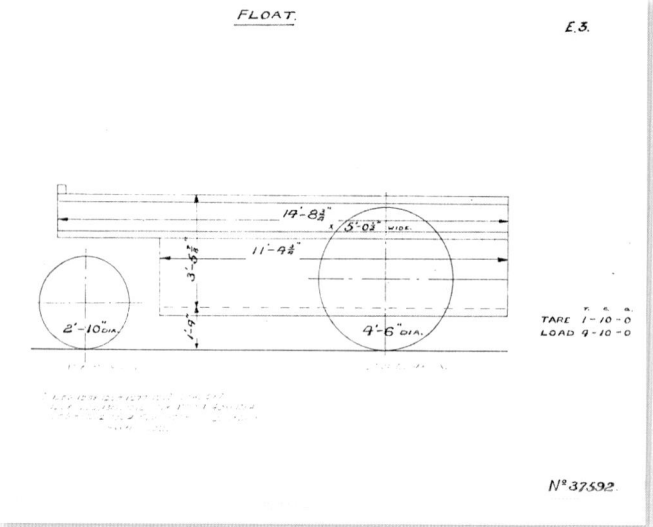

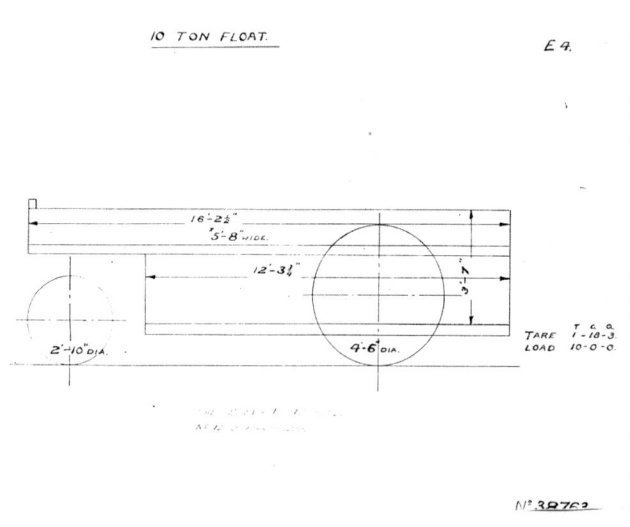

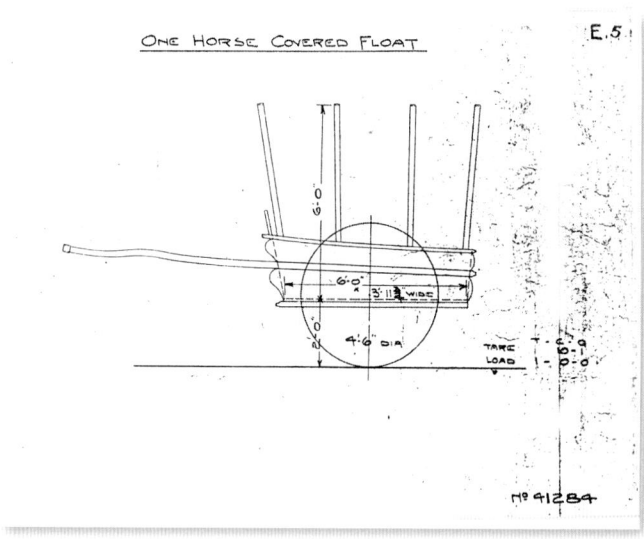

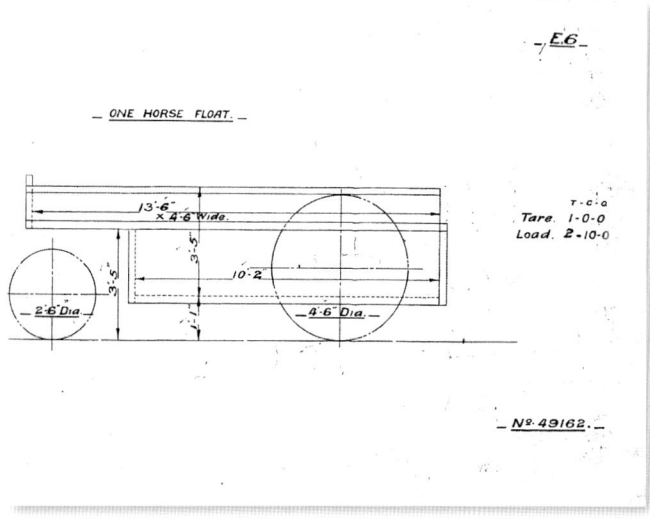

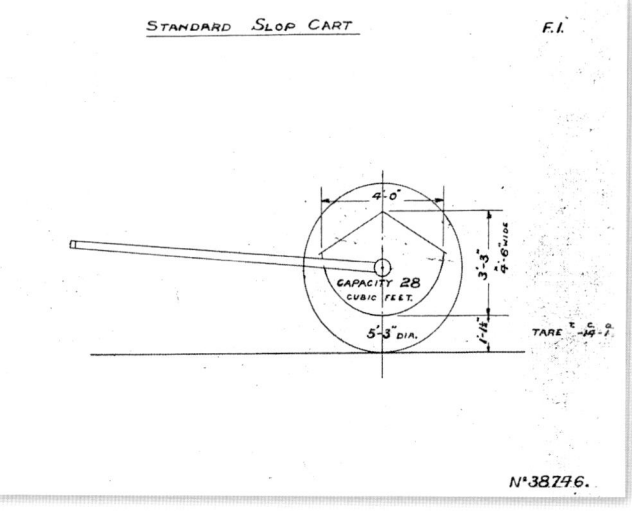

HORSE-DRAWN VEHICLES

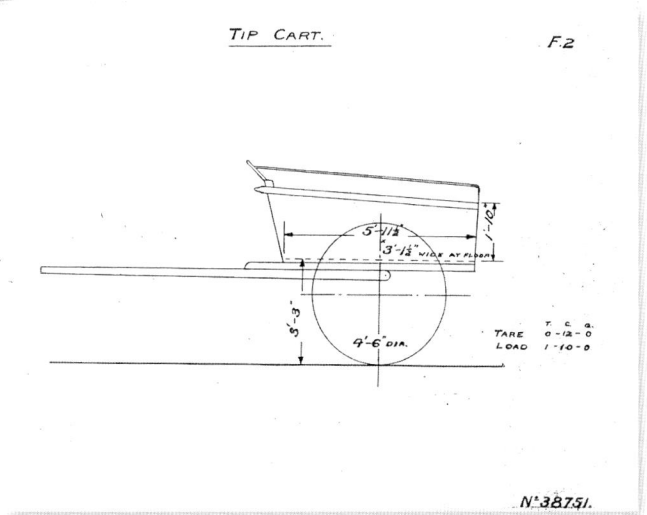

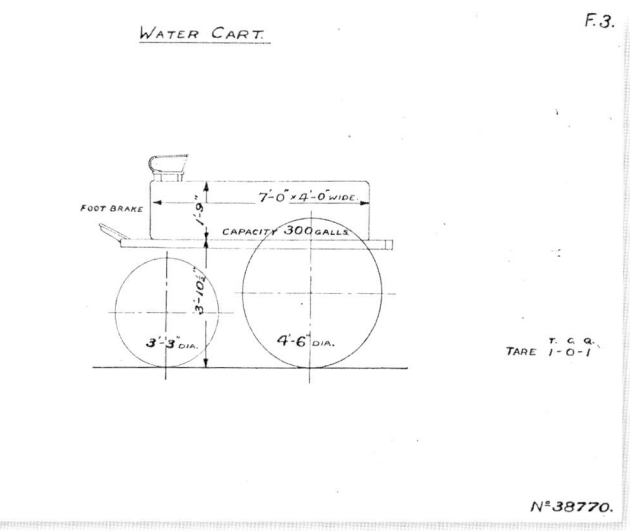

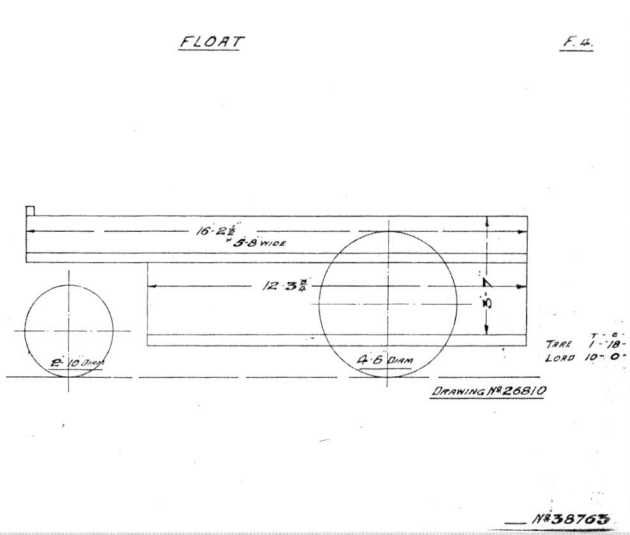

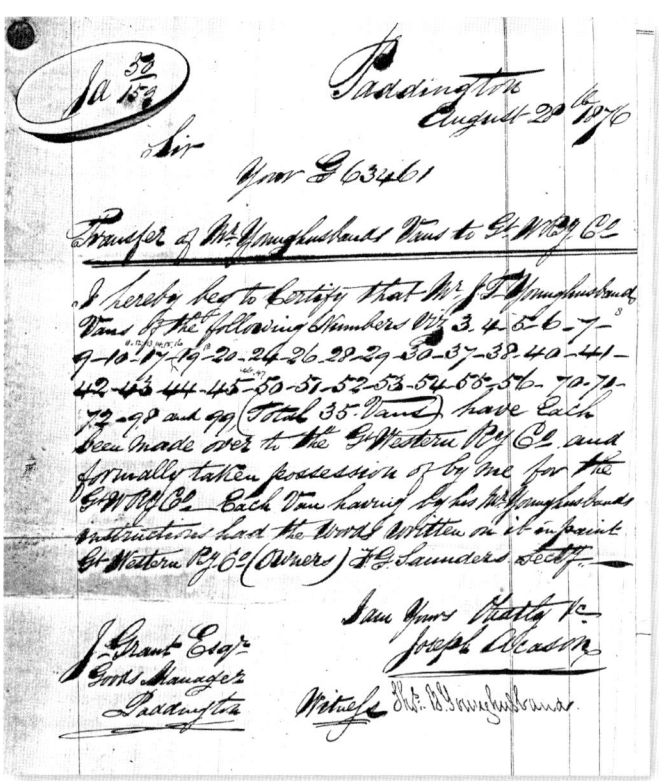

Horse-drawn vehicles ranged from fast one-horse (pony) express parcels delivery vans to the slow trundling four-wheel dray. The design of horse-drawn vehicles was traditional and well-tried, following the practices of contemporary road wagon building. Wood was the main constructional material with iron, and later steel, fitments. Wheels were wooden-spoked with iron tyres.

Under W L Newcombe's and James Grierson's goods managerships, the 'old' GW decided to perform cartage with its own equipment and opened a Road Wagon shop in 1870 within the new Carriage Works at Swindon (it was on the site of the original BG wagon shop). There, eventually, all its horse-drawn vehicles and, later, bodies and cabs for motor vehicles were built, as well as the many handcarts and barrows used across the system. To rapidly expand the GW cartage fleet, 35 pair-horse vans were bought from Younghusband for £1000 in 1876.

Just after the year 1900, diagrams of existing horse-drawn road vehicles were collected together with an index, to which new designs were added. Again, just like carriages and wagons, road vehicles were built under lot numbers at Swindon. At that time — long before the unified GW *Road Transport Department* was set up in 1922 — all horse-drawn cartage vehicles were under the control of the Chief Goods Manager at Paddington, with his 'horse department'. There were seven categories of vehicle in the road-wagon diagram index, given the letters A to G, namely:

(A 1-15) One-horse lorries;
(B 1-16) Two-horse and three-horse lorries;
(C 1-5) Timber carriages;
(D 1-15) Vans;
(E 1- 6) Floats;
(F 1-3) Miscellaneous (slop cart; tip cart; and water cart); and
(G 1) Light motor parcel van

wG1 is anomalous and related to the 12hp 15cwt Wolseley parcel van (fleet 40) purchased in 1906. Although the future of motor vehicles for cartage was unknown at the time, it was decided to set up a separate index when six Straker & Squire 1-ton chassis were purchased in 1909 and bodied at Swindon as parcel vans to operate in Birkenhead and Birmingham (Chapter 4).

Note that in those days 'van' meant a lorry with sides, hoop sticks and tilt ('tarpaulin-over'). The first motor vans were constructed in the same way with planked sides and tilts. Such vehicles were often employed without hoops and tilt as 'lorries with sides' — indeed Diagrams D4 and D8 are drawn without hoopsticks. The idea of a van being a vehicle having an integral enclosed body came into general use with later motor vehicles (although in fact there were some two-wheeled horse-drawn parcel vans with integral bodies). Note also that there were horse-drawn vehicles that, for some reason, were not given Diagram numbers, even though drawings and photographs show that they existed before the Index was drawn up; others that were designed and built afterwards do not seem to have been added to the list, unlike the indexes for wagons and carriages. Some are illustrated here, and others may be found in *Russell,* such as a vehicle for electric cables of 1906 which has most unusual springing arrangements (her Figures 148/9) and a wine and spirit lorry of 1919 (Fig 146).

Different variations in design of the same basic horse vehicle gave rise to different diagram numbers and Swindon engineering drawing numbers. Very often it related to how a vehicle was expected to be driven — from on the vehicle, or walking alongside on the road holding the leading animal's halter (the latter particularly when 'chain horses', attached in front by chain traces, were employed to assist a vehicle's normal complement of animals). For example, there were four versions of the basic 11ft 11ins long by 5ft 7ins wide one-horse flatbed lorry: (a) A7 (Paddington pattern) had a headboard and driver's seat (so-called 'dickey') perched above; (b) A8 was simply flat with no headboard nor driver's seat; (c) A10 (Bristol pattern) had just a headboard; and (d) A15 (Birmingham pattern) had neither headboard nor driver's seat, but did have a cover (two hoops and a short tilt) for the driver. What was called the Manchester pattern one-horse flatbed lorry was 12ft 6ins long by 6ft 0ins wide (A11). The GW cartage rule book stated that when a vehicle was fitted with a dickey it had to be used; the carman was not to drive from inside the vehicle nor from the shafts. On some vehicles, dickey seats could be quite high (up to 9ft 8ins) from the ground.

In most, but not all, cases the A-, B-, and C-groups were characterised by equal-size wheels (often 3ft 3ins diameter), the tops of which were lower than the underframe of the body. Smaller sizes were employed for heavier loads such as for the one-off Boat Lorry that was A4; and 2ft 0ins for the two-horse 6-ton lorry in B8. The rear wheels of vans (D group) at about 4ft 6ins diameter were larger than those on the forecarriage and their tops were higher off the ground than the floor of the vehicle and overlapped the sides of the body. Even so, the rear axle was in one piece passing across beneath the body, unlike 'floats' (see below). Within the D-group were two one-horse vehicles (D5) specially built in 1908 to convey pianos, where the floor was relatively low (2ft 6ins), requiring 1ft 9ins diameter front wheels and 2ft 0ins rear wheels. D7 was basically a one-horse van with racks from which to hang meat.

Floats were vehicles with normal-size wheels but low floors below axle height. There were single axle (2-wheel) floats as well as 4-wheel floats. To get the floor lower than the radius of the wheel, cranked axles had to be employed. In the case of 4-wheel floats, the body was brought up at the front to enable the use of a normal rotating forecarriage (rather like 'drop-frame' trailers used with articulated motors in later years). In E3 and E4, 2ft 10ins diameter wheels were at the front, with 4ft 6ins at the rear; the floor at the rear was 1ft 4ins above the ground. A special vehicle within the float-group was the two-horse E2 for carting plate glass. All vehicles having very small forecarriage wheels had to have the shafts angled up in order to bring them to a comfortable height for the horse. So-called 'windlass floats' had what we would now call a winch fitted at the front (on ships, a capstan rotated about a vertical axis; a windlass about a horizontal).

One-horse boat trolley of 1894, of which only one was built (Diagram A4). Angled-up shafts owing to low forecarriage and splinter bar. Cast iron disc wheels, 1ft 6ins in diameter, with large circular holes. The support trailer was attached 4ft behind the rear of the vehicle.
GWR/A G Atkins collection

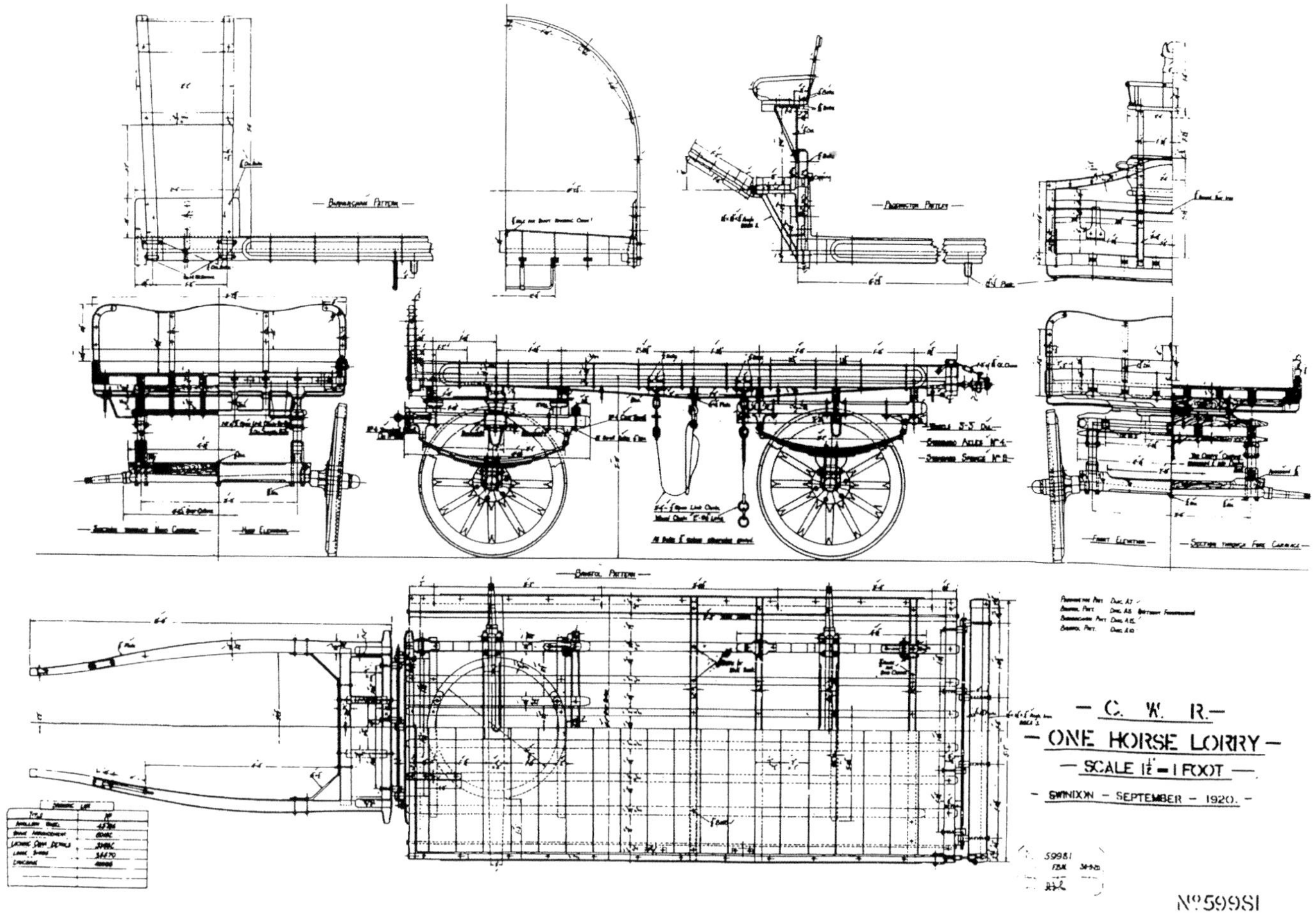

Engineering drawing and picture of one-horse lorry. Drawing dates from 1920 but the basic vehicle, shown on the bottom two rows, corresponds essentially with the picture from the turn of the 19th/20th centuries, except that the drawing shows later cast-iron artillery wheel hubs. A note below the front elevation states that Paddington, Bristol, Birmingham and Bristol (again) patterns correspond respectively to diagrams A7, A8, A15 and A10. The top row of drawings indicates options for a small driver tilt (Birmingham) and dickey seat (Paddington). The illustration shows seriffed writing along raves, 'LOAD NOT TO EXCEED 2-10-0' in block cast letters, and 'Tare 0-18-1' in script, on the front rave. Chains for attaching to horse harness towards front of shafts. *GWR/D J Hyde collection*

One-horse lorry to diagram A7 photographed in 1909. Brakes on rear wheels operated by foot pedal at driver dickey seat, so no skids nor chains to put round spokes. Shafts put up on to deck of lorry. 'Load not to exceed 2-0-0' on cast plate on front rave at left. 'Tare 0-18-3' in script on side of forecarriage. Footsteps for driver to reach dickey hanging from rod across headboard. *GWR/P J Kelley collection*

The goods warehouse at Hockley (Birmingham) with sacks of grain being unloaded from a one-horse lorry (Diagram A10/A15). The first floor door above the horse has a chute for transferring sacks down on to cartage vehicles. *GWR/D J Hyde collection*

Three-ton one-horse lorry fleet 3822 with shafts disconnected from splinter bar and laying on the vehicle. Tare 1-16-1 in script, and load in block letters, at front. 'A E BOLTER SEC^Y GWR PADDINGTON' on forecarriage. *GWR/D J Hyde collection*

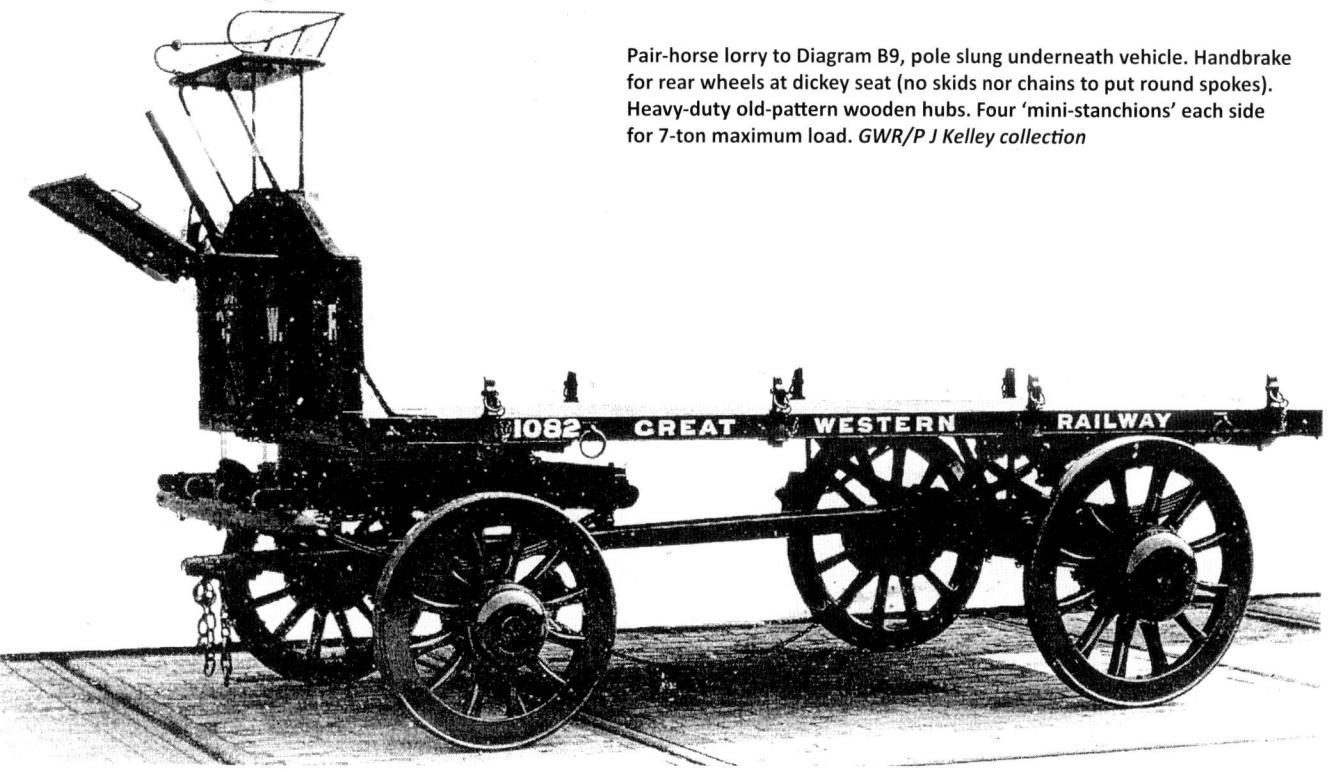

Pair-horse lorry to Diagram B9, pole slung underneath vehicle. Handbrake for rear wheels at dickey seat (no skids nor chains to put round spokes). Heavy-duty old-pattern wooden hubs. Four 'mini-stanchions' each side for 7-ton maximum load. *GWR/P J Kelley collection*

Three-horse 9-ton wagon with double shafts (Diagram B11). Rod under-trussing at sides of lorry. Heavy-duty old-pattern naves. Skids, wheel-spoke chains, etc, hanging down. Brake blocks on rear wheels operated by handwheel on side of vehicle. Wheel roller hanging on chain at rear.
GWR/P J Kelley collection

Left: Convertible timber carriage and stone lorry to Diagram C1. Load 4 tons. Shown with flat deck on bolsters to carry stone. With deck removed, it becomes a timber carriage, but with no pole as such. No brakes, but skid hanging on chain. There were 21 of these built.
GWR/A G Atkins collection

HORSE-DRAWN VEHICLES

40-ton boiler wagon, fleet 1089, built in 1894, for steel traffic at Wednesbury. Double shafts. The only one built, it has rod under-trussing beneath the deck that is not shown on the outline drawing for Diagram B14. Heavy-duty metal wheels. All bolsters (including that on the 'trailer') are fixed over the wheel axles. Big clasp brakeshoes on rear wheels operated by hand wheel on side at rear. Livery has 'Cº' after 'GREAT WESTERN RAILWAY' which is unusual. *GWR/P J Kelley collection*

15-ton crane lorry to Diagram B15. Clasp brakes on rear wheels operated by handwheel under 'RAIL''', but also with skid for metal wheels. Extended forecarriage with splinter bar attachments for double shafts; shafts are laying on the deck of the lorry interlaced with one facing forward and the other to the rear. Only one such wagon built. *GWR/P J Kelley collection*

Timber carriage (pole wagon). From tare weight of 1-4-0, it is to Diagram C2 with a 20ft long pole, to carry 4½ tons. Extended forecarriage to permit a level load to be as far forward as possible behind horse. For very long loads another stayed bolster could be added at the front so as to take an inclined load over the backs of the horse(s) [see *Russell*, Fig 202]. Rear wheels and bolster assembly slides along the pole to adjust length to suit load. *GWR/D J Hyde collection*

Below: Long roof truss chained to fully-extended pole wagon at Exeter. Diagram C3 or C4 (different-size wheels front and back, unlike other timber carriages). Heavy-duty old-pattern wheel hubs. *A G Atkins collection*

Two-horse timber carriage to Diagram C5 with 30ft-long pole and equal-size wheels of 3ft 3ins diameter. Shafts attached to an extension of the splinter bar on the forecarriage so as to allow long loads to extend in front of the vehicle or, with higher bolsters, over the horses. The length is adjusted by sliding the central pole through the rear wheel assembly and pinning the converging struts through holes in the pole (looped chains hold the pin). Wheel hubs are old pattern. *GWR/P J Kelley collection*

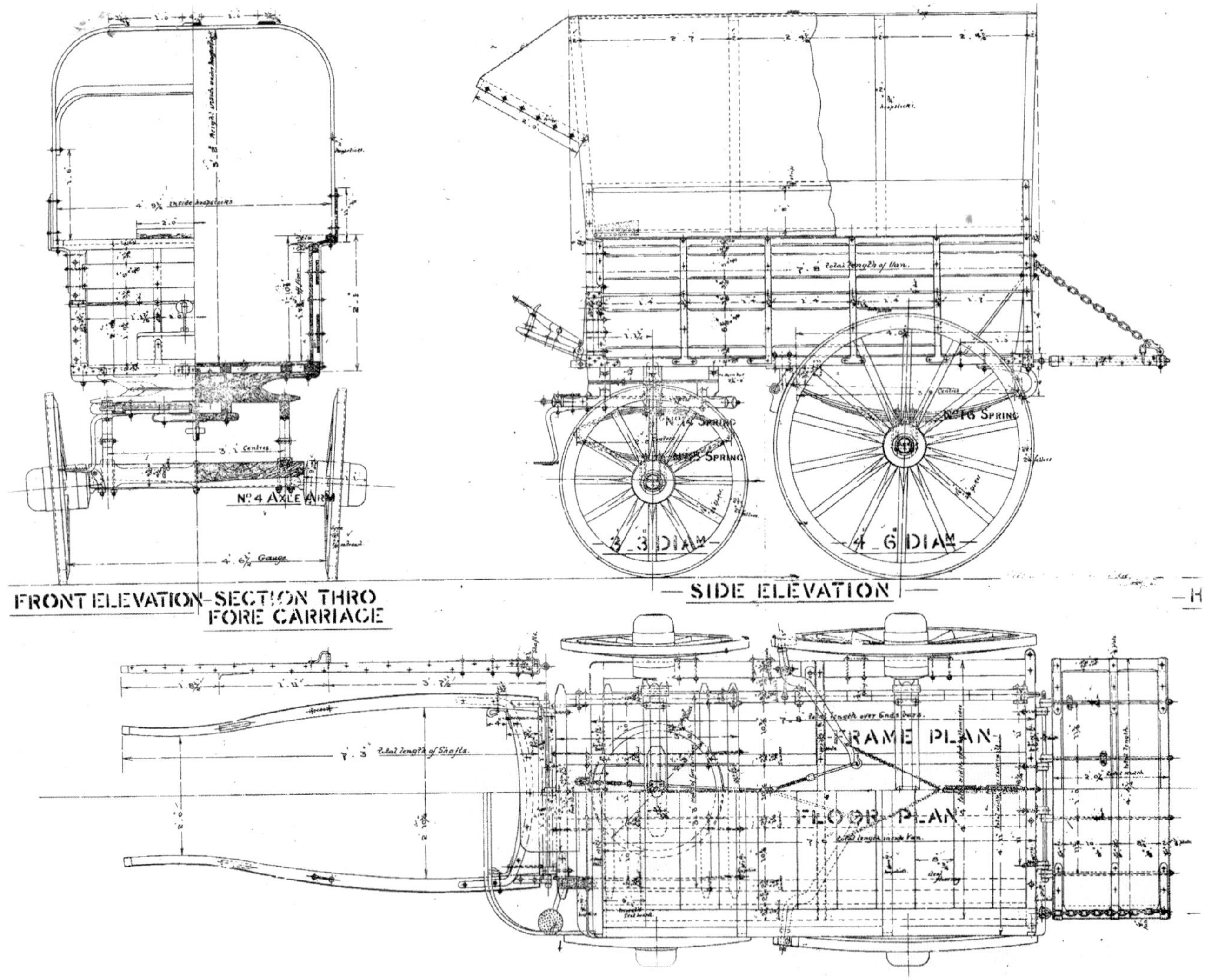

One-horse parcels van to Diagram D2 photographed after the introduction of the shirtbutton in 1934. Brake shoes on rear wheels operated by driver using foot pedal brake. 'Tare 0-16-1' in script on floor rave below fleet number. Drawing does not show side windows nor the artillery-type newer hubs on fleet 6295.
GWR/A G Atkins collection

Above: The depot at Bilston included a large open shed for bulky loads equipped with a 'Herbert Morris & Gastert' travelling crane, seen here loading a horse wagon to Diagram D4 in January 1925. The tops of the sides are widened out and supported by brackets. 'A E Bolter Secretary etc' just visible on forecarriage. Rear wheel obscures 'GREAT' in company name. New pattern iron artillery wheel hubs. Driver dickey with brake lever on. Apparently no chains/skids for wheels. *GWR/D J Hyde collection*

Left: One-horse van to Diagram D4. 'LOAD NOT TO EXCEED 2-0-0' on cast plate to left of rear wheel and company secretary, etc, on side of forecarriage. Top rail of body extended sideways with brackets, so no provision for hoopsticks. Brake on rear wheel operated by foot pedal from dickey seat. *GWR/P J Kelley collection*

Above: Panoramic view of Swansea(?) goods yard in August 1932 with a variety of horse and motor vehicles. Of particular interest is the newly-painted meat horse lorry fleet 2337 at the bottom right (Diagram D7). Notice that the 'T' in 'GREAT' is painted on the bottom of the second-from-front vertical 'hoopstick' so is not in the same plane as the rest of the company title. Yard weighbridge at bottom left. Ex-army AEC lorry at centre (fleet 426, registration AC7355, that had carried a bus body in the summer of 1927) loaded with dark-grey container, BX-23. *GWR/P J Kelley collection*

Left: Two-horse tilt van to Diagram D10 with a pair of greys. (Note that in the outline drawing in the Index the front hoopstick is shown vertical, but has been altered in pencil to correspond with the backwards-sloping front of the tilt behind the driver.) Van-boy standing on tailboard. Cream on brown livery but with 'GREAT WESTERN RAILWAY PARCEL VAN' (hardly visible in this picture) and '166.P. PADDINGTON STATION' in yellow. Letter 'P' after fleet number is unusual (is it a mistake and an extra 'P' in Paddington?). Outside gates of Paddington Mint stables. One-horse vans (D6 and D9) are similar and pencilled annotations to the Diagram Index book say that 369 in total were built. *GWR/P J Kelley collection*

Pair-horse lorry and 4-hoop tilt to Diagram D11. The rather slack tilt has a different number (in yellow) from the vehicle itself, on which lettering is in cream on brown. Brake shoes on rear wheels controlled by pedal at driver's feet. Pole between animals to which animals are attached by chains and to the splinter bar. Old pattern naves. Outside gates of Paddington Mint stables. *GWR/D J Hyde collection*

Another pair-horse lorry and 4-hoop tilt to Diagram D11, but now with a single chain horse ahead. Photographed outside gates of Paddington Mint stables. Old pattern hubs. *GWR/D J Hyde collection*

Pair horse wagon (to Diagram D12) with two chain horses in front outside the main gates of the Mint stables at Paddington in 1909. Chains attached to front of shafts. Collars of chain horses do not have hames and their reins are led through cruppers to pass between the pair of horses whose own reins are attached in the normal way. Heavy-duty old-pattern wooden naves. Tailboard used for loading. Among boxes on wagon are 'S J Wright & co Ltd/Ham & Bacon Curers/Taunton' and 'Sulis Water'. *GWR/D J Hyde collection*

The road wagon side of Hockley goods shed at the turn of the 19th/20th centuries with numerous horse C&D vehicles. 'GWR' lettering on tilts has serifs. *GWR/P J Kelley collection*

Right: 'Standard two-horse van' to Diagram D14, with 'semi-circular' (as opposed to vertical-sided) tilt. Livery cream on brown and vice versa, with seriffed lettering. Fleet 461, photographed on 14/9/1899. Note inclusion of 'company' at this period. Pole stowed beneath vehicle over axles. Skids and chains to go around spokes of rear wheel, and roller hanging behind rear wheel, in lieu of brakes. This design is also found without the driver dickey. *GWR/D J Hyde collection*

Below: The road-side of Taunton goods depot on 19/12/32 with broken window panes. 'Standard two-horse van' fleet 741 to Diagram D14. Notice that the base of the half-round tilt is wider than the width of the vehicle and sits on a plank supported by brackets at the positions of the hoopsticks. Van has artillery naves on wheels. Lorry fleet 2775 (Diagram A8) has old hubs. Mechanical horse in far distance. *GWR/D J Hyde collection*

D14-type van with semi-circular tilt outside warehouse at Hockley. Seriffed GWR lettering on tilt. *GWR/D J Hyde collection*

Two-horse plate glass float to Diagram E2. Cranked rear axle to pass beneath low floor. Forecarriage is very low and shafts are angled upwards. In March 1933 there were five such floats running with fleet numbers 1272/94/1300/08/09. *GWR/D J Hyde collection*

HORSE-DRAWN VEHICLES

Pedigree livestock being unloaded near the Albert St gate at Canton Sidings, Cardiff, for the Royal Welsh Show in August 1929. The GW Beetle from which the bull is being led must have leaked, hence the tarpaulin cover. Cattle float fleet 1280 to Diagram E3 awaits the bull with plenty of straw strewn around. There's a picture complementary to this on p259 of *GWR Goods Train Working* in which float number 1374 is being loaded. That vehicle had a winch (4280 here does not) and had old-pattern wooden hubs on the forecarriage wheels, but artillery-type at the rear. Here 4280 has wooden naves on both wheels. The tarpaulin sheet over the Paco/Beetle shown here has been removed in the other shot. The author grew up at the other (Cowbridge Rd) end of Albert St. *GWR/D J Hyde collection*

Two-wheel road water cart photographed at Redbrook/Chepstow(?) on 5/9/29. Old-type wooden wheel naves. Horse collar is chained to shafts and balance weight of cart is taken by large padded leather piece over animal's back. *GWR/P J Kelley collection*

Two-wheel tilt van fleet 1347 with 14-spoke wheels held in a suspension framework with low springs as stub-axle centreline is above floor of vehicle. Early pattern wooden hubs. 'G.W.R.' on tilt with 'square' full stops and 'Great Western Rail^y' in block letters along raves. Front of tilt is angled forwards, so windows are provided to help driver's vision. 'Load not to exceed 1-0-0' at driving position. Breast strap for horse attached to shafts on off-side, one of which is painted 'Tare 0-1' in script. 'G K Mills Sec^y GWR Paddington' along floor plank (Mills retired in 1910).
GWR/D J Hyde collection

Two-wheel tilt van fleet 1278 with 14-spoke wheels having early pattern wooden hubs. 'G.W.R.' on tilt with 'square' full stops and 'Great Western Rail^y' in seriffed letters along raves. Breast strap for horse attached to shafts on off-side, one of which is painted 'Tare 0-1-3' in script. *GWR/D J Hyde collection*

One-horse light van with integral body (not a tilt) and not in Diagram book. Photographed in 1890, with yellow on brown livery, fleet 143. Chain for passing around wheel spoke in lieu of brake, but no skid. Grab handles and step for driver on both sides. A similar van, now equipped with a lever brake acting on the rear wheels, may be found in *Russell*, Figure 102; although a later van it has the earlier fleet number 134. *GWR/P J Kelley collection*

Delivery van outside the Angel Hotel in Chippenham in the early 1930s. Another variation in van design consisting of a square framework but with canvas sides. Old pattern hubs on forecarriage wheels, but later cast iron artillery pattern at rear [postcard]. *Author's collection*

Various horse-drawn vehicles outside the former Bristol & Exeter Rly offices in Bristol. None of the flatbed lorries have dickeys; some have headboards and some not. Of vans parked at right angles to the gutter, the first at the end of the building in the middle is a one-horse van to Diagram D9, fleet 2063; the two-wheeler leaning forward on its shafts has five hoopsticks. Sign at right with pointing finger directs people to 'GREAT WESTERN RAILWAY/GENERAL OFFICES'. Roof of Temple Meads station at left with arches below. *GWR/D J Hyde collection*

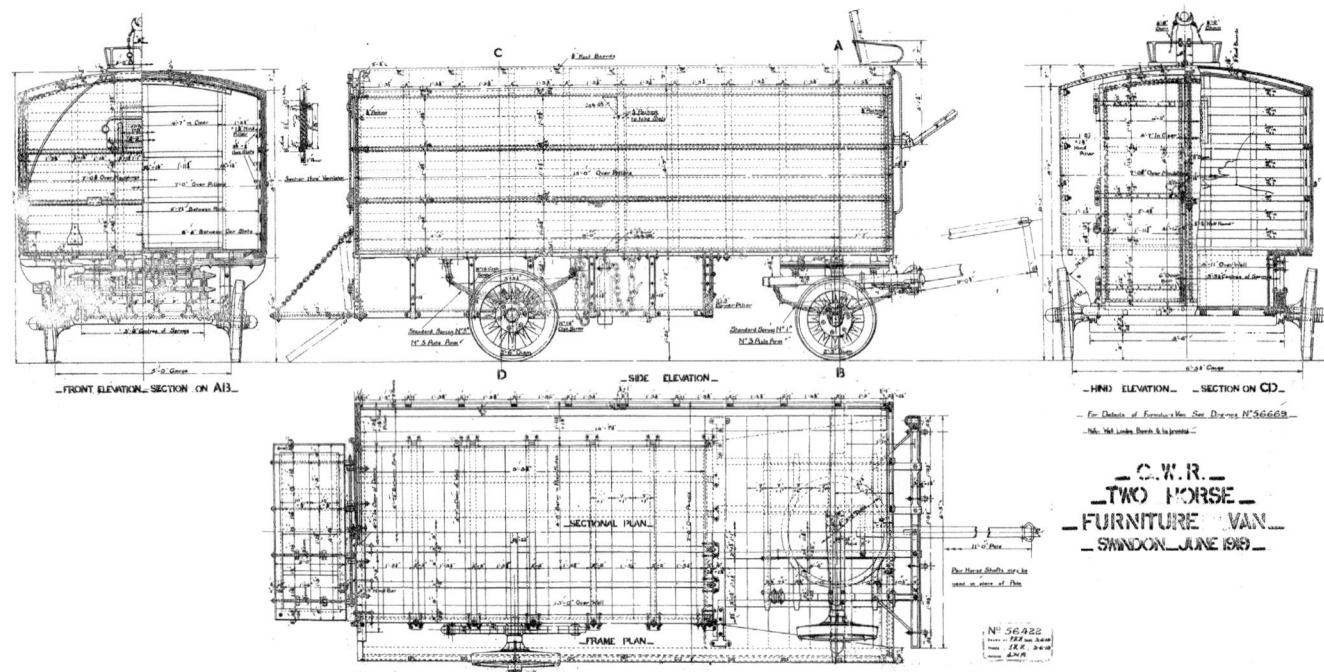

Above and left: Engineering drawing of two-horse furniture van, as modified in 1919, to have smaller wheels than before (a picture of the vehicle in its original state with 3ft forecarriage wheels and 4ft 6ins rear wheels with cranked axle may be found in *Russell*, Fig 213). Here the cranked axle has been replaced by one passing straight under the body with 2ft 6ins diameter wheels; the forecarriage wheels are 2ft 3ins in diameter. Dickey seat for driver on roof at front. Although there are now brakeshoes on the rear wheels controlled by a pedal at the driver's feet, a traditional chain and skid are provided.
GWR/P J Kelley collection

Right: A stone lorry designed in 1888 that was not given a Diagram number (C1 was a convertible timber carriage and stone lorry). Photographed in 1896. Very heavy springing and massive wheel hubs. Typical seriffed lettering of the period.
GWR/P J Kelley collection

G.W.R. TIMBER WHEELS.
TIMBER NAVES WITH BOXES

No AXLE	DIA OF AXLE	DIA OF BOX	LOAD	DRG. No
1	2" PARALLEL	3 1/8"	1T. 0C. 0Q.	—
2	1 5/8" PARALLEL	2 5/8"	8C. 0Q.	—
3				
4				
5	3 1/8" / 2 5/8" TAPER	4"	3T. 10C. 0Q.	36309A
6				
7				
8	1 3/4" PARALLEL	2 13/16"	10C. 0Q.	—
9				
10				
WHEELS FOR 10T. FLOAT HIND	3 1/4" / 2 13/16" TAPER	4 3/8" / 4 3/16" TAPER.		26931.
" FRONT	2 5/8" / 2 5/16" TAPER.	3 11/16" / 3 17/32" TAPER		"

ARTILLERY CENTRES

No OF AXLE	DIA OF SMALL END	DIA OF LARGE END	LOAD	DRG. No
1				
2				
3	2 1/4"	2 5/8"		39485.
4	1 5/8"	2"		41303 41306.
5	2 5/8"	3 1/8"		41204.
6	2 3/4"	3 1/4"		41205.
7				
8				
9	3 1/2"	4"		64528.
10	4 1/4"	4 3/4"		64239.
WHEELS FOR 40T. BOGIE LORRY.	4 13/16"	5 1/4"		6946. 6947.

K.E.F.

VEHICLE DRAWING & DESCRIPTION	WHEELS	TARE	LOAD	SPRINGS	TRANSVERSE SPRINGING	SPOKES	FELLOES & TYRE.
ONE HORSE VAN DRG. No 13978 "A" ISSUE (26.10.1897 ORIGINAL) 4 WHEELED. 5'-6" GAUGE.	WHEELS:- PROBABLY TIMBER NAVES ORIGINALLY "A" ISSUE SHOWS ARTILLERY CENTRES No 4 AXLE ARMS 3'-3" D. FRONT 12SP. 4'-6 D. HIND. 12SP.	17C. 1Q. 18C. 0Q. ? PENCILLED ON FAINTLY.	2T. 0C. 0Q.	FRONT:- STD SPRING No 1 HIND:- STD. SPRING No 5.	NONE.		
ONE HORSE VAN DRG. No 4302 (31.7.1889.). 4 WHEELED. 5'-6" GAUGE.	TIMBER NAVES 1'-1" LONG x 10" DIA. 3'-3" D. FRONT. 12SP. 4'-6" D. HIND. 14SP. No 4. AXLE ARMS	1T. 1C. 0Q.	2T. 10C. 0Q.	FRONT:- STD. SPRING No 1 HIND:- STD. SPRING No 5.	TRANSVERSE AT REAR OF HIND SPRING. STD. No 6 (2)		
PONY PARCEL VAN (DRG. No 15639). (11.6.1900.) 4 WHEELED. 4'-2" GAUGE.	TIMBER NAVES 8" DIA. 2'-8" D. FRONT 12SP. 3'-8" D. HIND 14SP. No 2. AXLE ARMS.	8C. 0Q.				1 1/8 x 1 7/8"	2 1/4" DEEP 2" WIDE. 5/8" THICK TYRE.
TWO HORSE TROLLEY DRG. No 6881. (10.12.1889.). SHAFTS INDICATE HORSES IN TANDEM. 4 WHEELED. 4'-10" GAUGE.	TIMBER NAVES 1'-2" LONG x 11" DIA. 3'-3" D. FRONT 14SP. 3'-3" D. HIND 14SP. No 3. AXLE ARM.	1T. 7C. 3Q.	4T. 10C. 0Q.	FRONT No 1A HIND No 3	No 2 ACROSS & ABOVE BACK AXLE CASE.		
10 TON TROLLEY DRG. No 28171A. (28.11.1905.). TWO HORSE 4 WHEELED. 4'-8" GAUGE.	TIMBER NAVES 1'-2 1/2" LONG. x 11" DIA. 2'-0" D. FRONT. 12SP. 2'-0" D. HIND. 12SP. No 6 AXLE ARM.	1T. 15C. 3Q.	10T. 0C. 0Q.	FRONT No 1A. HIND No 3A.			

The wheelbase of timber carriages was adjusted to suit the length of the load by sliding the rear wheel assembly along the long central pole and locking in place. Timber wagons were sometimes called 'pole wagons' — not to be confused with the 'pole' between horses when double shafts were not used on two-horse vehicles.

From pencilled annotations dated 1909 in the road-wagon Diagram Index, there is information on the total number of vehicles built in some of the groups at that time: A1, 25; A2 and A3, 53; A4, 1; A8, 343; A11, 19; A14, 1 (fleet 3822); B1, 1; B2, B3 and B4, 5; B5, 15; B6, 107; B7, 2; B8, 1; B9, 7; B10, 12; B11, 13; B13, 1 (fleet 1092); B14, 1; B15, 1 (fleet 1088); C1, 21; C3, 7; C4, 1; D1, 21; D2, 137; D3, 39; D4, 17; D5, 2; D6, D7, D9 and D10, 369; D8, 28; D11, 499; D12, 17; D13, 9; E1, 1; E2, 2; E3, 22; and E4, 1 (fleet 1269). Additional vehicles built after 1909 increased the numbers in a group. For example, in 1933, five fleet numbers 1272/1294/1300/1308/1309 are given for 2-horse plate glass floats (E2) compared with two in 1909. Again 39 fleet numbers, 1256/58/65/77/78/80/84/87/98/99/1313/16/18/30/49/50-54/56-62/64-66/73-79/81/86, are given for E3 in contrast to 22 in 1909. Some horse-drawn floats would later be adapted so as to be drawn by tractor (Chapter 6).

Other annotations show that the 4-ton timber carriage in C2 was upgraded to 4½ tons in 1913 by altering the cross section of the 20ft long pole from 4½ x 4 inches to 5 x 4½ inches, but the 15-ton horse lorry in B13 was downgraded in 1924, with loading limited to 10 tons distributed, 9 tons over the back axle and 8 tons carried centrally.

Four-wheeled vehicles were able to be turned since the *forecarriage* (that contained the front axle) was attached to the underside of the vehicle by the so-called *futchels* to form a turntable. At the front of the forecarriage was the *splinter bar* that transmitted the pull of the animal to the vehicle. Attached to the splinter bar were shafts or chains for a single horse; and for two horses side by side either double shafts were employed for heavy loads, or for lighter loads the animals were separated by a central pole attached to the wagon to which they were coupled by chains. Different harnesses would be employed depending on the means of coupling the horse(s) to the splinter bar. When not in use, to save on parking space, shafts would be put vertical and poles would be slid beneath the vehicle where also sack trucks and other equipment were stowed. Lengths of shafts and poles reflected the size of the animal expected to be employed. The harnessing of three-horse vehicles was formed from a pair-horse wagon with the central third horse attached by chains in front; four-horse vehicles had two horses chained in front with a spreader bar between the chains to keep the animals apart and to even out the load. In the case of two-wheeled wagons, the lengths of shafts, and where they were attached to the harness of the animal, were important for the balance of the vehicle and how easy it was for the horse to turn. *In extremis* a single-axle vehicle, very overloaded at the rear, might lift a harnessed horse into the air.

Below and opposite: **Blueprints of shafts.**

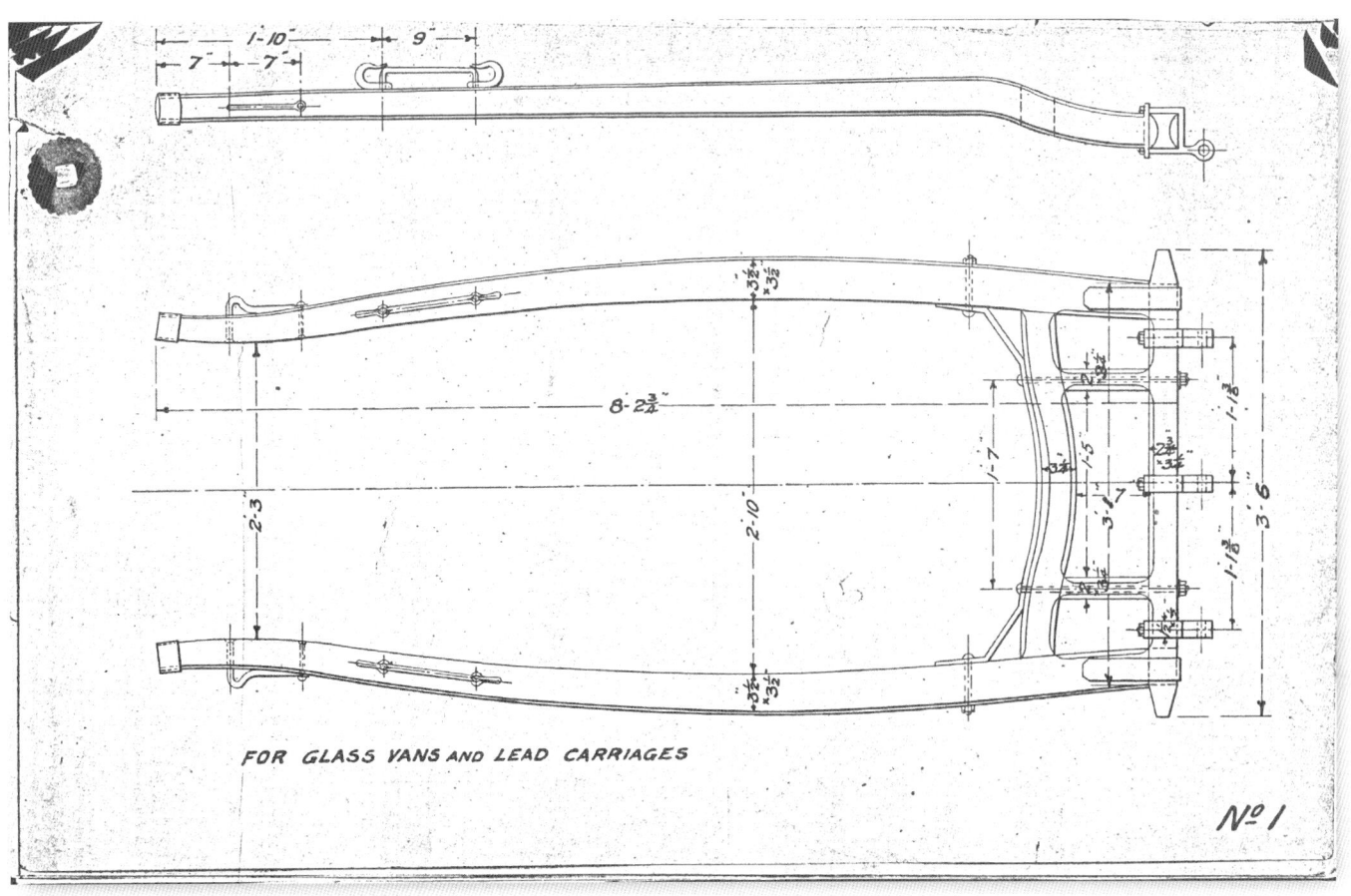

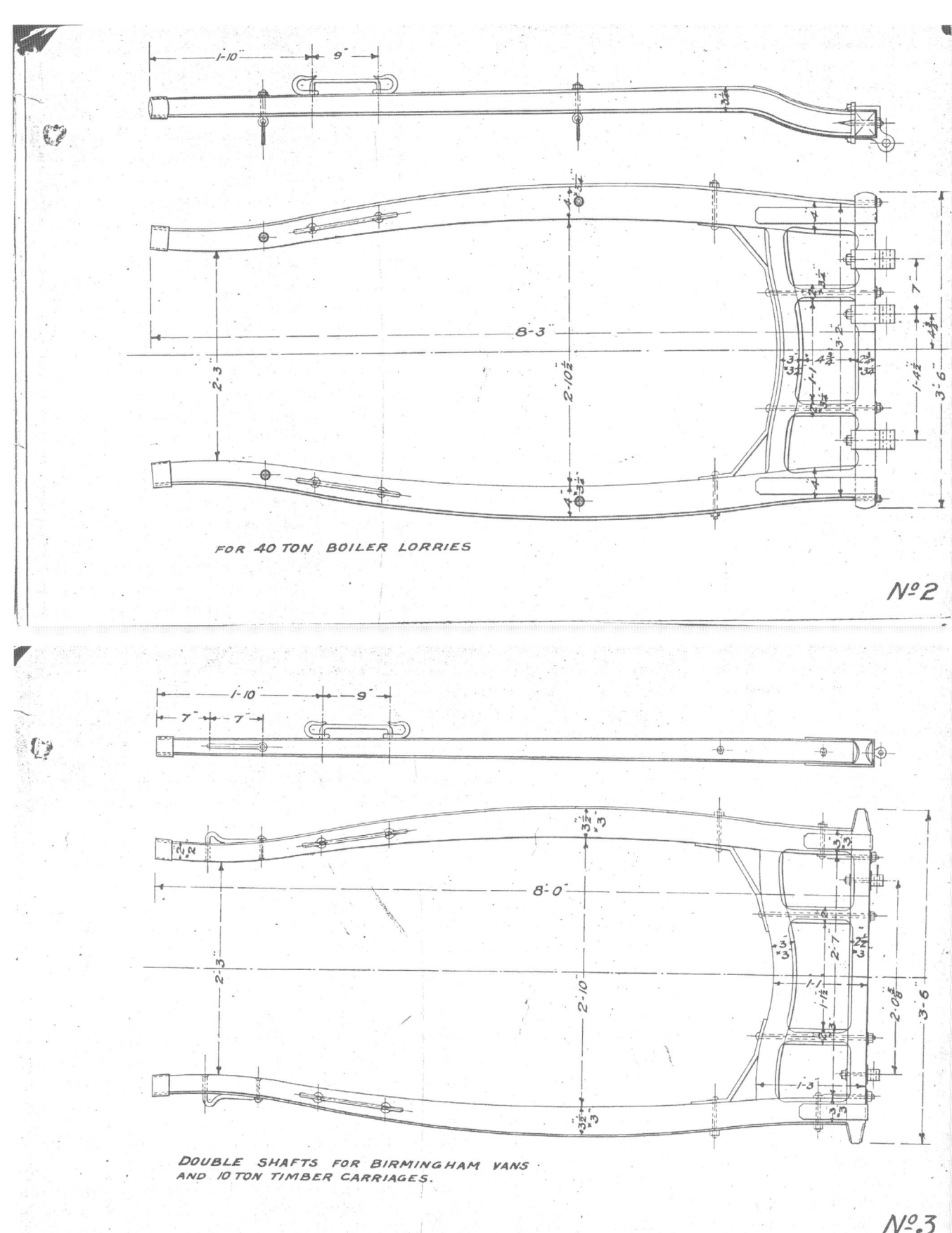

FOR 40 TON BOILER LORRIES — Nº 2

DOUBLE SHAFTS FOR BIRMINGHAM VANS AND 10 TON TIMBER CARRIAGES. — Nº 3

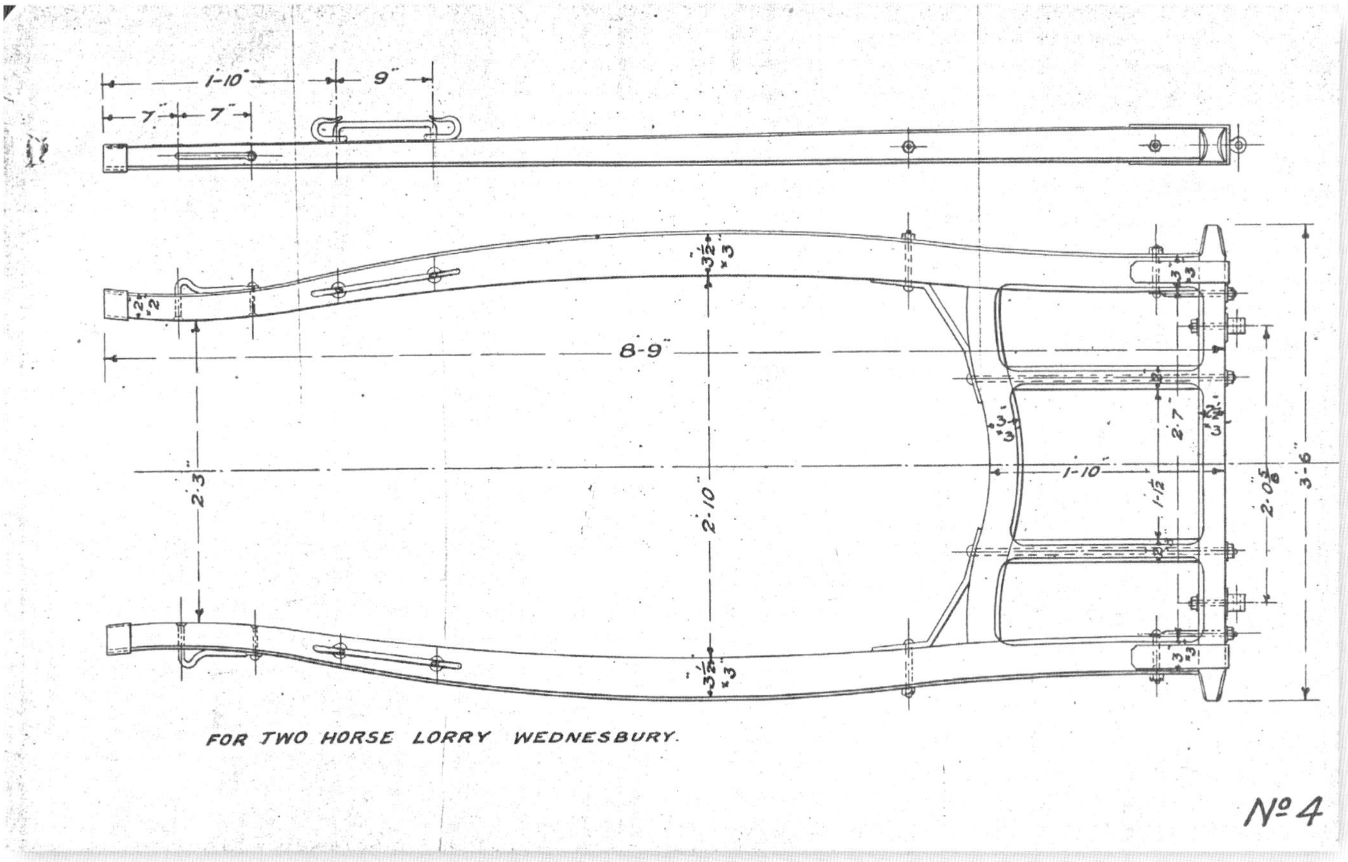

FOR TWO HORSE LORRY WEDNESBURY.

No 4

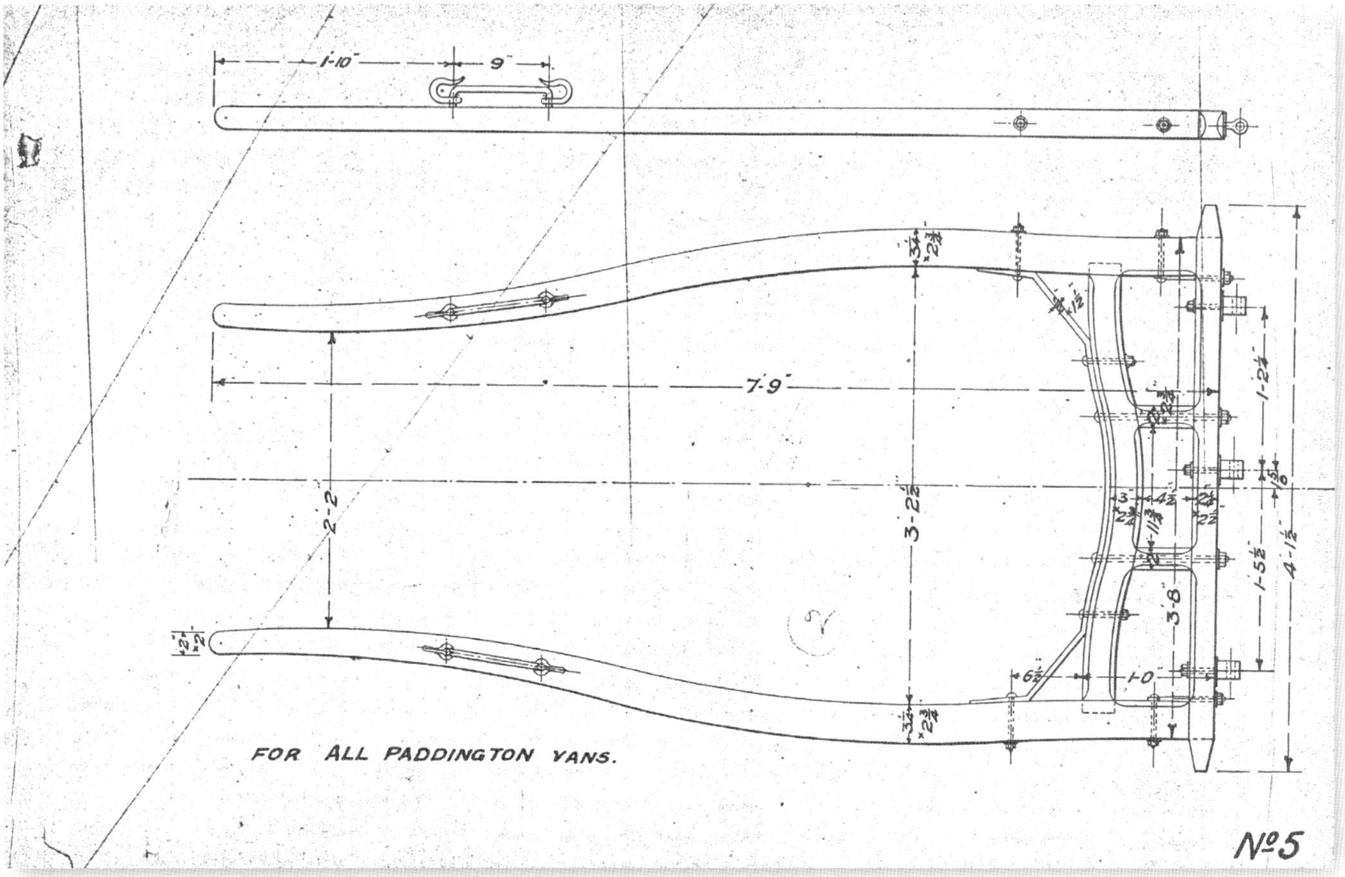

FOR ALL PADDINGTON VANS.

No 5

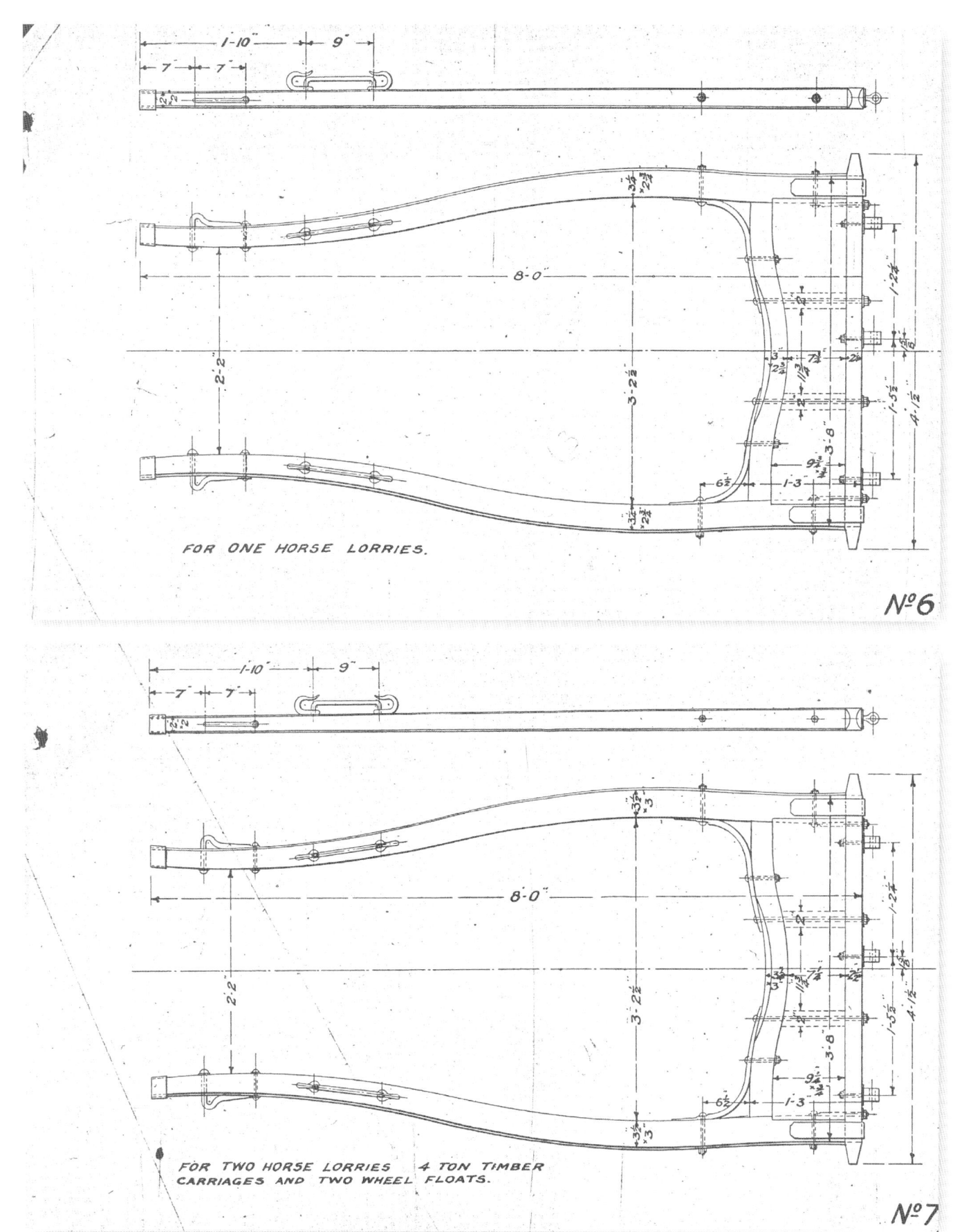

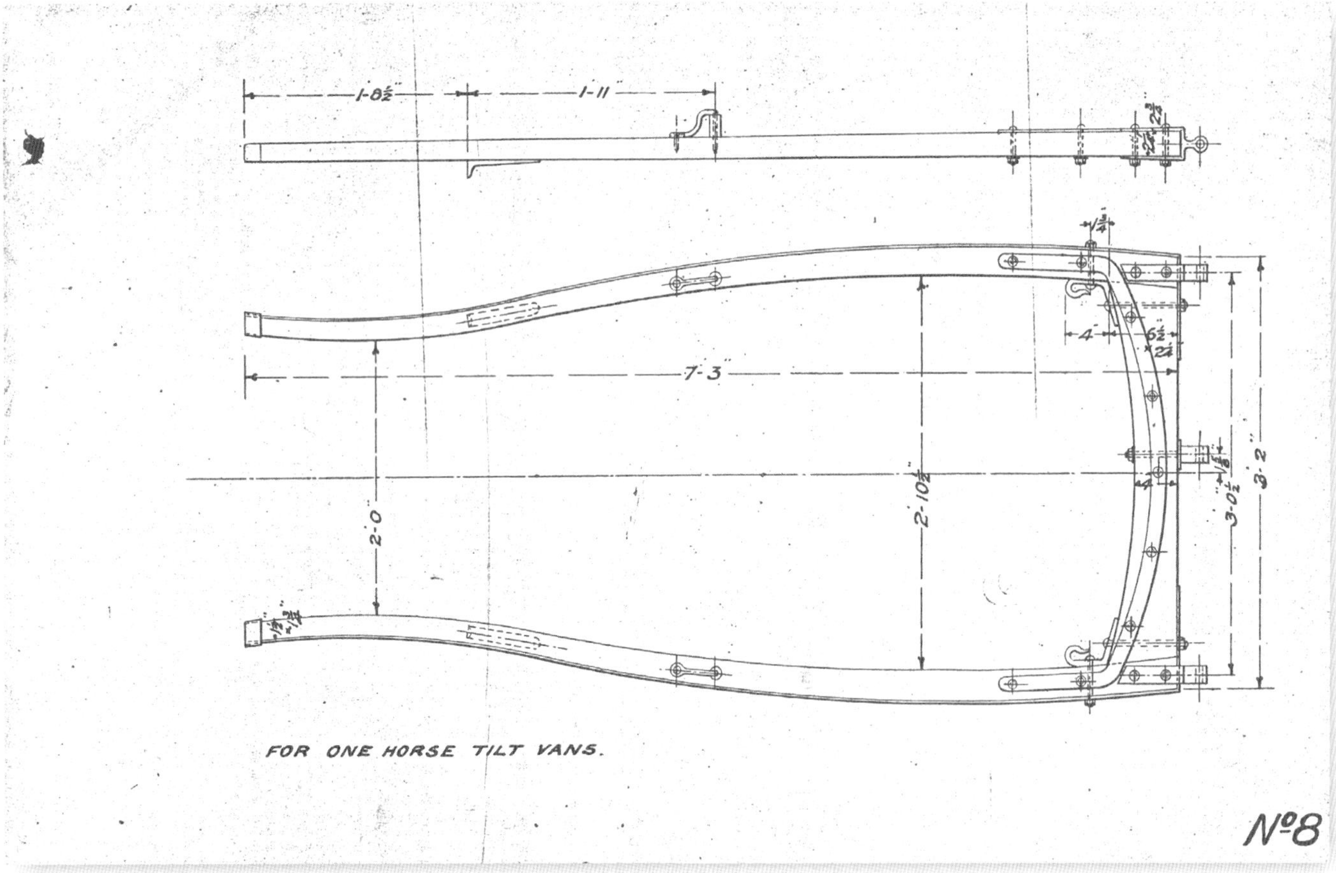
1-8½"
1-11"
7-3"
2-0"
2-10½"
3-0½"
3-2"
FOR ONE HORSE TILT VANS.
No8

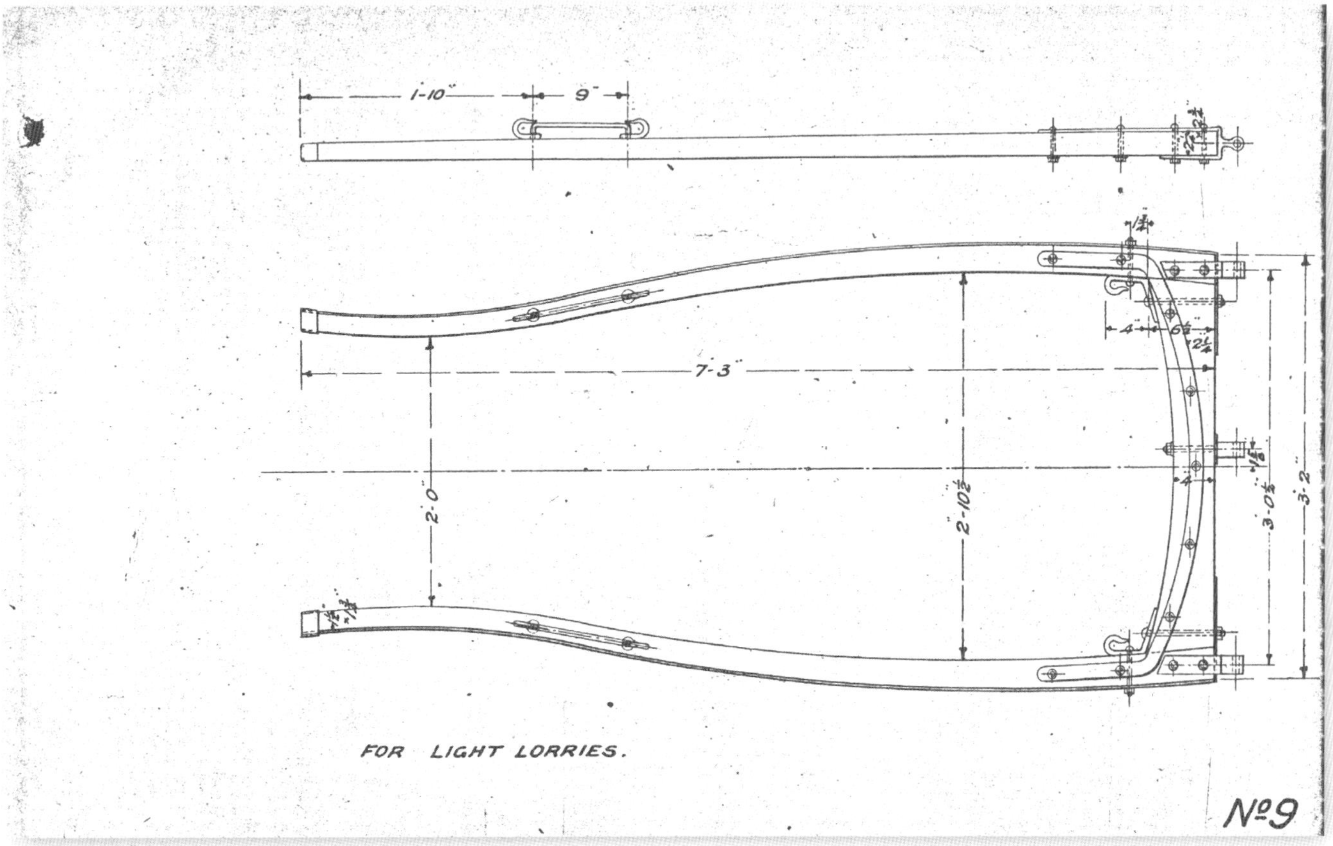
1-10"
9"
7-3"
2-0"
2-10½"
3-0½"
3-2"
FOR LIGHT LORRIES.
No9

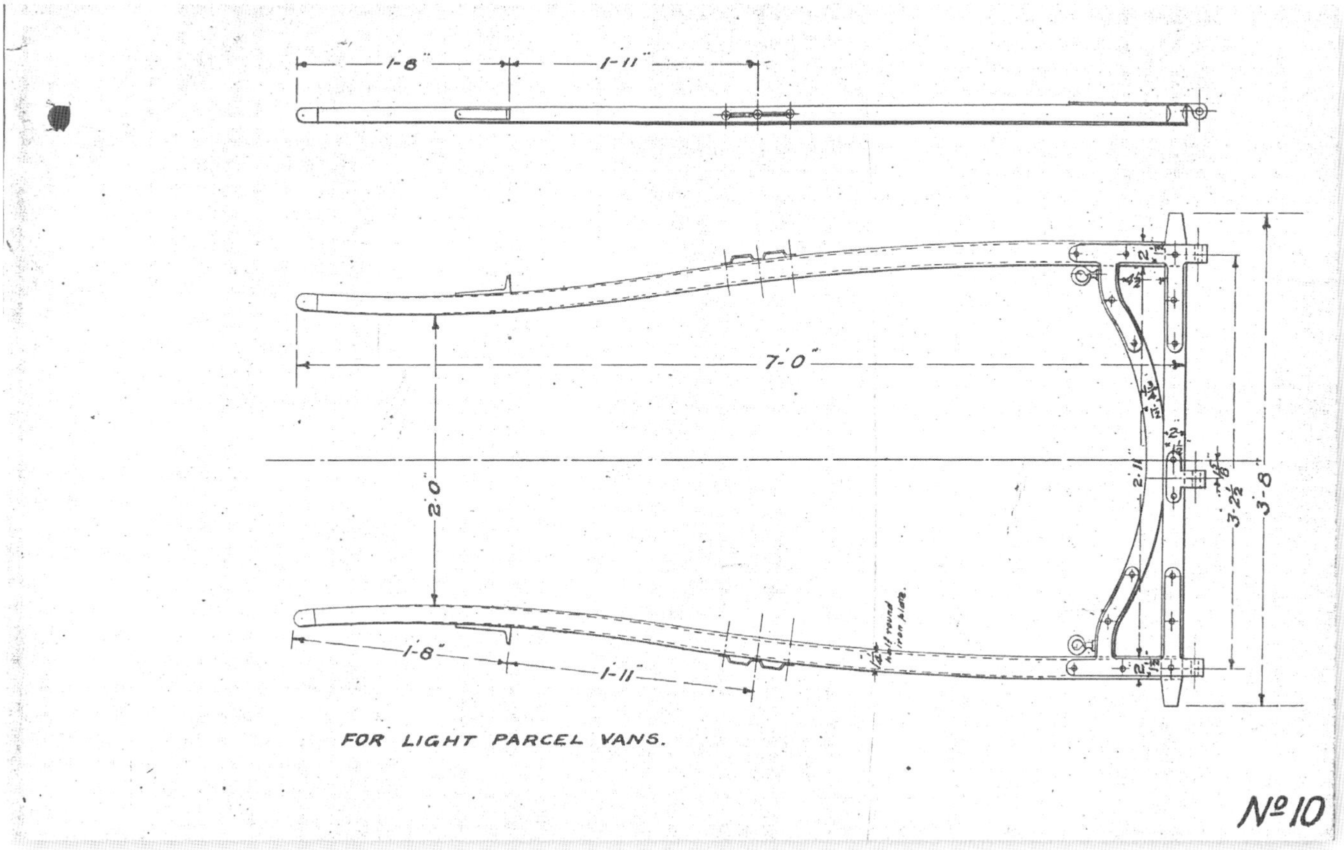
1-8"
1-11"
7-0"
2-0"
2-11"
3-2½
3-8
1-8"
1-11"
FOR LIGHT PARCEL VANS.
№10

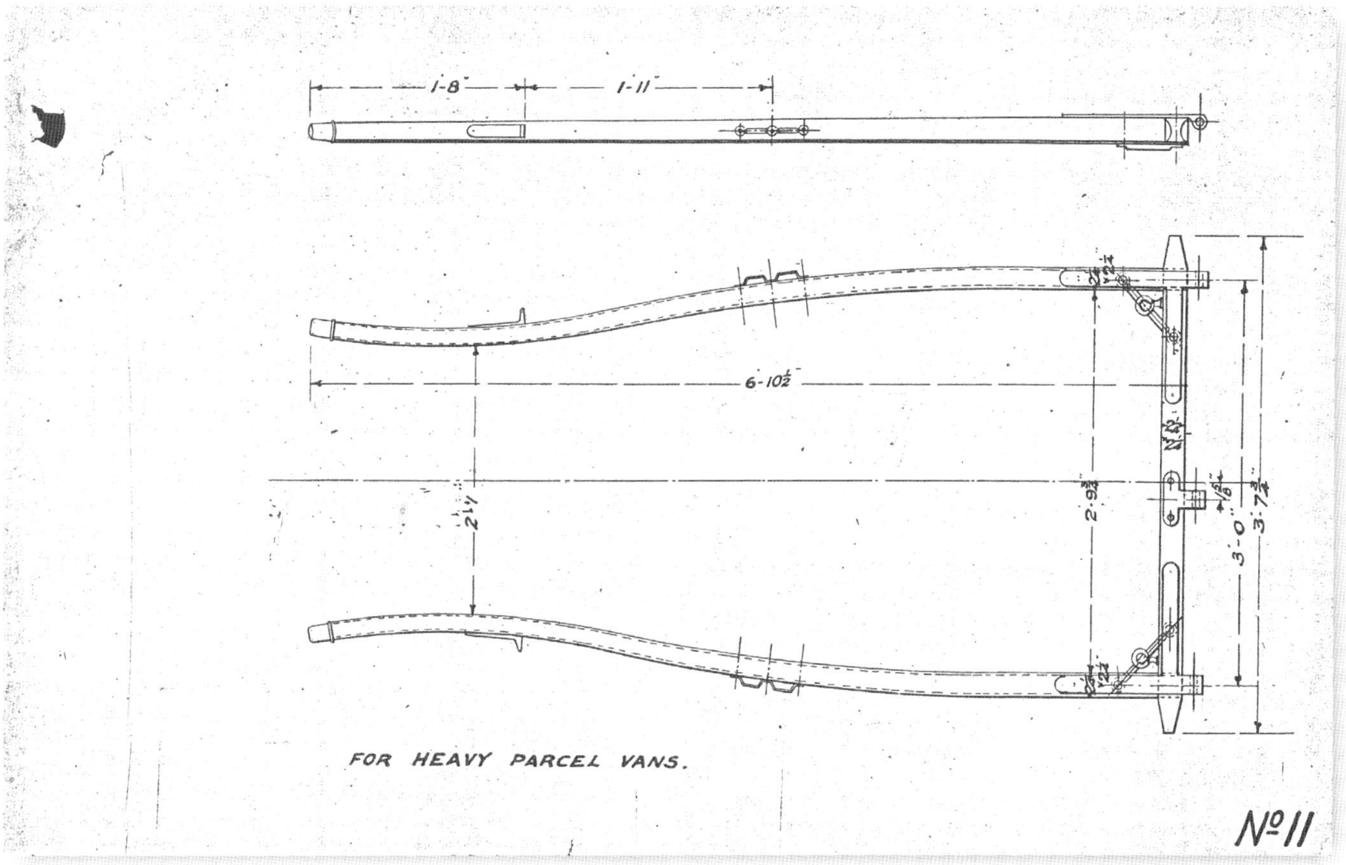
1-8"
1-11"
6-10½"
2-9¾
2-1½
3-0"
3-7¾
FOR HEAVY PARCEL VANS.
№11

G.W.R. Road Wagon Dept. — Renewal Account.

No.	Date	Amount £	DESCRIPTION OF WORK.	Lot.	Expenditure to June 19 1909	28 days ending July 17
			Brought forward			
			London Goods			
			1 Ton Gas Lorry — Paddington	849		7.—
			General Goods			
			1 One horse Lorry — Bristol	855		
			2 Windlass Float — do	857		
			6 Standard Lorries (to carry 3 tons) — 3 Leeds, 3 Bradford	859		
			1 One horse Lorry — Stourbridge	861		
			2 do do — Oxford	862		
			2 One horse Lorries — do	863		
			1 do do — Bury	870		
			1 do do — Neath	972		
			2 do do Lorries — Bristol	970		

G.W.R. Road Wagon Dept. — Additional Account.

No.	Date	Amount £	DESCRIPTION OF WORK.	Lot.	Expenditure to June 25 1909	23 days ending July 23	28 days ending Aug 20
13	1908 Feb 10	65	**London Parcels** 1 Lorry for Motor Lorry — Paddington	616			15/6.11
			1 next level Tail Van — Oldham Junc	625			
13	June 8	112	**General Parcels** 2 Parcel Collecting Vans — Dublin	605		26	46.10.9
19	July 20	50	2 Lowlevel Parcel Tail Vans — Slough	607			47.19.9
11	Oct 19	56	1 One horse Street Tail Van — Hayes	620			
26	Aug 10	56	1 2 Fold Street Tail Van — Solihull	622			
		211	**London Goods** 1 Two horse Lorry & 4 pair horses from London Carting (Mitchell & Boardes)	636			
7	Oct 12 Aug 10	96	**General Goods** 2 One horse Lorries — Bristol	594	60.15.11	6.12.11	
6	1909 Feb 10	60	1 do — do	596	10.2.-		13
19	June 15	75	1 Handbrake	597	11.9.3	3.16	1.6.5
		100	1 One horse Van	600	11.16	23.2.8	60.3.1
11	May 6	300	1 do do — Stafford Road Reading	601	94.19.3	29.9.1	15.8.10.6
14		70	1 Motor truck, not Loco Stowell Cloff Worcester	602	5.11.8	1.3.3	9.14
19	1910 Feb 10	60	1 Float — do	603		56.4	80.7.7
19		60	1 One horse Lorry	604	14.4.7		25.1
13	June 15	90	2 do — Dublin	605			11.39.1
13		100	2 do do — Neath	601			
		50	1 Two horse Lorry — do	609			23.3.0
19	July 20	168	3 One horse Vans (Storage & fittings etc) — Hayes	610			55.3.7
13		42	1 Two horse Lorry (Tow) — Bristol	611			9.0
19	Oct 19	55	1 One horse Lorry — Solihull	613			1.3
25	May 11	17	1 Two horse Lorry — Frome	621			
10	Oct 18	600	12 One horse Lorries — Cardiff	623			
		300		629			
41		200	— Witney	620			
	Aug 10	100	do	641			
25		80	1 Float	613			
			Carried forward		76.11.4	598.12.11	

Road Wagon Dept Accounts.

Construction of horse vehicles was for places all over the system. For example, in 1915 for Bath, Bilston, Birmingham, Blaenavon, Bristol, Clevedon, Ebbw Vale, Frome, Hockley, Kingswear, Launceston, Lawrence Hill, Leeds, Liverpool, Manchester, Oakengates, Oswestry, Oxford, Plymouth, Shrewsbury, Tavistock, Wednesbury, Weston-super-Mare and Uxbridge. The order for Liverpool was for twenty one-horse lorries. Note the inclusion of Leeds where, before the Grouping, the GW had offices as it had at stations in the likes of Leicester, Sheffield and so on in foreign territory. Note also the construction of two one-horse lorries for Dublin in 1904 (lot 606) costing £45 each; six 'standard lorries' in 1909 as renewals (lot 859) — 3 for Leeds and 3 for Bradford; a timber carriage for Leeds costing £63 in 1909 (lot 851) under additional vehicles to the fleet; a stone carriage for Bridgwater costing £65 and a crank axle cart for Clevedon costing £44.

The Swindon Road Wagon shop had its own smithy, and a small rolling machine for the tyres of wheels. A wheel was made up from circular arcs (felloes) of ash wood that together formed the rim, connected to the hub by oak spokes. Wheels were dished to give lateral stiffness, and the ends of axles were angled downwards so that those spokes between hub and ground were always vertical as the wheel rotated. Angling of wheels encouraged the vehicle to travel straight. According to Blackmore's article in the February 1937 *GW Magazine*, the method of fitting tyre to wheel at Swindon was the exact opposite of the usual wheelwright practice where the wheel was made correct to size, but the tyre undersize, before the tyre was heated uniformly in a giant gas-ring until it slipped over the wheel and was shrunk on by rapid cooling with water. Instead, at Swindon, the wheel was made slightly larger in diameter but the tyre rolled dead to size. After heating the tyre so that it encircled the wheel, the two were placed in a hydraulic 'radial vice' that applied pressure all round so that a wheel of a specified dimension could be manufactured.

Two designs of wheel hubs (naves) are found. Early designs were fairly substantial cylinders of wood of just over 1ft in diameter into which the spokes were directly morticed. Hubs were bored to take the greased axlebox (really just a lubricated tubular metal sleeve). Parcel van hubs were smaller and essentially the same but finished off with metal rims. From about 1910, the GW began to use so-called 'artillery-type' wooden wheels that, for their designed use with gun carriages, had much greater lateral strength than conventional wagon wheels, and could be more readily re-spoked if damaged in war. In this design spokes were not mortised into the hub, but rather fitted together (mitred) all around the nave to leave a 3ins diameter hole through which a cast iron centre (bored for the greased axle) was inserted from the inside of the wheel to meet a corresponding iron cap on the outside. The outside diameters of the iron bosses were 10ins and both were nut-and-bolted together from either side of the wheel directly through the ends of the spokes (six bolts for 12-spoked wheels; seven for 10-spoke). (When the standard-size boss was used on very small wheels, it made them look as if they were solid.) On repair, older vehicles were re-wheeled with the new design, resulting in some cases of 4-wheel vehicles having different hubs on two axles. Artillery wheels had been used on steam wagons, and the shape was later used on motor vehicles just before and after WW1 where the whole wheel was pressed out of steel.

No brakes were fitted on the first horse-drawn vehicles. Instead, a chain was hung from the body in front of the rear wheels, which would be wound round a spoke and tied back to

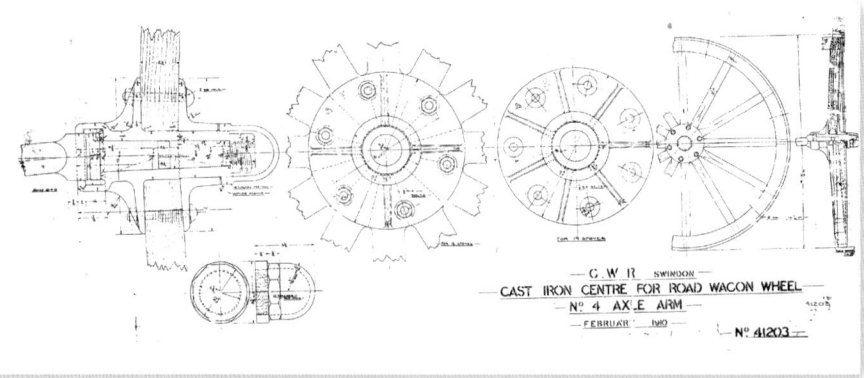

Above: **Cast iron wheel centres.**

Left: **The wheel section of the Road Wagon shop at Swindon in January 1915 showing part-assembled artillery-pattern wheels.**
GWR/P J Kelley collection

Above: Horse parcel van fleet 6286 roped and chained to G11 Hydra 42299 of 1899 *en route* to Plymouth in 1947. The van is probably to Diagram D2 and has artillery hubs. The *Road Motor Department* and its successors (*Road Transport Dept* and *Road Motor Engineer's Dept*) had two passenger well wagons for its own use, namely 42289/90 to Diagram G16, coded Hydra. *J H Russell*

The sawmill at Swindon with a log suspended from the Stothert & Pitt overhead 10-ton gantry crane. *J H Russell*

prevent movement when parked. In addition, skids (tapered blocks of wood) were chained to the wagon and were to be put under the rear wheel to chock it from rolling either up or down a hill. The safe way of 'skidding' a wheel was to chain the spoke first (Kelley, p9). When the vehicle was moving, the harness of the horse helped control the speed downhill. The skid could also be used to control speed and some heavy vehicles had a roller behind the rear wheels to prevent runaways. Brake blocks acting against the rear wheels began to be fitted to parcel vans at the turn of the 19th/20th centuries and later became common on other horse-drawn vehicles. They were applied by the carman either by footbrake or by lever handbrake depending on the design of the vehicle; on heavier wagons brakes were sometimes applied by rotation of a hand-wheel.

Wheel bearings in the hubs of horse-drawn wagons were plain.

Left: **The Road Wagon shop at Swindon with all sorts of horse vehicles in various states.** *GWR/D J Hyde collection*

Below: **The Road Wagon shop at Swindon at the turn of the 19th/20th centuries showing the multiplicity of other items manufactured there (tables, chairs, ladders, wheel barrows and so on). Lettered train destination boards at bottom right. Various road vehicles in background including passenger stage coach at middle top right.** *GWR/D J Hyde collection*

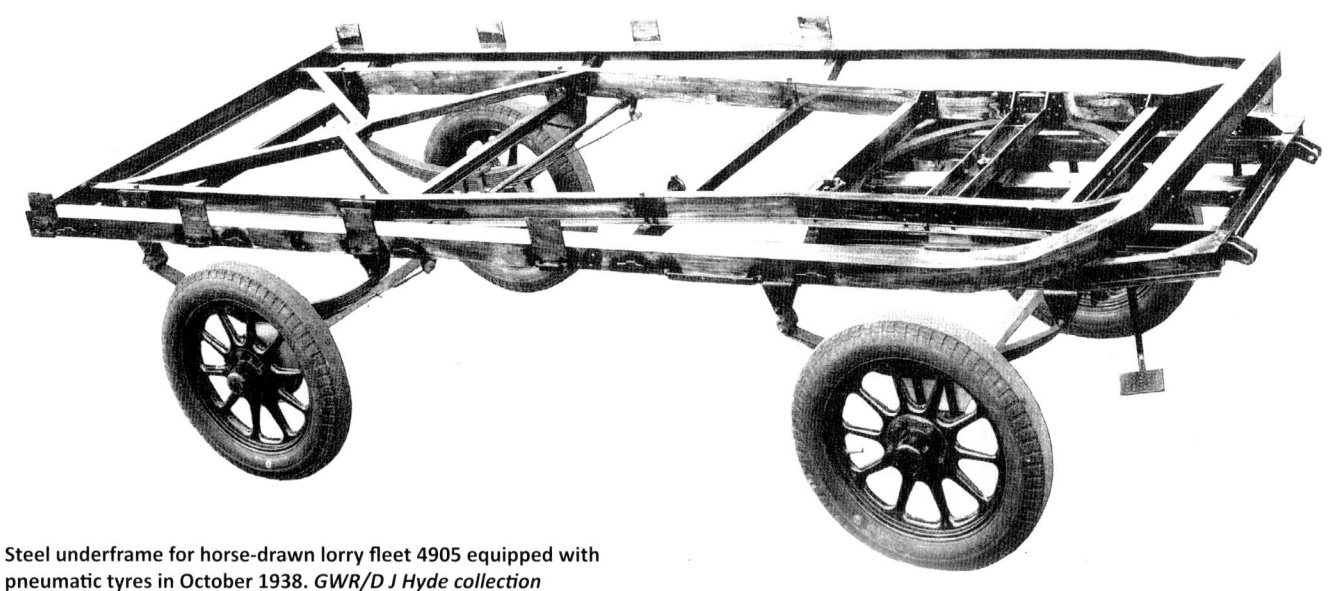

Steel underframe for horse-drawn lorry fleet 4905 equipped with pneumatic tyres in October 1938. *GWR/D J Hyde collection*

New Work Order 3468 1937.

Bulkeley, in 1921, gave details of tests done on horse vehicles, some of which were fitted with ball bearings and some left plain. Animals climbed a 580yd long hill with gradients of 1-in-16 to 1-in-23. The pulses and respirations of the horses were taken before and after the climb, and the time taken for the animal to return to normal conditions; the time to travel up the incline was also noted. Starting from rest, the tests showed that the effort required to start a traditional plain-bearing cart loaded with 15 cwt was able to start a ball-bearing-fitted cart loaded with 33cwt. At the end of a day's work, the reduction in friction made a horse less fatigued. However, it wasn't until much later that a GW horse-drawn vehicle was built which had ball-bearing wheels. An experimental horse-drawn van was put into service at Oxford in 1937, which also incorporated other 'modern' features, such as pneumatic tyres, electric lighting and motor car hub brakes. The driver's seat was recessed into the body with a projecting canopy and a scuttle dash in front, thus protecting him from the weather. Five similar vehicles were built in 1938, some as open flat lorries.

Some idea of the costs of construction of horse wagons, and how costs increased with time, may be gleaned from the following: for London cartage in 1882, William Dean (Loco Superintendent) was asked by the Horse Committee to construct 12 pair-horse pole vans at an estimated cost of £44 each; 1 piano van (£50); and one parcels collecting van (£44). In 1904 a pair-horse tilt parcel van cost £60/7/3d; and six one-horse goods vans £288/4/4d, i.e. £48 each. In 1912, a float for glass to be stationed at South Lambeth was £65; one-horse vans were £50 each; 2-horse vans £65 each (£100 in 1919); one-horse lorries £50 each (£75 in 1919); two-horse lorries £65 each; a 3-horse van £72; a 4½-ton timber carriage for Tyseley £60; a 10-ton timber carriage £90; a 10-ton lorry £75; crank-axle cart (2-wheel float) £44; and a pony van £56. In 1922, two one-horse covered goods lorries were built in the Road Wagon shop to Diagram A9 for Leamington and Bristol; three one-horse goods lorries to Diagram A10 for Oxford,

Long wheelbase one-horse flatbed lorry designed with pneumatic tyres and internal-expanding drum brakes on rear wheels (operated by driver using lever to pull on wires seen below vehicle). 'Tare 0-16-2' in script below frame of small tilt to cover driver. Photographed 7/5/47. *STEAM Swindon*

the cost of the three being £71/19/7; one to Diagram A11 for Bristol; and two to Diagram A15 for Swindon. The value of equipment may also be gauged by sums (given in Chapter 9) paid to agents when their vehicles were taken over.

Some cartage vehicles were owned by joint companies such as the Shrewsbury & Hereford, and after the Grouping some rationalisation took place, such as two single-horse drays being withdrawn from joint ownership at Tenbury Wells and absorbed into GW stock.

There were also internal users of horse-drawn equipment, such as the mechanical and civil engineers' departments, not only before motors were introduced but even as late as 1944 (Chapter 8). In 1911 it was necessary to run off water along a section of the Kennet & Avon canal near Semington and, to prevent loss of water, a temporary bay was to be formed using a 66ft long baulk of pine weighing 6½tons. The log was carted on a timber carriage from the goods yard at Devizes to the canal wharf, rolled into the water and towed to Semington. Another pole wagon was built on lot 278 in 1919 to be used along the Kennet & Avon canal.

There were 577 horse-drawn vehicles at Paddington in 1908. In 1913 the company's total fleet was 3,610 horse wagons and the GW's total grew to 4,027 by absorption at the Grouping and by purchase of Agents' equipment. Up until 1934 replacement of cartage horses by motors had been on an ad hoc basis, but thereafter a deliberate policy arose of completely motorising the cartage fleet at certain stations. It is significant that it was in 1934 that the three-wheeled 'mechanical horse' and articulated trailer was introduced on a widespread basis at a large number of goods stations across the system, and this type of vehicle figured prominently in the all-motor cartage fleets. There were 3,700 horse-drawn wagons in 1935, and it had dropped to 2,827 vehicles in 1939. Repairs of old road vehicles went on, of course, particularly wheels. In 1939, for example, 445 horse-drawn vehicles were repaired at Swindon. In 1940 there were entries in New Work Orders for the Road Wagon shop 'to make good damage to GW horse-drawn road vehicles due to enemy action'. To help save on petrol during WW2, 24 new one-horse drays were built between December 1940 and August 1942 on lot 774 (no new horse vehicles had been built since 1935). The next lot, 775, concerned the manufacture between May and August 1941 of 12 one-horse drays in which 'parts recovered from vehicles damaged by enemy action at Small Heath [were] to be utilised'. In August 1943 12 single-horse lorries were built for returned empties traffic at a cost of £1380, and 30 more in 1946 at £4500, all to Swindon drawing No 119870/Slough drawing HV49 (on the formation of the *Road Transport Department* in 1922, which took over responsibility for horse-drawn vehicles from the Paddington 'horse department'. Slough incorporated the existing Swindon road-wagon drawing numbers into its own numbering scheme for motors, so that a given horse-vehicle diagram was known by two numbers). Note that in the New Work Order for returned empties, reference is made to 'sheet bows' that presumably means hoopsticks. At the end of 1947, the number of GW horse wagons and carts had dropped to 2,357.

The idea of using redundant horse lorries as trailers to be towed by motor tractor is described in Chapter 6. Chapter 8 also explains that when horse-drawn floats and other vehicles were converted to be drawn by tractor, they received fleet numbers prefixed by the letter 'T' to conform to the way motor trailers were numbered; *no* horse-drawn vehicle had a T-prefixed number. An intriguing NWO for March 1955 in BR days was to 'Construct and Paint 4-wheeled low-loading horse trolley with drawbar, fitted with wheels having solid rubber tyres to sketch and photographs supplied, and despatch to The Irish Traffic Superintendent, Waterford, Ireland'.

CHAPTER THREE

HORSES & STABLING

As explained in Chapter 1, goods cartage using GW equipment and horses had been established in 1855 at Hockley, on the opening of the broad gauge line from Birmingham to Wolverhampton, at a time when elsewhere on the GW customers were expected themselves to collect and deliver goods — GW agents being employed for cartage in only a few of the larger towns. The GW Board of Directors set up a *Committee of the Horse Establishment* to oversee affairs at Hockley, and it would not be until 1883 that Paddington became as important as Birmingham, after which the GW Horse Superintendent was moved to London.

At Hockley there were veterinary and rest facilities, and a department for making harnesses and other equipment. Hockley supplied horses for many GW bus services such as that between Ilfracombe and Barnstaple (see *Russell*). James Grierson (from 1857 Chief Goods Manager at Paddington and then the first General Manager of the enlarged GWR in October 1863) was asked in 1867 to investigate rumours that company horses at Birmingham were being overworked or otherwise improperly treated. He went fully into it with Mr Allen the Superintendent of the Horse Department at Hockley, Mr Bill the District Goods Manager, the Hockley Station Master and others. Mr Allen had been in charge of horses since 1855 when the depot was first established. Careful enquiry was made as to the time at which horses went out in the morning and returned in the middle of the day, the amount of work they were required to perform, and the time at which they returned to the stables in the evening. No complaint had been made for many years and there was no evidence of improper working; the staff paid every attention to the health of the animals. There was however criticism of stable provision; there was accommodation for 101 horses at Hockley, exclusive of three loose boxes but, including 'store stock' (horses kept in reserve), there were 130 horses at the station. Thirty had to be kept in rented stables near the depot, which was unsatisfactory. There had been repeated applications to the Board for more stabling and eventually £375 was voted for the purpose, but when Mr Grierson sent in his report in August 1867, building of the extra stables had yet to commence.

Rail 250/680

Great Western Railway
General Manager's Office
Paddington Station
London W. August 1867

Gentlemen,

In accordance with your instructions given at the last Meeting of the Board for me to report if the complaints which were said to have been made as to the overworking or other improper use of the Company's Horses particularly at Birmingham I have to state that I have visited that Station and have gone fully into the question with Mr Allen the Superintendent of the Horse Department, Mr Bell the Goods Manager of the District, the Station Master, and others.

I find that at Birmingham there is at present Stable Accommodation for 101 Horses exclusive of three loose boxes and there are including Store Stock 130 Horses at the Station. At present 30 Horses are kept at various stables rented in the neighbourhood of the Station which is very objectionable and repeated applications have been made to the Board for further accommodation and eventually on the ___ day of ___ they authorized Stables to be erected at a cost of £375 which are not yet commenced, but if done would afford sufficient accommodation for all the Horses at present kept there by the Company.

I made careful enquiry as to the time went out in the Morning at which they returned in the middle of the day, the amount of work they are required to perform and the time at which they returned to the Stables in the evening, and I am satisfied that the Horses are not overworked, but on the contrary not only Mr Allen but the Goods Staff pay every attention to the proper working and health of the Horses.

I made strict enquiries so as to ascertain whether there are any grounds for complaint in the subject and was assured by all parties including Mr Allen that no complaint had been made nor had any case arisen for making any for several years past, nor can any explanation be given as to how rumours which were referred to at the Board had arisen.

I annex Extracts from the Books shewing the number of hours which the Horses were out on three days which I required to be taken out at random from the Books and which I am sure will shew satisfactorily that the Horses are not overworked.

I am Gentlemen,
Yours faithfully
J. Grierson.

Monday July 29th 1867

No Team	No Horses	Time at dinner H. M.	Time in at night H. M.	No Team	No Horses	Time at dinner H. M.	Time in at night H. M.
1	2	Not in	7 30	17	3	Not in	7 20
2	2	" 0	8 10	18	2	Not in	7 15
3	2	1 40	7 40	19	2	2 20	7 50
4	2	1 15	7 30	20	2	3 15	8 0
5	2	3 0	7 30	21	2	2 25	6 45
6	2	Not in	8 20	22	3	Not in	7 0
7	2	1 55	7 15	23	2	2 15	7 45
8	2	1 15	7 15	25	1	2 45	6 45
9	2	1 15	7 20	26	2	Not in	7 0
10	3	2 0	8 15	28	2	2 50	7 20
11	2	2 25	6 15	31	2	2 30	7 0
12	3	2 10	7 0	33	2	2 25	8 0
13	2	1 15	7 20	34	2	Not in	7 0
14	1	" 45	6 30	44	1	1 45	6 45
15	2	2 20	7 20	45	2	2 40	6 45
16	2	2 30	7 45	46	2	2 10	8 15

Monday July 29th 1867 continued

No Team	No Horses	Time at dinner H. M.	Time in at night H. M.	No Team	No Horses	Time at dinner H. M.	Time in at night H. M.
47	2	1 45	7 30	64	2	Not in	7 45
51	2	2 20	7 45	65	1	2 30	7 10
52	3	2 35	6 45	66	1	2 20	7 10
55	2	2 0	7 45	68	1	2 5	7 5
57	2	2 50	7 15	72	3	Not in	7 0
58	2	Not in	7 10	161	2	2 15	7 30
62	2	2 0	7 0				

Wednesday 31st July 1867

No Team	No Horses	Time at dinner	Time in at night	No Team	No Horses	Time at dinner	Time in at night
1	2	2 5	7 30	25	1	2 5	7 0
2	2	Not in	8 30	26	2	Not in	7 30
3	2	Not in	8 0	28	2	2 5	7 40
4	2	1 0	7 45	31	2	1 50	8 30
5	2	Not in	7 20	32	2	Not in	8 30
6	2	2 20	8 30	33	3	Not in	6 45
7	2	1 0	7 0	44	1	2 0	7 0
8	2	2 5	7 45	45	2	2 10	8 30
9	2	4 0	8 0	46	2	2 15	8 15
10	3	Not in	8 0	47	2	Not in	8 15
11	2	Not in	7 0	51	2	Not in	7 0
12	3	Not in	7 30	52	3	2 45	7 15
13	2	1 20	7 15	55	2	1 35	7 30
14	1	Not in	7 0	57	2	Not in	7 10
15	2	2 30	7 40	58	2	1 45	7 15
16	2	1 50	7 45	62	2	1 55	7 15
17	3	Not in	8 15	64	2	2 50	8 0
18	2	2 20	7 20	65	1	Not in	7 30
19	2	2 15	7 10	66	1	2 30	7 30
20	2	2 30	8 0	68	2	2 5	7 40
21	1	Not in	7 30	72	3	1 50	6 15
22	3	Not in	7 30	161	2	2 30	7 30
23	2	1 40	7 45				

Friday August 2nd 1867

No Team	No Horses	Time at dinner H. M.	Time in at night H. M.	No Team	No Horses	Time at dinner H. M.	Time in at night H. M.
1	2	1 35	7 20	25	1	1 45	7 40
2	2	Not in	7 20	26	2	Not in	7 10
3	2	2 25	7 15	31	2	2 0	6 15
4	2	1 25	7 30	33	2	1 50	8 0
5	2	2 0	8 0	34	3	1 50	7 15
6	2	2 25	8 30	44	1	2 0	6 0
7	2	1 50	7 30	45	2	1 55	7 10
8	2	1 30	7 45	46	2	Not in	8 20
9	2	1 55	7 40	47	2	1 50	8 0
10	3	2 15	7 40	51	2	2 0	7 15
11	2	2 0	7 10	52	3	Not in	7 20
12	3	Not in	7 20	55	2	2 0	7 45
13	2	1 45	7 20	57	2	2 25	7 10
14	1	2 10	7 10	58	2	2 0	7 50
15	2	2 55	7 30	62	2	1 45	7 20
16	2	2 30	7 30	64	2	Not in	7 40
17	3	2 15	7 45	65	1	Not in	7 15
18	2	1 55	7 30	66	2	1 55	7 40
19	2	1 45	7 45	68	1	1 50	7 0
20	2	1 55	8 0	72	3	1 40	7 20
21	1	2 0	7 15	161	2	2 35	7 0
22	3	2 10	7 30				
23	2	2 5	7 40				

Later, Grierson sent a detailed report to the Board in February 1869 about the company's stock of horses, their management and the quantity of provender supplied compared with other companies. By that time, the GW had a total of 297 horses, of which 120 were stationed at Hockley in Birmingham and the remainder distributed mainly around the Northern and West Midland districts. Comparative figures were given for the average purchase cost of horses, viz: £37/7/0, GW; £34/10/0, GNR; £44/10/0, LNWR; and £48 (J C Wall, B&E agent). [When the GW depot at Brixham was provided with horses in 1908, they were priced at £55 each.] The average weekly cost of horses including fodder was £1/0/9½d (GW); 15/¼d (GN); and £1/2/7½d (Younghusband — one of the GW's contractors in London). Since nearly one half of GW animals were based at Hockley, a fairer comparison was with the other principal carriers in Birmingham, viz: the Midland Rly, Pickfords, and Messrs Crowleys (Grierson's letter stated that the LNWR had no horses of their own for carting in Birmingham). It was found that the GW fed their horses 44½ lbs of fodder per day; the MR 34lbs; Pickfords 41½ lbs; and Crowleys 41lbs, all with variations in the mix. Mr Grierson asked Mr Leney (another of the GW's horse contractors in London) to go to Birmingham with Mr Lambert (later to become GW Goods Manager) to examine the condition of horses belonging to the company and to other carriers. Mr Leney concluded that the quantity of food given to GW horses was too much and that they could do their work, and remain in as good condition, on less food including substitution of maize (Indian corn) for oats. Mention was made in the letter that horses on the joint Shrewsbury and Hereford line were fed by the GW, but on the joint Birkenhead line by the LNWR. Data for 1868 showed that much more food was given to the S&H horses than those on the Birkenhead line, even though the work done was no different and the horses in no better condition. The S&H ration was reduced gradually to the Birkenhead level and no deterioration in condition or performance was found.

Other topics raised in the letter were (a) the number of 'rest horses': the GW kept 7½% of its total stock which was rather less than other companies — Younghusband kept up to 29% at rest but this reflected the very heavy work they did; and (b) depreciation: the initial quality of bought-in animals, and the work they had to do, governed the average length of service of GW horses which was, at that time, about 6 years. Taking into account the amounts received for worn-out and disabled horses, carcases and manure, a depreciation rate of 16% was employed by the GW. The letter concluded that costs of shoeing, harnesses and veterinary attendance was about the average of other companies.

In order to give the Superintendent of Horses, Mr Allen, more time to inspect GW animals across the system, a new person was appointed to take charge of provender. There were 13 GW-owned horses at Birkenhead, Chester (6), Liverpool (4), Saltney (5), Shrewsbury (7), Warrington (1), and Worcester (7). Closer to home, there were about 30 horses at Wolverhampton; Bilston had 6 including 2 shunting horses; Kidderminster 6 plus 3 shunting horses (it was considered a fire risk to use shunting locomotives near the local carpet factories and wool stores); Wednesbury 8; and West Bromwich 15. Dudley and Swan village also had a few GW horses.

As mentioned above, horses used by the broad gauge GW at Paddington Station were provided by contactors such as J T Younghusband & Son who also later supplied horses for both Smithfield underground depot (opened 1869) and Poplar depots (1878), where they were accommodated in rented private stables (at Poplar, rented from the North London Rly). Another contractor for horses and harness was S & E Leney of Norwich who supplied 250 horses for London GW cartage in 1869 and later 300 for goods work together with 52 horses for parcels work. Drivers, carmen and van-boys were appointed by the GW.

Among the various provisions, horses would be walked from their stables to GW premises to start work under rules (such as dismissal of grooms for cruelty). Rent was £94/10 per year for every horse, and 1/- per horse per week for stabling at the Bull & Mouth coaching inn, that later became the GW Receiving Office at St Martin's le Grand leased by the GW. Under Schedule A: trollies, vans and carts under 30cwt, and travelling at less than 5mph, would work for 12 hours/day (the time being calculated from the time the horses reached GW premises) and were expected to go out on 2 journeys/day totalling 18 miles daily from Paddington. Schedule B shows the distribution of stabling at Paddington, at the Bull & Mouth coaching inn, at Crutched Friars, at GW offices in the Strand and at Holborn.

Having determined to perform cartage itself in London, the GW decided in 1875 to build new stables at Paddington and Smithfield for 288 and 120 horses respectively. Stables (initially on two floors) at Paddington were in South Wharf Road parallel with, but some distance behind, what was then the arrival side of the station (and are now part of St Mary's Hospital). They were called the 'Mint stables' because of the nearby 'Mint' public house: the records of the Sun Fire Insurance Co in the London Metropolitan Archives show that in 1839 the landlord of the pub was William Henry Smith.

Additions to the GW stud in 1881 were five horses stabled at Cilely colliery, one of the mines owned by the company at that time to supply loco coal (see *GWR Goods Train Working*). The Horse Committee in March 1882 approved an additional stall to be added to the stables at Great Bridge (Birmingham) at a cost of £17/9/0, and that two extra shunting horses be provided at Great Bridge and at West Bromwich. In anticipation of the GW itself performing more and more of its London cartage, the Horse Committee recommended that Mr Leney's contract be terminated and that steps be taken for the purchase and accommodation of GW horses in London.

The government had a voluntary registration scheme with owners of large studs of horses that could be requisitioned for military purposes. According to the agreement of March 1889, there were 100 'heavy, medium and light' draught horses from Paddington, and 50 from Hockley for which a retainer was paid to the GW. Under the Army Horse Reserve Agreement of 13/3/1913, the GW was obliged to supply 221 horses in return for cost price plus 50%. Action was taken as soon as WW1 broke out, and an additional 40 light draft horses from Paddington, and 12 from Hockley, were commandeered. [In the so-called *Subsidy Scheme* for motor vehicles after WW1 the government paid to manufacturers

Dated 7 December 186_

The Great Western
Railway Company

— and —

Mr. Sam Leney

Contract for the hire of
250 Horses for the Company's
London Cartage Business.

Be it remembered that before the date and execution of the within written Contract it has been found necessary for the within named Sam Leney to pay a considerably higher Rent for Stables than was contemplated when he tendered for the said Contract, and that the Company have therefore agreed to allow and pay to him in addition to the sums of money payable under and by virtue of the said Contract the further sum of Three hundred pounds per annum as a contribution towards such Rent by equal quarterly payments during so long as he shall perform all the engagements on his part contained in the within written Agreement he the said Sam Leney rendering to the Company a quarterly account (duly vouched) of the Rent so paid by him and of the contribution from them due in respect thereof.

Witness   Sam Leney

Articles of Agreement

made this seventh day of December One thousand eight hundred and sixty six **Between** The Great Western Railway Company (hereinafter called "The Company") on the one part and Sam Leney of Thorpe Hamlet Norwich Contractor (hereinafter called "The Contractor") of the other part.

The Company, on the one part, and the Contractor, on the other part, mutually and reciprocally agree, the one with the other, faithfully to perform and fulfil, on the part of each, the stipulations clauses and agreements hereinafter contained that is to say —

Contractor to provide and Company to hire 250 Horses.
1. **The** Contractor shall provide and supply, each working day throughout the year, and the Company shall hire and pay for, two hundred and fifty Horses in good working condition fit and suitable in every way for the daily performance of the usual and ordinary work of the Company as Carriers in London. Such Horses shall be in all respects of the description and in accordance with the Specification in Schedule A hereunto annexed. Should a larger number than two hundred and fifty be required at any time during the continuance of this Contract, for the purposes of the Company's work as such Carriers as aforesaid, the Contractor shall provide such extra Horses, not exceeding fifty, for such period as the Company may at any time, and from time to time, require the same for such

Number of extra Horses not to exceed 50.

---

extra work **Provided** That the Company shall not be bound to take any such extra Horses from the Contractor, but may hire the same from other parties upon any terms they think proper.

Suitable Harness to be provided.
2. **Each** Horse shall be fitted with proper Harness suited in all respects for the work which may be required by the Company to be done, and which harness shall be maintained in a thorough state of repair, and kept clean and shall have polished brass mountings having on the usual place the letters "G.W.R." and all the said Horses shall at all times be kept by the Contractor well fed, clean, in good condition, and fit for the daily work and shall be under the control and subject to the approval of the Superintendent for the time being of the Goods Department at the Paddington Station of the Company or any other person who may be appointed by the Company for the purpose; and on every occasion when the said Superintendent, or such other person as aforesaid, shall at any time object to any Horse or Horses supplied by the Contractor under this Contract as being disabled, vicious or otherwise unfit for the work required, and shall give notice in writing thereof to the Contractor such Horse or Horses shall be immediately removed and another or others shall be immediately supplied in place of the same so that the Company shall always have Two hundred and fifty Horses in good working condition to do the daily work usually done by Carriers and required for the Company's carrying trade in London, and if within twenty four hours of

Horses to be kept fit for work.

Horses objected to by the Superintendent to be removed.

Company to be at liberty to hire of other persons if Horses are not removed upon Notice.

[Page 10 - top left]

such Notice the Contractor shall fail so to remove and replace such Horse or Horses, the Company shall be at liberty to hire another Horse or Horses at the expense of the Contractor to replace every such Horse as aforesaid and to deduct the amount of such hire from any monies due, or to become due, to the Contractor under this Contract.—

[margin: Horses to be brought to and taken from their work by Contractor]

The Horses to be supplied under this Contract shall be taken to their Work by the Contractor at his expense to the Goods Station at Paddington aforesaid; the "Bull and Mouth" Receiving Office, St. Martin's le Grand; and to such other place or places as the said Superintendent or other person as aforesaid from time to time directs and as many men as may be necessary shall be supplied by the Contractor to take the Horses to and from their work at the respective times of commencing and completing the same. The times when the Horses are required to be employed and to be taken away, shall be in the sole discretion of the said Superintendent or other the person appointed by the Company as aforesaid; and the Contractor and his Servants shall at all times and in all things attend and conform to such regulations as by the said Superintendent, or other person, as aforesaid, may from time to time be issued, and be applicable to the said Horses or Servants under this Contract. The Company's van boys will, if required, assist in this duty under the superintendence of the Contractor's Servants, but the acceptance of such assistance by the Contractor shall relieve the Company from all liability in respect to such service so gratuitously rendered. Schedule B hereunto

[margin: Times for Horses to be at work to be at discretion of Superintendent]

[Top right]

annexed, shews the manner in which it is proposed to commence the ordinary daily working of the Horses under this Contract, but the Superintendent, or other person, as aforesaid, may from time to time, alter or vary such working in such manner as he may consider the exigencies of the service require.

[margin: Company to appoint Drivers and Carmen]

All the Drivers and Carmen shall be appointed by the Company, but if the Contractor shall at any time consider that his Horses are not properly used by such Drivers and Carmen, the Contractor shall complain to, and report his objection in writing to the said Superintendent or other person as aforesaid who shall at once investigate and decide on the matter; and in the meantime and until such decision, such Driver and Carman shall be suspended from duty. And if such Superintendent, or other person, shall consider that the Contractor has good cause of complaint, he shall remove such cause of complaint immediately, or remove the Driver or Carman from their employ; and if the said Superintendent, or other person, shall consider and decide that the Contractor has no cause of complaint, then the Contractor may appeal from such decision to the Board of Directors of the Company whose decision in all such cases shall be final and conclusive between the parties. And in the event of any Driver or Carman, being once dismissed for cruelty to his Horses, or any other offence affecting this Contract, he shall not be allowed again to return to his duty.—

[margin: Contractor's complaint to be at once investigated by the Superintendent]
[margin: Contractor may appeal to the Board]

[Bottom left]

[margin: Horses hired of other persons in lieu of Contractor's Horses to be paid for by Contractor]

5. If at any time it shall become necessary for the Company to hire Horses from other persons than the Contractor, in consequence of the Contractor not supplying the number and description of Horses hereinbefore contracted for, then the sum or sums which the Company shall pay for such hire shall be borne by the Contractor, and may be deducted from the sums payable to the Contractor under this Agreement.

[margin: Loss or damage by Horses to be made good by Contractor]

6. In case any damage or loss shall arise to the Company through the neglect or default of the Contractor or his Servants, or any damage or loss shall arise, or be occasioned to the property of the Company, or to the property of any other person or persons entrusted to them, and for which the Company may be liable, or be called upon to pay by reason or in consequence, directly or indirectly, of the viciousness, incapacity, or fault of the said Horses, or any of them, all such losses shall be made good to the Company by the Contractor, and the amount thereof may be deducted from any sums due to the Contractor under this Agreement; provided that the Contractor shall not be liable or responsible for any damage or loss which may be occasioned by, or happen solely from, foul driving by the Company's Servants; but any damage so occasioned shall be borne by the Company.

[margin: Contractor not to be liable for consequences of foul driving]

7. If any accident or damage shall arise to any of the Horses or Harness, to be supplied by the Contractor under this Agreement, solely from bad or unskilful driving, or solely from the fault of the Servants of the Company, the Contractor shall be entitled to receive from the Company and the Company shall pay to the Contractor, such sum as may be fair and reasonable for such accident or damage

[margin: Damage to Horses or Harness by default of Company's Servants to be paid for by Company]

[Bottom right]

[margin: Amount to be paid for yearly hire]

8. The Company shall pay to the Contractor, in full, for the daily use and hire of the aforesaid Horses and Harness, for keeping the same continually in good order and condition as aforesaid and for all other charges of the Contractor attending the execution of this Contract the price or sum following; that is to say, at, and after the rate of Ninety four pounds ten shillings per Annum for every one of the Two hundred and fifty Horses coming within the description set forth in the Specification hereunto annexed.—

[margin: Contractor to have the use of Stables at "Bull and Mouth" during Company's tenancy]

9. The Company shall allow the Contractor to have the use of the Stables of the Company, at the "Bull and Mouth" Receiving House aforesaid up to Michaelmas next, or longer if the Company's tenancy shall be extended therein; and the Contractor shall pay or allow to the Company the sum of One shilling per Horse per Week for every Horse which the Company may require to be kept from time to time at such Stables, the number of such Horses to be ascertained at the end of each week.—

[margin: Accounts to be rendered fortnightly]

10. The Contractor shall deliver his accounts to the Company and the Company shall adjust the same every fortnight, and the amount due upon such accounts shall be paid every fortnight, on or before the last day of every fortnight succeeding that for which payment is asked

[margin: Term of commencement of Contract]

11. This Contract shall commence and continue in force for the term of three years from Twenty fourth June One thousand eight hundred and sixty 9; and after the expiration of that period of three years the same shall continue as a Contract from year to year; subject nevertheless

Determination of Contract.

to be determined by the Company at any time after the expiration of the said three years, upon giving to the Contractor three calendar Months previous Notice in writing of the intention of the Company to determine the same by delivering such Notice personally to the Contractor or by leaving the same at his last known place of abode or business and the Contractor may by a like Notice in writing to be given by him to the Company addressed to the Secretary and left for them at the Paddington Station aforesaid determine the said contract at any time after the expiration of the said three years; and on the expiration of any such Notice when given the said contract shall be at an end except so far as may be necessary to determine the rights of the parties previously to such determination.

12. Contractor to give a Bond for performance of Contract.

The Contractor shall give a Bond with two Sureties to be approved of by the Company or the Security of a Guarantee Society approved of by the Company, in the penal sum of Three thousand pounds conditioned for the faithful performance on his part of this contract and shall be liable to pay to the Company the sum of Ten Pounds per day until such security shall be given and in default in any respect on the Contractor's part of the observance of this contract the said penal and other sums shall be recoverable by the Company as liquidated damages both from the Contractor and his Sureties.

13. Arbitration Clause.

If any difference (other than such as is specially provided for by Article 4) arise between the parties hereto as to the intent or effect of this Contract or as to any breach, or alleged breach thereof or as to any damages payable thereunder, or as to its incidents or consequences the same shall be referred to arbitration pursuant to the provisions of the Common Law Procedure Act 1854.

14. Name of Single Arbitrator.

Mr Seymour Clarke shall be the single Arbitrator mutually agreed on between the parties for the purposes of the last preceding clause.

As witness the Common Seal of the Company and the hand and seal of the Contractor the day and year first above written.

Schedule A.

A Specification of the Horses referred to in the foregoing Agreement

Description of Horses:

First — Horses for Spring Trollies, Vans and Carts

The Horses for the draught of Spring Trollies, Vans and Carts, shall be such as are suitable and in ordinary use by Railway Companies for their work and capable of drawing at one time, an average load of not exceeding Thirty hundredweight to each Horse used and to do a fair average day's work, at a speed not exceeding five miles per hour averaging twelve hours a day (the time to be calculated from the time the Horses reach the Company premises, until they leave their work at said premises) and capable of going such distances as the necessities of the Company's work may from day to day require

from each Horse or Team employed, and in case of need performing two journeys daily from Paddington or an average distance of Eighteen miles daily for each Horse employed.

Second — Horses for Wagons and Trollies.

The Horses for the draught of Wagons and Trollies shall be such as are suitable, and in ordinary use by Railway Companies, for their work, and capable of drawing at one time an average load of not exceeding Thirty five hundred weight for each Horse used and to do a fair average day's work, at a walking pace, averaging twelve hours a day (time to be calculated as aforesaid), and capable of going such distances as the necessities of the Company's work may from day to day require from each Horse or Team employed: and in case of need of performing two journeys daily from Paddington, or an average distance of Eighteen miles daily for each Horse employed.

The foregoing Specification represents the average daily working of the Horses, and the Company on their part will, as far as practicable, adhere to it: but they are not to be liable for any payment for excess in time, weight, distance or otherwise.

Schedule B.

Number	Vehicles Description	Number of Horses at Work Daily
Paddington		
26	1 Horse Vans	26
84	2 Ditto	168
3	4 Horse Wagons	12
5	Chain Horses	5
Bull and Mouth		
11	1 Horse Vans	11
9	2 Ditto	18
Crutched Friars		
6	1 Horse Vans	6
1	2 Ditto	2
Strand and Holborn Offices		
2	1 Horse Vans	2
	Total	250 Horses

Signed Sealed and delivered by the said
in the presence of

Sam Levy

ARTICLES OF AGREEMENT

Made the *seventh* day of *March* 1889, between *Henry Lambert* of *Paddington Station London* the General Manager of, and on behalf of the *Great Western* Railway Company, hereinafter called "the owners," of the one part, and the Inspector-General of Remounts, War Office, London, S.W., for and on behalf of Her Majesty's Principal Secretary of State for the War Department (who, and the Principal Secretary of State for the time being of the same Department, are hereinafter included in the term Secretary of State) of the other part.

1. If at any time during the continuance of this Agreement, the Secretary of State shall be of opinion and shall so certify in writing under his hand that the country is in a state of national danger, or if a Proclamation shall be issued under the Reserve Forces Act, 1882, then while such Proclamation continues in force, or such certificate remains unrevoked, the Secretary of State shall be entitled to purchase at the price or prices in that behalf mentioned in the Schedule hereto, all or any of the horses of the classes mentioned in the said Schedule, but not exceeding as regards any class the number opposite the same in the said Schedule.

2. The owners shall, within forty-eight hours after receipt, from the Secretary of State, of notice to purchase as aforesaid ~~any such horses, place~~ the same at the disposal of the War Department at the stables mentioned in the said Schedule, and all horses so delivered or placed at the disposal of the War Department shall be serviceably sound and suitable.

3. All horses at the time of purchase will be subject to inspection by some officer on behalf of the Secretary of State, and no horse need be purchased unless the same shall in the opinion of such officer be practically sound and suitable.

4. Any part of the number of horses for the time being liable to be purchased on such contingency as hereinbefore mentioned may at any time be withdrawn from this Agreement—

   (a) By the Secretary of State on notice to the owners.

   (b) By the owners with the sanction of the Secretary of State, on repayment of Ten shillings per horse for the part so withdrawn.

If any part be so withdrawn as aforesaid by the Secretary of State, the owners shall not be required to repay any sum previously paid as hereinafter mentioned in respect of horses so withdrawn.

5. The owners shall, from time to time, upon receipt from the Secretary of State of notice in that behalf, permit an inspection at such time, not later than ten days from the date of the notice, and at such place as may be mutually agreed, of all horses in their possession.

6. The owners will, during the continuance of this Agreement, maintain to the satisfaction of the Secretary of State a sufficient number of serviceable horses between the ages of 6 and 10 years, and of the classes mentioned in the Schedule hereto, to allow of a selection to be made therefrom of all or any of the horses for the time being liable to be purchased under this Agreement on such contingency as aforesaid.

7. In consideration of the owners' agreements herein contained the Secretary of State will forthwith pay to the owners the sum of Ten shillings per horse on the total number of horses mentioned in the Schedule hereto, and will henceforth, on every 29th September during the continuance of this Agreement, and if the necessary funds be provided by Parliament for that purpose, pay to the owners for their agreements herein contained for the then following twelve calendar months the sum of Ten shillings per horse, on the total number of horses then liable to be purchased under this Agreement on such contingency as aforesaid.

8. This Agreement may be determined after the 29th September, 1889, by either party giving to the other at least six calendar months' notice in writing terminating on the 28th September in any year.

9. Any notice by the Secretary of State under this Agreement may be delivered at the owners' above-mentioned address, or at any of the stables mentioned in the Schedule hereto.

AS WITNESS the hands of the parties the day and year above written.

Signature on behalf of Owners   (sd) *Hy Lambert*

Signature of Witness   (sd) *J. L. Wilkinson*
                         Paddington Station
                         London

(sd) *J. G. Marcwill*
Major-General
Inspector General
Remounts

To Messrs ...

True Copy
J. G. Marcwill
Inspector General Remounts

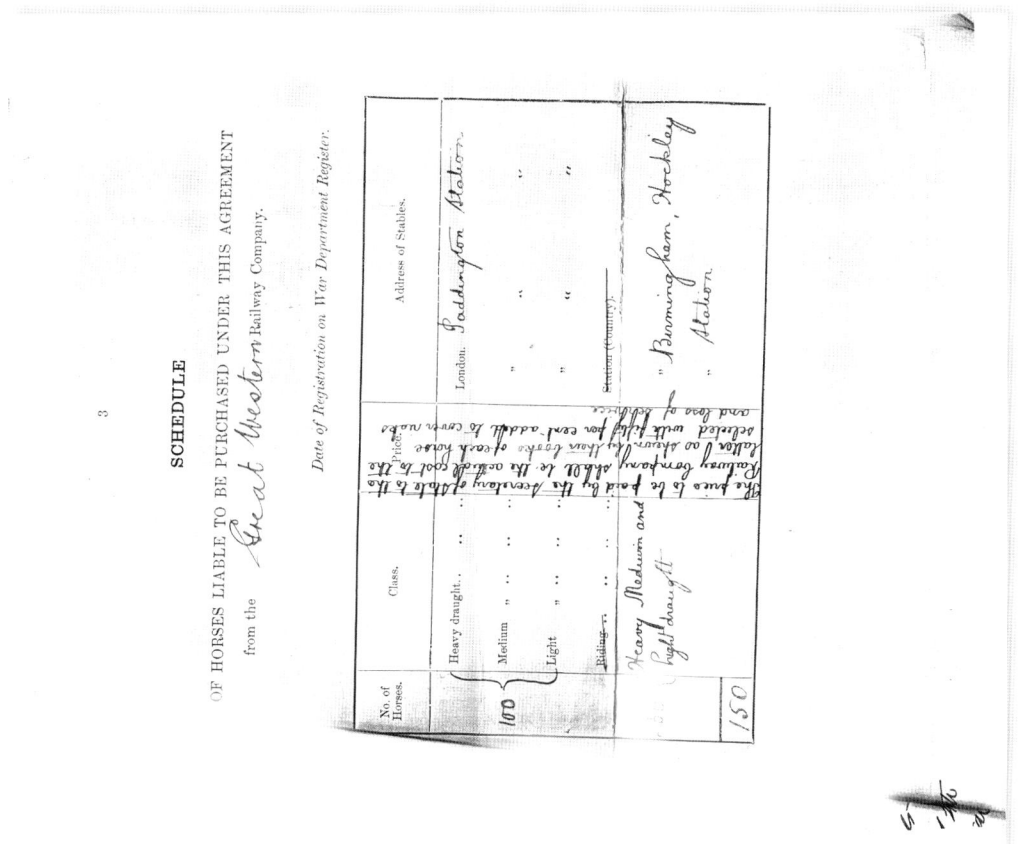

something like a third of the construction cost of certain motor chassis in order that vehicles could be taken over in time of war. A number of Thornycroft A1 chassis in the mid-1920s bought by the GW were under this arrangement, as was the Morris 6-wheeler Plynlimon bus (later tractor), fleet 1115.

By the turn of the 19th/20th centuries, the type of horse mostly employed on C&D cartage across the GW was known as the *London Van Horse.* It was lighter than the shire horse, more active and was suited to town roads. Heavy dray ('cart') horses used on goods cartage were at least 16 hands high and weighed about 17cwt (a 'hand' is equal to 4 inches and the measurement is from the ground to the withers which is the ridge between the horse's shoulder blades); parcel van horses might be 15 hands high and weigh 10cwt. The GWR's horses (both mares and geldings) were purchased at five-to-six years of age, in batches as required, and were good for anything from six to twelve years' cartage service. In the *GW Magazine* for Sept 1936, a picture is shown of the then oldest horse in GWR service — a roan mare purchased in March 1917 and still in service at Hockley; the May 1940 *Magazine* tells of the passing of 'Lion', a big bay horse, purchased in 1921, that worked at Thame from 1923 to 1940. The average price for a railway dray horse in 1900 was about £60. A large proportion of GW horses came from North and Central Wales and all would be already broken to harness on farm work.

Every horse was known by a number branded on the offside forehoof (offside being away from the gutter when driving on the left of the road). The number was shown on a card above each stall in the stables; often the carman would have an unofficial name for his animal. The number of the long-serving horse at Hockley mentioned above was No 1859, given to her in 1917.

After a batch of horses had been purchased subject to inspection by the GW vets, they were allocated to depots. Each new animal was harnessed to a pair-horse van in company with an experienced horse and tried out on the road. After new horses had become accustomed to town environments, they were selected for the type of work best suited to their strength and mobility. The more powerful horses on C&D duties usually worked singly and were expected to haul loads of 30 to 35cwts at walking pace; lighter horses worked in pairs, with 3 tons 10cwts being expected in reasonably flat urban areas. Loads would be different in hilly districts. The lightest and fastest animals were engaged in parcels work, at about 5mph. For the movement of very heavy loads, 3- and 4-horse vehicles were employed, often with special trailers. The 1900 *Railway Magazine* said that '........ a unique and noteworthy feature of the cartage service [at Paddington] is the employment of four-horse vans of nine-tons carrying capacity.......'.

Horses worked not more than a 10-hour day. There was a considerable variation in the number of horses on duty, particularly in the big towns and particularly in the days when the cartage fleet had few motor lorries. In the early years of the 20th century at Paddington, for example, some eighty horses were allocated each day to make deliveries to the Billingsgate (fish), Covent Garden (fruit and vegetable) and Smithfield (meat) markets. For this work, a start had to be made as early as 3.0am, the main exodus of the day

Right: **This passenger-carrying submarine was collected from J Yatton & Co of Carr St, Limehouse, in London E1 to put on rail. In the vicinity, only the yards at Bow Road (LTS/Met District Joint and GE) and Old Ford (NL) yards – or the GW Poplar depot in Millwall docks – would have had sufficient crane power for loading. It travelled over the North London/West London lines to Shepherd's Bush (WL) goods yard, from where it is seen being carted the few hundred yards by a three-horse team to the Japanese-British Exhibition at White City in June 1910 for a 'pleasure ride sideshow'. The raised covered walkway from Shepherd's Bush passenger station to the exhibition grounds may be seen in the right background.** *GWR/D J Hyde collection*

Above: **A boiler on a 40-ton trolley hauled by four horses at Paddington old yard in March 1911. The vehicle, fleet 1091, is similar to the Diagram B-14 wagon with trailer shown earlier, but has metal wheels rather than wooden.** *GWR/D J Hyde collection*

Left: **A 4½-ton timber carriage to Diagram C2 has built-up front stanchions to enable a load of long iron bars to be carried over the backs of the horses in the shafts of the vehicle. Photographed at Paddington new yard in March 1911.** *GWR/D J Hyde collection*

being between 8.0 and 9.00am. Before WW1, 22 cartage staff came on duty at 5.00am; 71 up to 7.30am; 218 at 8.00am; and 26 at 9.00am. The authorised number of carmen and van guards at Paddington at that time was 910 men and boys.

Before the widespread introduction of motor vehicles, the majority of GW horses in London were to be found at Paddington Goods, with additional horses (but in smaller numbers) stabled at Poplar, Victoria & Albert Docks, Smithfield, and later South Lambeth. Country centres over a large area of the southern part of the GW system were kept supplied with horses from Paddington. Telegraph codes relating to cartage horses included *Indus* — The following horse or horses ill. Wire instructions: *Stirrup* — Send vet immediately to examine; *Belfry* — Undermentioned horse hence by passenger train as follows. Wire when you are returning your sick or lame horse; *Lima* — Can you spare a horse for a few days?; *Lough* — Shunting horse ill. Send relief; *Loon* — Cannot send relief horse. Hire if absolutely necessary.

Extra stabling at Paddington was obtained in 1892 by erecting new stables for 97 horses near the approach from the Harrow Road to the goods depot; in 1897 by converting a former stores building near Westbourne Bridge into a 31-stall stable, to which 15 additional loose boxes were added in 1898; by purchasing, and converting, the buildings of All Saints Schools in Francis Street in 1900 to accommodate 41 animals; and increasing accommodation at the Mint stables where, after 1910, it was on three floors connected by ramps. Over 600 horses could be accommodated there: 50 in the basement, 261 on the ground floor, 228 on the first floor and 66 on the top floor. Note that at all stables across the GW, some horses would be sick and some kept in reserve, so the total number accommodated would not all be working simultaneously. In 1907, a 6-stall stable was added to existing accommodation at Kensington Warwick Road.

The peak size of the GW horse stud was about 3,500 in the early years of the 20th century. Just before WW1 the London studs were: Paddington, 72 on parcels, 485 on cartage, 32 shunting, 10 chain, 1 trap, 87 sick and 38 resting, totalling 725 horses; Poplar, 49 cartage, 3 chain, 3 sick, 5 resting, totalling 60; and Smithfield, 141 cartage, 9 shunting, 4 chain, 9 sick, 8 resting, totalling 171 animals.

Multi-storey stables could be found at other GW goods depots, especially in large towns where the cost of land was expensive (Cardiff Newtown, for example). As cartage agents were dispensed with and the company began to perform its own cartage, new stables or additions to existing stables were built around the system (see Chapter 9). For example, new stables at Westbury in 1899 for 3 horses; additions for 6 horses at Lawrence Hill (Bristol) in 1904; new 6-stall stables at Devizes and at Brixham (where the building cost £454) in 1908 and a 4-stall stable on the up side at Littleton & Badsey; at Hockley in 1910 nine loose boxes for sick horses were added and a 6-stall stable at Crumlin (LL) in the same year; a 6-stall stable at

Upstairs at the Mint stables, Paddington. Horse at right being groomed by man with brush in his hand. Block and tackle below to bring fodder to upper levels. *GWR/D J Hyde collection*

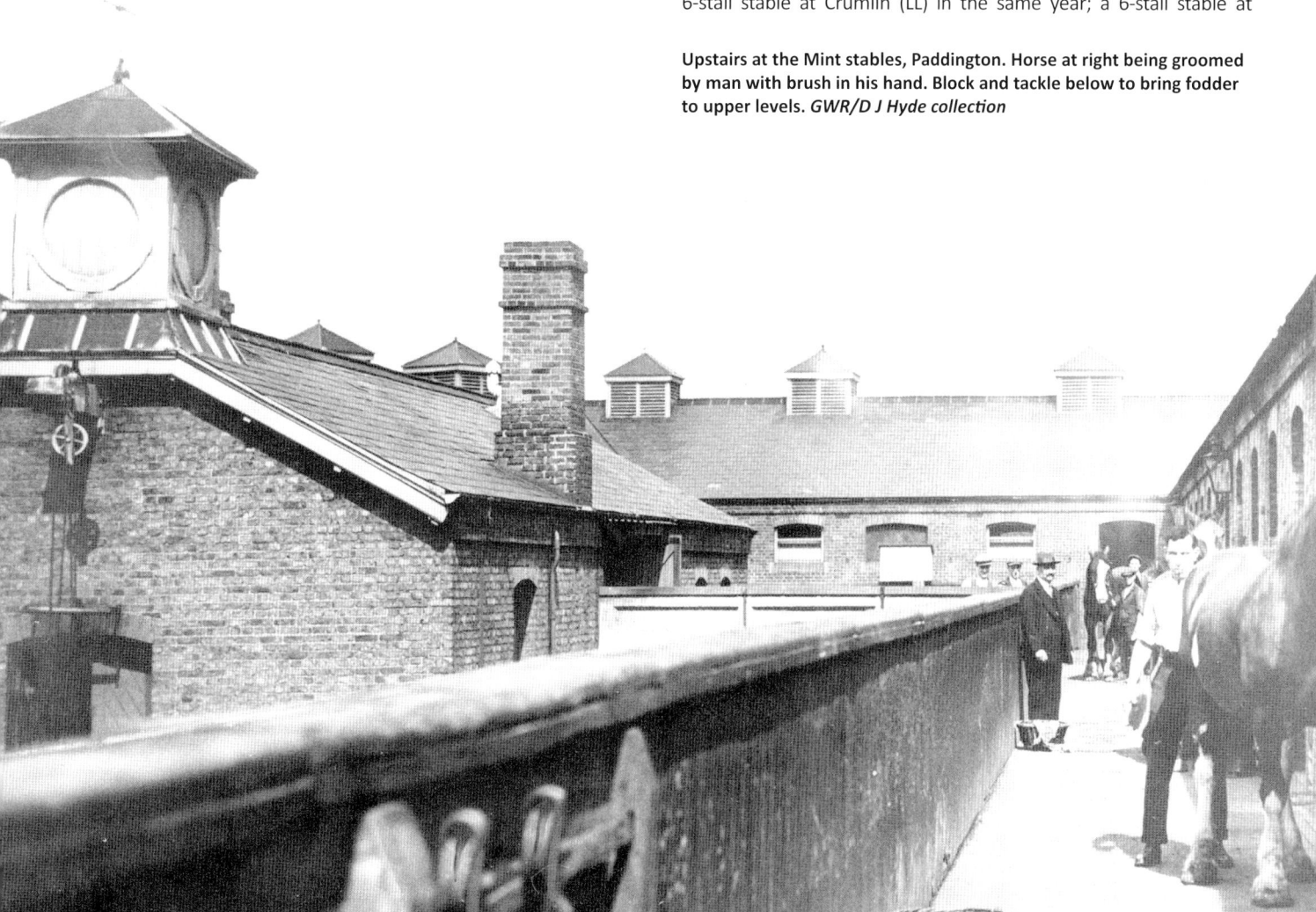

Martock in 1911; a 4-stall stable at Clevedon and 20-stall stable and cart weighbridge at Weston-super-Mare, both in 1911/12; an additional 11 stables at Handsworth in 1912; a 42-stall stable, loose boxes, provender store, drying room, and covered paved area for 8 carts at Oxford in 1912.

Building of stables was managed by the Chief (Civil) Engineer but could be contracted out to firms of builders. At that time, smaller sets of stabling cost about £500 to complete and larger much more (£5000 at Oxford in 1912). It depended on location, whether the company owned the land, and how much extra work was involved (new fencing, shortening of existing sidings to make room in the yard, and so on). In 1928, it was reported that

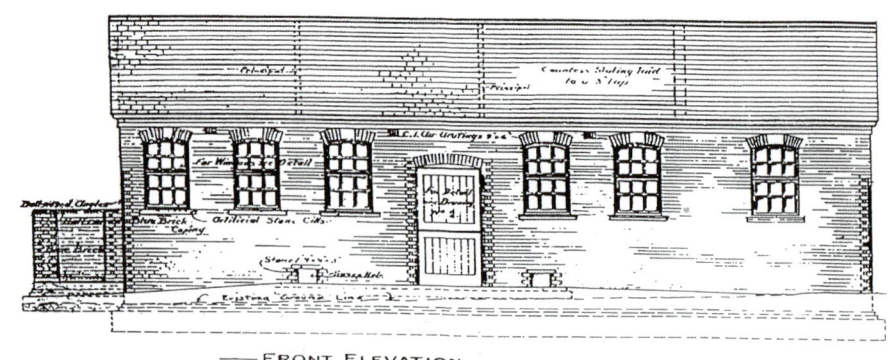

Right: **Stables built at Devizes station in 1908.** *Author's collection*

Below, left and right: **'Scenes at Paddington Stables during the Strike of May 1926'** was the title of this pair of pictures showing the same woman groom getting different horses ready for duty. *Author's collection*

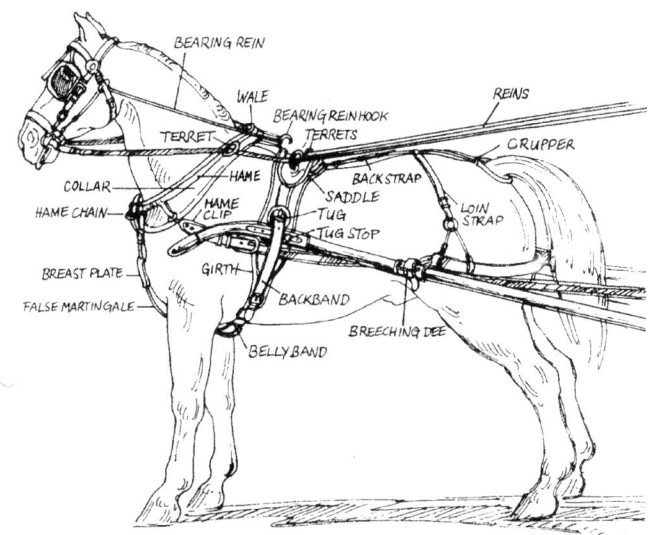

Above: **Horse nomenclature.**

Above: **Horses loaded in trailer fleet 116 ready to be taken to Castle Bar convalescent home from Paddington, using a Thornycroft lorry as tractor** *GWR/D J Hyde collection*

the Goswell Rd (Smithfield) stables were in a dangerous condition and needed to be rebuilt, including demolition of the top floor.

At many larger stables around the system, there would be a farriers' shop. Horses had to be shod surprisingly often, a month being good service for a set of shoes in regular daily use, but a horse with uneven tread may have required new shoes every fortnight. Horse shoes (fabricated from iron bar) were fitted in the farriers' shop. Shoes were made in a limited number of different, but not widely varying, sizes. Each shoe had seven nail holes — four on the outer and three on the inner side. The nails, which were three inches long, were not straight but slightly tapered in a way to help shoeing.

Great importance was attached to the harness fitting the horse properly and carmen were to report problems with collars, galling or rubbing harness to the horse foreman/station master/goods agent. Horse collars were wider at the bottom than the top, and were put on upside-down with the widest part going over the horse's head. Collars for dray horses had *hames*, two brass projections sticking up above the top of the collar, through which the reins were run. When a 'cartage establishment' was created at Brixham in 1908, a set of harnesses was priced at £6. While minor repairs to harness and shunting chains would be done locally at stations around the system, sets of harnesses requiring major repairs had to be sent to the Saddler Foreman at Hockley or, later, to the harness shop at the Mint stables. In addition to keeping an eye on the harness, it was the duty of drivers constantly to be on the alert to detect any signs of sickness in the animals. Lameness of one sort or the other was the most common complaint. In London, it was said that general illness occurred among young horses before they got used to conditions. A large float (low-floored ambulance cart), fitted with first-aid essentials, was kept in the stable yard at Paddington ready to be sent anywhere required in London to bring back injured/sick horses to the veterinary department. (Years later in 1940, a Scammell 'mechanical horse' 3-ton drop frame AL trailer coded *Dyak OU* was fitted with a horse ambulance body.)

Below: **Horse ambulance built on Scammell 3-ton drop-frame AL trailer chassis on 9/10/41. Fleet T-2151, code *Dyak OU*. Full brown and cream livery. Attendant's compartment with window over jockey wheel with door and steps to gain access on other side. Brown-encircled GWR shirtbutton painted directly on to cream sides above waist. This rear view shows that there is a trolley inside on the floor which runs up the ramp if the animal can't walk.** *GWR/P J Kelley collection*

There were two horse hospitals at Paddington — one at the extreme western end of the goods yard (isolated from the stables) having 32 loose boxes, where severe cases were dealt with; and the other at Westbourne Park stables with 30 loose boxes, where improving animals (and all cases of lameness) were accommodated. In addition, there was a convalescent centre at Castle Bar (West Ealing) near the GW sports ground

HORSE DEPARTMENT.

INSTRUCTIONS TO STATION AGENTS

AND OTHERS HAVING THE CHARGE OF HORSES.

HORSES.

1. All the Company's horses, harness, and vehicles are under the control of Captain Milne, the Horse Superintendent (whose office is at Paddington).

No horse must be removed from one Station to another, under any pretence whatever, without the authority of Captain Milne being first obtained.

2. In all cases of removal, the number card, and the collar in which the horse has been working, must be sent with it.

3. The number card of each horse must be kept in the tin case provided for it, and be placed over the stall in which the horse stands. Should one of these cards get defaced, it must be sent to the Horse Superintendent, who will cause a renewal to be supplied.

4. The monthly return (Form No. 842) of horse stock, harness, and vehicles, and horse shoeing report must be made to the Horse Superintendent on the first day of each month. Great care must be taken to see that the numbers and other particulars are properly entered, and it is important for the horses to be correctly classified.

The Station Agents are held responsible for seeing that the printed instructions for stable management are hung in each stable; and they must, by personal supervision, enforce the due observance of the instructions. At the stables in London and Birmingham the Horse Foremen will be responsible.

5. In all cases of sickness or lameness to the Company's horses, a report must be sent at once to the Horse Superintendent upon the Form supplied for that purpose (No. 3246).

DEAD HORSES.

6. Each Station Agent will be instructed from time to time of the names and addresses of the contractors appointed for removing dead horses, or of the other arrangements which may be made for that purpose.

PROVENDER.

7. All requisitions for Provender must be made (through book No. 605) to the Horse Superintendent. They will be due at his office on each alternate Thursday. The date and quantity last supplied must be entered in the space provided for the purpose, and should there be any surplus stock on hand at the time of ordering, the requisition should be made less that quantity.

A supply for fourteen days ending on a Monday must be ordered each time, except for those Stations specially instructed to order weekly, at the following scale, viz.:—

SUMMER ALLOWANCE.			WINTER ALLOWANCE.		
Hay (cut) ...	16 lbs.	per horse per day.	Hay (cut) ...	16 lbs.	per horse per day.
Oats	8 "		Oats	8 "	
Maize	6 "		Maize	6 "	
Beans	3 "		Beans	5 "	
Bran	2 "		Bran	2 "	

The date for changing these allowances at the beginning and close of each winter will be fixed by the Horse Superintendent.

The quantities given do not apply to the Barnstaple and Ilfracombe Coaching Stud, or to small horses used in parcels carts, traps, etc. For these horses a scale, varying with the circumstances in each case, will be specially advised by the Horse Superintendent.

The provender must be weighed on its receipt, and should a deficiency of any of the component parts be discovered, the circumstance must be at once reported. Great care must be taken to prevent waste and misappropriation.

PROVENDER SACKS.

8. Immediately on receipt of a supply of provender, the Station Agent must shoot as much of it as the Bin accommodation will admit of, pack up the empty sacks and forward them to the Provender Stores, taking care to insert upon the direction the number of the sacks and name of the sending Station, that credit may be given the Station for them. Every care must be taken to keep the provender dry and protected from vermin.

Provender sacks must not be lent, or used for any other purpose.

VEHICLES.

9. To ensure the easy running of the vans, trollies and other vehicles, it is necessary they should be kept greased and clean. Care must be taken to prevent vehicles being disfigured by overflow of grease from axle boxes and locks of fore carriages. Neglect in this respect entails extra wear-and-tear to both vehicles and horses. When not in use, vehicles must, if possible, be placed under cover.

When vehicles are not in use the poles must be put over the bed of the vehicle with the chain attached to the splinter bar. Each pole is painted with the number of the vehicle to which it belongs, and must be kept with the proper vehicle.

STABLEMEN & SHUNTING HORSE DRIVERS.

10. The Horse Superintendent will appoint in London and at Birmingham all Stablemen and Shunting Horse Drivers employed by the Company. At other Stations such men will be appointed by him on the recommendation of the respective Traffic Officers.

STABLE STORES.

11. When ordering Stable Stores, a requisition (Form 206) must be made out and forwarded to the Horse Superintendent, who will, if the requisition be approved, certify the order, and forward it to the Store-keeper, that he may supply the stores direct.

The old articles or empty tins must be sent to the Stores, Swindon; and the name of the sending Station must be entered upon the direction label.

HARNESS AND OTHER REPAIRS.

12. Slight repairs to harness, or shunting chains, may be done locally; but when more than slight repairs are necessary, the entire and complete sets must be sent to the Saddler Foreman at Hockley, an advice on Form No. 206 C being sent at the same time to the Horse Superintendent, Paddington.

In getting sundry small repairs executed at Stations, no alteration must be made in the style or pattern, nor must any interference be made with the harness arrangement.

When ordering change collars, the length required must always be given, and any peculiarity as to the fitting of the old collar sent for repairs must be explained.

In sending in harness for repairs the name of the sending Station must be inserted on the label.

These rules do not apply to harness for horses in London or Birmingham. All repairs at those places will be carried out at the respective stations by the Staff of the Horse Superintendent.

ACCOUNTS.

13. Accounts for horse-shoeing, Veterinary charges, or slight repairs to chains or harness, must not have any other description of charges mixed up with them. They must be obtained immediately after the expiration of each month, and if correct, certified and forwarded to the Horse Superintendent, who will return them to the Station Agents, signed by himself.

Accounts for horse-hire incurred in consequence of the Company's horses being sick or off work must be dealt with in like manner, but this rule will not apply to accounts for horses regularly or ordinarily hired for shunting or cartage purposes.

MANURE.

14. Stable manure must be regularly removed. When there is an accumulation at places at which there are no instructions for disposal, the Station Agent must advise the Horse Superintendent of the best offer per ton which he can obtain; and authority for sale will be given.

A return (Form 3630) of the manure sold each month, accompanied by the machine tickets of the weight, price per ton, and the name and address of the purchaser must be sent to the Horse Superintendent on the first day of each month; who will deal with the matter through the Accountant's office at Paddington.

MEDICINES.

15. The Station Agents will be instructed from time to time of the names and addresses of the Veterinary Surgeons appointed by the Company to attend to the horses in their respective districts.

Where special Veterinary arrangements are not made necessary horse medicines may be obtained upon application to the Horse Superintendent. They must be kept under the care of the Agent, who is only to deliver them out as they are required; and it is his duty to carry out the following instructions according to each particular case.

NOTE.—Empty Cases and Bottles must be returned to the Hockley Goods Station, consigned to the Horse Foreman.

Coughs and Colds.—Give a cough ball, and rub the throat well down to the breast with liniment.

Influenza.—As this disease varies much in its form, and requires skilful treatment, a Veterinary Surgeon must be called in; the case being reported to the Horse Superintendent. The symptoms first observable are generally slight shivering, accompanied by a staring coat, pulse weak, belly tucked up, cough to a varying extent, loss of appetite, and often a heaving of the flanks. The animal should be clothed up; and, if possible, kept from other horses.

Colic.—Give a colic drink, and, if required, one Physic Ball; chilled water to drink. If in an hour pain in the bowels is still shown, rub them well with liniment or mustard.

Sore Shoulders and Backs.—Bathe the parts well with warm water, apply lotion, and attend to the collars.

Grease.—Clip the hair clean out of the heel, and wash well with soft soap and warm water; then apply the astringent lotion.

Worms.—Worm powders may be applied for when necessary. If possible, a description of the worm the horse has been seen to part with must be given. A little common salt or bruised rock salt should be given occasionally in a bran mash.

Physic.—This should not be administered without a well-defined cause, and when it is necessary to give it, the horse must be prepared the day before by having nothing in the way of food but bran mashes. If the medicine does not operate in twelve hours, the horse should be walked out (clothed). He must be stopped from work for at least three days after, and during this time he must be kept on soft diet, and have chilled water to drink.

Diuretic or Staling Balls.—Give one when necessary, but not systematically.

Tonic Balls.—Give one occasionally, if the horse is not feeding well, and if there appears no special reason for his refusal of food. This medicine must not, however, be given systematically.

Rock Salt.—A portion of Rock Salt must be kept in each manger. A supply can be obtained on application.

Mashes.—A bran mash may be given to each horse on Saturday nights.

Horse-Shoeing and Lameness.—In all cases of sudden lameness, and especially after shoeing, where there is no visible cause, the shoe must be taken off by the shoeing smith, and the foot thoroughly examined. If on rapping the foot, the horse is found to flinch in one part more than another, the nail holes must be well opened out, and the foot put into a bran poultice. Prompt attention to sudden lameness often avoids a long illness.

JAS. GRIERSON,

General Manager.

with 20 loose boxes and a large roomy shed in which horses could move under cover. During the winter months 24 horses could be tended there in stables: in the summer as many as 40 could be dealt with using outdoors grazing. Elsewhere around the system, local veterinary surgeons (known to the station masters and agents) were appointed to attend to the GW's horses. Where such special arrangements were not in place, horse medicines were requested from the Horse Superintendent at Paddington.

When the stud at Paddington became bigger than that at Hockley, James Grierson, the GW General Manager in Circular No 774 of 1 January 1883, advised that 'Captain Milne, the company's Horse Superintendent, has now been removed to Paddington and communications must be addressed to him there instead of being addressed to Birmingham as heretofore'. Mr R Eaglesham was appointed veterinary surgeon in 1897, and assistant to Mr R H Cartwright, the GW Horse Superintendent, in 1901. On the formation of the *Road Transport Department* in 1922, Mr A Twist was Horse Superintendent. Eaglesham retired in 1938 and was succeeded as Chief Veterinary Officer by Mr E O'Neill who had been the company vet for the northern part of the system based at Hockley, from where he also supervised the Bristol stud. Mr E B Ince became veterinary surgeon in the London area at this time.

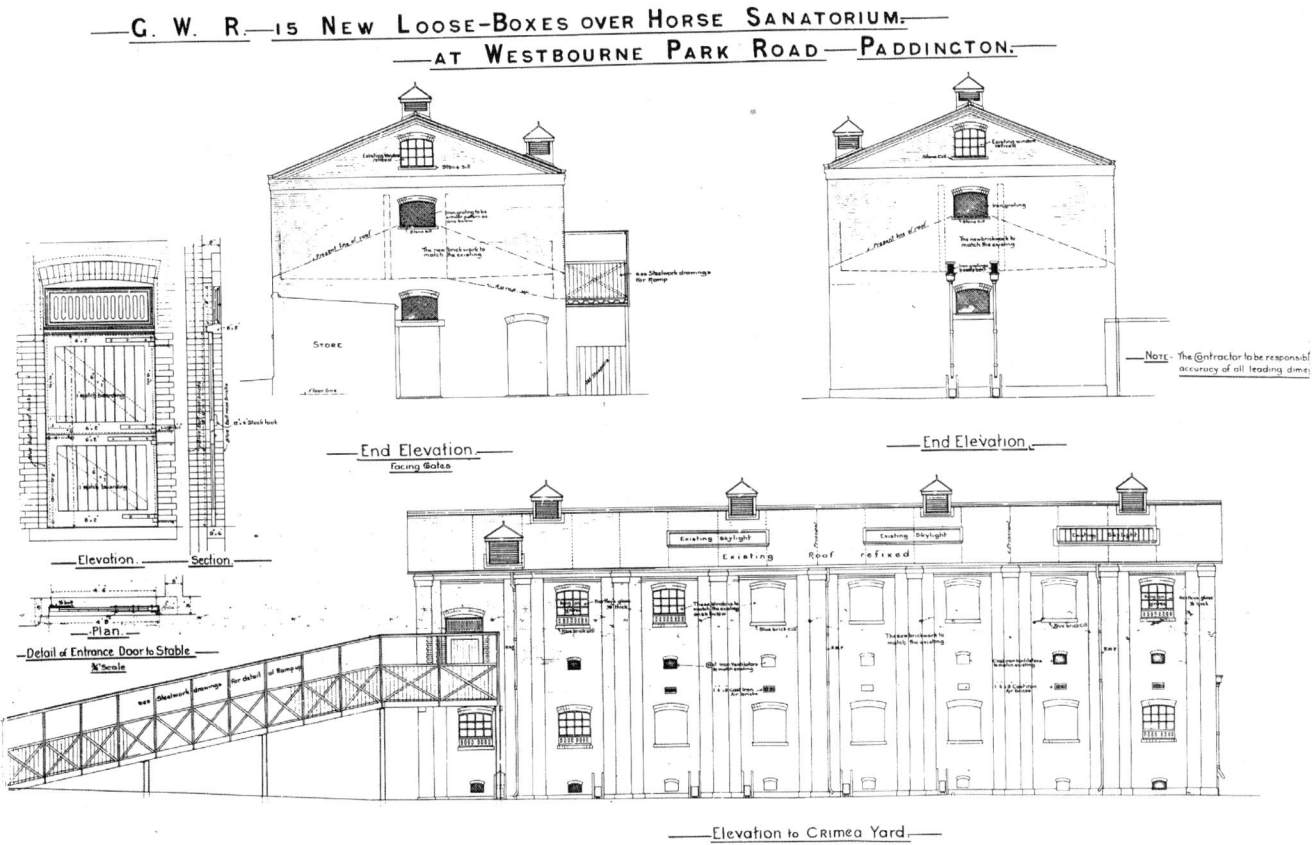

Fifteen new loose boxes built over Westbourne Park Horse Sanatorium, the original roof line of which may be seen in the end elevations. Details include blue bull-nose bricks to match old brickwork. New steelwork ramp. *GWR/D J Hyde collection*

There was a great variety of jobs at GW stables. Perusal of the Rates of Pay document for 1921 in Chapter 14 lists stablemen, ostlers, horsekeepers, horse dressers, horse removers, manger washers, collarmen and harness cleaners among others. Stablemen cleaned the stalls, looked after bedding and the feeding of the horses. Feeding was an important feature of the daily routine at all stables across the system. When the stud at Hockley was the biggest, provender was obtained from Handsworth — a few miles along the main line from Hockley towards Wolverhampton; the Horse Committee in 1882 approved spending £3/10/0 to seed two fields belonging to the company near Hatton station for grazing and £10 for repairing fences and cleaning ditches around those fields. But once the GW determined to do its own cartage in large towns, a Provender store with the latest steam-driven equipment for cutting hay into chaff and so on was opened at Didcot in 1884, from where fodder was dispatched by train all over the system. Electricity was installed in 1901 to drive the machinery (it also provided current for point motors and signals at Didcot). The standard feed mixture made up at Didcot for country horses consisted of 22½% oats, 10% beans, 20% maize, 41½% hay and 6% oat-straw (chaff). For London horses, a slightly different mixture containing 2½% more oats and 2½% less hay was issued. The daily allowance of mixed provender varied between 27lbs to 32lbs, depending on the individual horse. On Saturdays and Sundays bran and long hay were additionally fed to all GW horses. These allowances may be compared with those given in Grierson's letter of 1869 mentioned above. Six thousand sacks were required for each weekly supply across the whole GW territory, and altogether there were 14,000 provender sacks in circulation. Every week in the years before WW1, Paddington alone received about 1,000 sacks of oats, 220 sacks of beans, 480 sacks of maize, 110 tons of hay, 16 tons of oat-straw and 18 tons of bran, to which should be added 40-50 tons of straw for bedding. Enough fodder for about a week was kept in reserve at most GW stables. According to the well-known article on the Didcot Provender Store written by WH Stanier in the 1906 *GW Magazine*, over 9,000 acres of farmland were required to grow all the hay, oats and beans distributed over the GW system. In order to encourage home production at that time, the GWR Directors made it the practice that all provender should be British-produced. In 1909 it cost about £70,000 to feed all the GW horses. Complaints were made in the 1935 Goods Department Report that the cost of provender had risen in price so much that savings, which should have accrued from improved operational practices by the cartage department, were not being achieved. (Complaints were also made about the cost of petrol and tyres for the motor fleet!)

DELIVERY ROUNDS and DRIVERS

The majority of drivers of horse-drawn wagons served their apprenticeship as GW van-guards, being gradually trained and advanced from that grade to chain-horse drivers, then by successive stages to carmen (van or lorry) with one-horse, pair horse, three-horse, and four-horse teams. Working practices instilled in the drivers of horses included instructions not to start hurriedly or pull up quickly; that effort must be made to keep the horses cool; that horses must not be allowed to make their own pace; that they should be driven at walking pace up and down hills; and on no account were they to be allowed to drink from public water troughs. Street accidents causing injury to horses were infrequent, which an article in the 1909 *GW Magazine* attributed to the judgement and care exercised by drivers, although 'the advent of the motor-car has added materially to the difficulties of driving in congested districts'.

Above: **Potato traffic underground at Moor St Birmingham, with forecarriage of lorry (Diagram A15) turned at rightangles. Later pattern artillery iron wheel hubs. Small tilt for driver at front. GWR-labelled nosebag. Wheel skids and chains hanging down for looping round wheel spokes (in lieu of brake blocks).** *GWR/D J Hyde collection*

Left: **Carter Bert Miles and lad porter Bill Brooks in 1922 with the one-horse lorry issued to Devizes station in 1908 and used for town deliveries.** *W Brooks*

Deliveries in Wolverhampton. At the gutter, there is a skid on a chain under the rear wheel of this horse lorry built to Diagram A15. The tailboard is down and carrying part of the load. Skids for unloading and a sacktruck are slung under the vehicle at the rear (skids sticking out beyond the tailboard). Cast iron artillery wheel hubs. *Wolverhampton Arts and Heritage*

40

Subject.	Interpretation.	Code.
Customs	Following consignment for Irish Free State marked Duty Paid. Advise Senders duty will again be demanded on landing Ireland. Ascertain whether under drawback or ex bonded warehouse. Wire reply.	*Drawbon*
,,	Following consignment ex you......... contents declared as foreign manufacture. Wire actual country of origin with full details, under the respective Export List headings.	*Origa*
Delay	Wire full particulars of delay.	Niger
,,	Report fully by next train with reference to delay, as follows.	Palm
,,	Wire train, date and time of arrival and departure of following, explaining any delay.	Magi
Delivery	We are now asked to deliver following traffic to firm named. Wire if we may do so.	Donkey
,,	Following received different from invoice. Wire if we may deliver.	Finch
,,	Secure charges on following consignment before delivery.	Vik
,,	Your enquiry respecting following. Correct as received. You may deliver.	Gazel
,,	Arrange for special delivery of.	Ash
,,	Wire date and proof of delivery.	Pod

41

Subject.	Interpretation.	Code.
Delivery	Following delivered on date named, and signed for by.........	Hawk
,,	Undermentioned out for delivery to-day. Proof later.	Kish
,,	If unable to deliver the following, dispose of to best advantage.	Eagle
,,	Can you deal with undermentioned traffic at station named for delivery? If not, say which is the nearest available station.	Pink
,,	Following entered per our invoice (or Waybill) said not delivered. Give date, proof of delivery, and explanation of any delay. If not to hand state transfer point at which last checked.	Mullet
,,	Following said to have been sent you on or about undermentioned date by station named. Wire particulars of receipt and proof of delivery if effected.	Fox
,,	Following entered to you, and supposed to have been crossed in transit. See Consignee, and ascertain if you received and delivered correct marks and numbers, and wire me.	Salad
,,	Following on hand for want of better address. Send full particulars at once, to enable delivery to be effected. Now addressed.........	Bream
,,	Your enquiry re undermentioned. Following is address of.........	Cheta

42

Subject.	Interpretation.	Code.
Delivery	Following entered as under must not be delivered but held for further instructions. Wire whether Consignee advised; if not, do not advise.	Jackal
,,	Following on our invoice or waybill should have been entered "paid." Deliver free; clearance authority will be sent.	Ape
,,	Wire if we may deliver the following goods claimed by undermentioned and see Senders if necessary.	Sepoy
,,	Consignee resides outside delivery limits. Duly advised.	Hen
,,	Cannot trace delivery. Wire full description, marks, and contents, and say who complains.	Chicory
,,	Deliver free and debit me.	Thrush
,,	Wire if Consignees advised or recognised.	Argot
,,	Can you arrange cartage to address given of following traffic, carried at S. to S. rate? If so, wire charge for that service.	Drake
,,	Wire immediately whether following consignment can be accepted by Consignee by Road Motor, and unloaded immediately on arrival.	Roadmo

Subject.	Interpretation.	Code.
Delivery	Road Motors left at time shown below with the following consignments. Arrange return load, and wire when leaving and particulars of load.	Backmo
,,	Expect Road Motors with goods for	Exmo
,,	If following not delivered immediately Sender threatens to throw on Company's hands.	Panther
,,	Received and delivered as entered, no excess here.	Redex
,,	Following consignment hence in truck .... Expedite delivery, and wire time sent.	Trend
,,	Sender declines to give instructions.	Tarsus
Detaching	Be prepared to detach undermentioned leaving here next to engine on following train.	Cloth
,,	Be prepared to detach undermentioned in middle of following train.	Climb
,,	Be prepared to detach undermentioned leaving here in the rear of following train.	Cow
Detention	Detain undermentioned until you receive further instructions.	Turnip

When out on the road, the carter was the driver in charge. Very occasionally on particularly busy rounds there was a second carman acting as 'book-keeper' to look after delivery sheets, consignment notes and collection and custody of any money due to the GW. The van-guard assisted in loading/unloading and looked after the vehicle and horse when the carman was away. When journeying, the van-guard rode on the back part of the load or the vehicle. It was his duty to keep the iron and brass-work of the harness clean and bright, and leather clean and pliable. A van-guard was not to drive when younger than 17 years of age. In both world wars, during which there was a shortage of staff, drivers asked for and received extra pay for operating vehicles without van-guards (see Chapter 5). During WW1, owing to shortage of cartage staff away in the forces, instructions in the *Towns & Villages* book were suspended so that, for example, traffic from Hadley, New Hadley, Trench and Wombridge (all LNW stations in Shropshire)–to Oakengates (GWR) was re-routed to Oakengates (LNWR).

Blackmore reminisced in his article in the February 1937 *GW Magazine*, about ".....the carman in a sleeved waistcoat sweeping aside a rug from across his knees, slipping whip into holster, jumping to the ground and hitching his reins all, seemingly, in one movement; or the same figure with both hands to bridle, backing his wagon against a parcel-office platform amid a great scuffling of hooves and a rattle of tail-board chains...."

In Victorian times in London and some other large towns, authorised cartage routes along which whisky and other valuable goods were carried were watched by police and railway officials to lessen the risk of robbery. Cartage vehicles had to go over a weighbridge when leaving and returning to depots. Employees were not to purchase goods for others, nor stop at public houses, coffee houses, etc, except on railway business or during meal times. Staff on duty were not to smoke on or off GW premises. The carman was issued with a 'pouch, tarpaulin, net, sack, nosebag, bucket, sack truck, pulley, roller, scotch, rope, chin and packing' for which he was responsible. Buckets, nosebags and sack trucks had to be slung under the vehicle when not in use. Lamps had to be lit at proper times. On long journeys buckets were supplied for water. Horses were not to be worked when in a heated condition (overheating resulted in colics, colds and other ailments). Skids were required to unload heavy C & D articles; three pairs were supplied to Huntspill Sidings (Bridgwater) by the Road Wagon shop in 1941.

When roads were favourable, heavy teams normally travelled at 4mph, and a 3-horse wagon would carry 6 tons; 2-horse, 4 tons; 1 horse wagon or lorry, 1 ton 10cwt. Light teams travelled at 6mph, and a 2-horse van carried 3 tons 10cwt; 1 horse van, 1 ton 10cwt. In hilly districts permissible loads were reduced.

The GW was very proud of its London four-horse teams. Indeed, great pride was taken in all the railway horses, and they were regularly entered in local shows. For example, in June 1922 Parcel Carman Davis driving the GWR horse van was awarded 1st prize at the Minehead Horse and Harness Parade with Carman Tudbull winning the 3rd prize. At the London Carthorse Parade held in Regents Park on Whit Monday, 1932, eighteen Great

Decorating a well-groomed GW horse for a show. Beautifully cleaned and dubbined leather bridle having a snaffel bit with curious second ring. Hames of horse collar visible to right of carter's head.
GWR/P J Kelley collection

Horses ready for a show. A pair of dappled greys photographed in front of the Royal Waiting Room at Windsor station on 28/6/47.
GWR/D J Hyde collection

Western teams were entered from Paddington and Smithfield; fifteen first and three second prizes were gained (there would have been about 800 horses in the parade). At Birmingham in 1934, in the 'railway class', Great Western staff secured the first prize for the best horse and cleanest harness employed on parcels work, and the second prize for horses on goods work. The *GW Magazine* often reported horse parades at various centres at which GW carmen participated. Competing in the 1937 London Van Horse Parade in Regents Park on Easter Monday 1938, Paddington Parcel Carman T Hoare received first prize for his horse and van, and the RSPCA medal for the best undocked horse in the parade (docking was to cut short the horse's tail). There was even an intra-depot competition at Hockley to find the best-groomed and decorated horses.

As more and more motor vehicles were added to the cartage fleet, the question was posed as to whether it would ever be possible to have depots with no horse-drawn vehicles at all. There was great concern about the loss of the 'spare horse lorry' whereby incoming carters could attach their horses to a loaded dray and leave the depot with the minimum of delay. To provide spare motor vehicles in the same proportion as spare horse lorries would be prohibitively expensive. Hence all the efforts with 'demountable bodies' described in Chapter 6. In reality, according to Pragnell (*GW London Lecture & Debating Society*, 1931/2, paper 263) the demountable machinery received little use since the cartage rounds were long (an average of only two trips per day), so that with only a small percentage of spare motor strength, the idle time was equal to or superior to the horse. Consequently, in 1930, it was decided to completely motorise South Lambeth goods station. It was the first on the GW and was followed in 1934 by Smithfield goods depot. In 1934 too, Swansea lost its remaining 32 horses (but some were reintroduced later) and the stations at Brixham, Buckfastleigh, Chester, Haverfordwest, Ilminster, Malmsbury, Penzance, St Austell, St Ives, Shrewsbury, Staines and Wiveliscombe all soon became fully motorised. It is significant that it was in 1934 that the three-wheeled 'mechanical horse' and articulated trailer was introduced on a widespread basis at a large number of goods stations across the system and this type of vehicle figured prominently in the all-motor cartage fleets.

All stations had to return a monthly *Salaries and Wages Return* (Form 6334). The Superintendent of Road Transport stated in 1931 that charges to be debited to Horse and Motor Cartage at stations where both were employed should be in the following proportions: 1-ton vehicle = 1 horse; 1½-ton = 1½ horses; 2-ton = 2 horses; 4/5-ton = 2½ horses; 6/8-ton = 2½ horses; and a 10-ton motor = 4 horses.

Left: **Horse lorry to Diagram A10 decorated for a carnival parade at Devizes.** *D J Hyde*

Below: **Women worked as carters in WW2.** *D J Hyde collection*

Complete replacement of horses by motors meant that stables became redundant, and sometimes they would be converted to garages. When a stud of horses was only reduced in number, it was sometimes possible to reorganise stabling, such as at Hockley where the stables on the main site were demolished and converted to other use, and all the remaining horses accommodated in stables at the nearby Hockley Basin. [In 1928, there were 461 horse-drawn vehicles at Hockley, 270 horses and 41 road motors.]

The number of horses (including those used for shunting) was 3,386 in 1913, and 2,731 in 1923. In 1925 there had been a small increase in the stud of horses used for short distance cartage work in towns, owing to the overall increase in railway goods traffic in the 1920s. [In passing, it is of interest that the GW was still running 18 horse buses as feeders to rail services (for a list see page 174 of the 1922 *Railway Year Book*); the size of horse for bus work came in between the cart horse and the van horse.] By 1935, however, the number of cartage horses had dropped to 2,000: by 1936 to l,773 (of which 500 were stabled in London); by 1937 to 1,690; and by 1938 to 1,476. On the outbreak of war in September 1939 the need for economy in the use of petrol meant that the horse stud had risen again by over 100 animals to 1,584 by the end of that year (and an order was given to the Road Wagon shop in November 1940 by Mr J Auld (ex-Loco Superintendent of the Barry Rly who became Docks and, after Stanier left for the LMS, Principal Assistant to Collett) 'to adapt GW horse-drawn vehicles for Swindon's War Weapons Week'). In 1945 the number had fallen to 1,105 horses and to 1,018 in 1947. In that year before nationalisation, the following areas were still using horses: Birmingham 245; London 242; Bristol 186; Cardiff 121; Plymouth 43; Swansea 41; Newport 31; Gloucester 30; Worcester 23; Exeter 20; Central Wales 16; and Liverpool 15.

During WW2 working hours were curtailed at many depots during the mid-winter months, to fit in with the blackout arrangements. The work of stablemen usually took place during early morning and late evening when blackout was necessary. With windows and doors strictly covered, this limited the ventilation and fresh air that were required for the horses' health. However, the problem was eventually overcome to restore nearly-normal stable conditions, and instructions were issued to carmen as to what to do should an airraid occur when out at work. Other instructions were issued to all stations and depots early in the war regarding emergency treatment of injured or gassed animals, and the method of dealing with gas-contaminated harness and tackle. In anticipation of delays in the supply of provender, special reserves of food and bedding were put in at the larger stations. When Plymouth Millbay station was bombed in 1941, the goods shed, goods offices and stables were destroyed by fire and 32 horses were killed.

Grounded bodies for storage could be found all across the system and the Road Transport Department used many for oil and supplies. Even so, an interesting order to the Swindon Road Wagon

SHUNTING HORSES	
Location	Class of Drivers
Bridgwater	3
Bristol	1
Cardiff	1
Challow	3
Cradley	2
Croes Newydd	1
Dorchester	3
Dudley	2
Dunball Wharf	3
Evesham	3
Gloucester	2
Great Bridge	2
Hartlebury	3
Hayle	3
Hereford	2
Kidderminster	2
Leamington	2
Netherton	2
Newport Dock St	1
Newport High St	1
Oakengates	2
Oswestry	3
Paddington	1
Rowley Regis	2
Ruabon	1
Saltney	2
Shifnal	3
Shrewsbury	2
Stourbridge	2
Swan Village	2
Swindon	2
Tipton	2
Warwick	2
Wednesbury	2
Wellington (Salop)	2
West Bromwich	2
Withymoor	2
Wolverhampton	1
Worcester	2
Wrexham	2
Yeovil	3

shop in 1942 stated 'prepare and despatch to Melksham the body of condemned horsebox No 833 for use as stabling accommodation'. The value of the body was given as £4; making it weatherproof cost £4/10/0; and demounting and loading up, 16/-. In 1946, an order from David Blee (Chief Goods Manager) requested the CME's department to 'De-infest Temple Street stables, Bristol'.

Chain Horses and Shunting Horses
Chain ('trace') horses were employed to help loaded cartage vehicles up steep hills. A well-known example relates to the Pitsford Street hill at Hockley goods depot, where 3-wheel Karrier Cob light tractors were introduced as replacements in 1932 (see Chapter 6). A chain horse was kept at Smithfield to assist loaded vehicles coming up the helical exit road from the underground depot. As narrated in *GW Docks & Marine*, horses were often seen in difficulties near the Welsh Back wharf in Bristol, having slipped down either in hauling a heavy load up the incline from Baldwin Street, or on to Bristol Bridge. To help, the GW and Midland Rly had a shed near the bridge where 2 or 3 trace horses were stabled along with men to deal with heavy loads.

Chain and shunting horses were looked after exactly the same as those used for cartage. The contactor Younghusband provided shunting horses and drivers in London up to about 1890. The conditions at Smithfield, where shunting horses worked underground with poor lighting, were considered severe. In 1913, the GW had 124 horses on the books for shunting; in 1939 there were only 22 and this level remained with minor changes through to nationalisation. The 1915 edition of the *Instructions to Shunt-Horse Drivers and Horse-Keepers* is reproduced on pp84 *et seq* in *GWR Goods Train Working*.

The horseman usually looked after two horses with a 'chain horse boy', and might move wagons in and out of goods sheds and perform other movements (e.g. at Bridgwater, according to Leslie King, recovering the slip coach if it overran the passenger platform!). In the busy larger depots, the jobs done by shunting horses had been eliminated by the installation of capstans and reels, whereby wagons could be moved around by hitching up to a wire driven by the capstan (see *GW Goods Services*). Where replacement of steam locos by petrol or diesel shunting engines was tried out (a 40hp 8-ton Simplex petrol rail tractor in 1922 at Hockley goods station and at Wednesbury), the capital cost meant that it could only be justified in large depots, so that there was still need for the shunting horse in places where it was necessary to move wagons around fairly often, yet uneconomical to provide locomotive shunting 'on tap'. As described in Chapter 6, the GW used a number of tractors kitted out for shunting in areas where the rails were level with the surrounding roadway.

CHAPTER FOUR

'MECHANICALLY-PROPELLED' GOODS VEHICLES BEFORE 1920: PARCELS TRAFFIC

TWO Acts of Parliament at the turn of the 19th/20th centuries that amended earlier Acts enabled 'mechanically-propelled' (i.e. self-propelled) road vehicles to be considered as replacements for horse-drawn cartage vehicles. The *Locomotives on Highways Act* of 1896 removed both the old 4 mph speed limit on vehicles under 3 tons in weight and also the obligation of having a man with a red flag (the 'pilot') precede the 'locomotive' (that was part of an 1865 Act). Even so, manufacturers found it difficult to produce commercial vehicles economically until the *Heavy Motor-Car Act* of 1903 came into force which allowed vehicles up to 5 tons in weight to be used on common roads without a pilot. The 1903 Act, that had a direct influence on the growth of the GWR motor fleet, required all mechanically-propelled vehicles to be registered and carry number plates, and to be taxed (Appendix 2).

Towards the end of the 19th century, railways had been connected to practically every district where sufficient traffic could be obtained to justify the construction of branch lines, but there were still areas that remained isolated. One of the aims of the *Light Railways Act* of 1896 was to help farmers in such remote places get their dairy products to market by allowing the construction of railways that were cheaper and less substantial than standard lines. Local authorities were permitted to financially assist such schemes. However, the powers were not taken up to any great extent as it was difficult to raise capital, and the cost of land and works was still relatively high, as was maintenance after construction. In any case, the Act that got rid of the red flag was passed in the same year as the Light Railway Act, and enabled equivalent services to be provided by road at less outlay, with lower running costs, and not be confined to a fixed track (often single line). So it seemed that self-propelled vehicles would enable far-outlying districts to be linked up with the railway in relatively short journey times.

The GW tried three experiments with various forms of mechanically-propelled goods transport.

Steam propulsion

The first was in 1902 when a Thornycroft 'undertype' steam-driven lorry was put on trial with and without a trailer on C&D work at Hockley Goods Depot in Birmingham. Such vehicles had performed well in the recent Boer War. (There were two basic types of steam lorry, those with a vertical boiler ('undertypes'), and those with a horizontal boiler similar to those on most railway locomotives — 'overtypes', see Appendix 3.) F C A Coventry (then Assistant to the Manager of the Carriage works at Swindon and in charge of road motors) had visited the makers at Basingstoke in 1902. An engineering drawing of the 4-ton steamer is given in a 1952 *Railway Magazine* article by Dent (pp 627-632) with other details of its operation, in particular that it was preferable to use the steam wagon alone owing to difficulties in manipulating the trailer in confined spaces. According to an article by Coventry in the transactions of the 1910-11 session of the *Swindon Engineering Society,* the experiment at Hockley was not a success — and the vehicle was returned to its makers — largely owing to traders' objections and to the realisation by the Goods Department that the advantage of greater speed of the more-costly steam lorry over horse vehicles was nullified in practice by the time taken for loading and unloading (this 'idle time' was a factor that reappeared in the 1920s when deciding where best to utilise motor lorries, and ultimately led to the use of trailers behind tractors and motors).

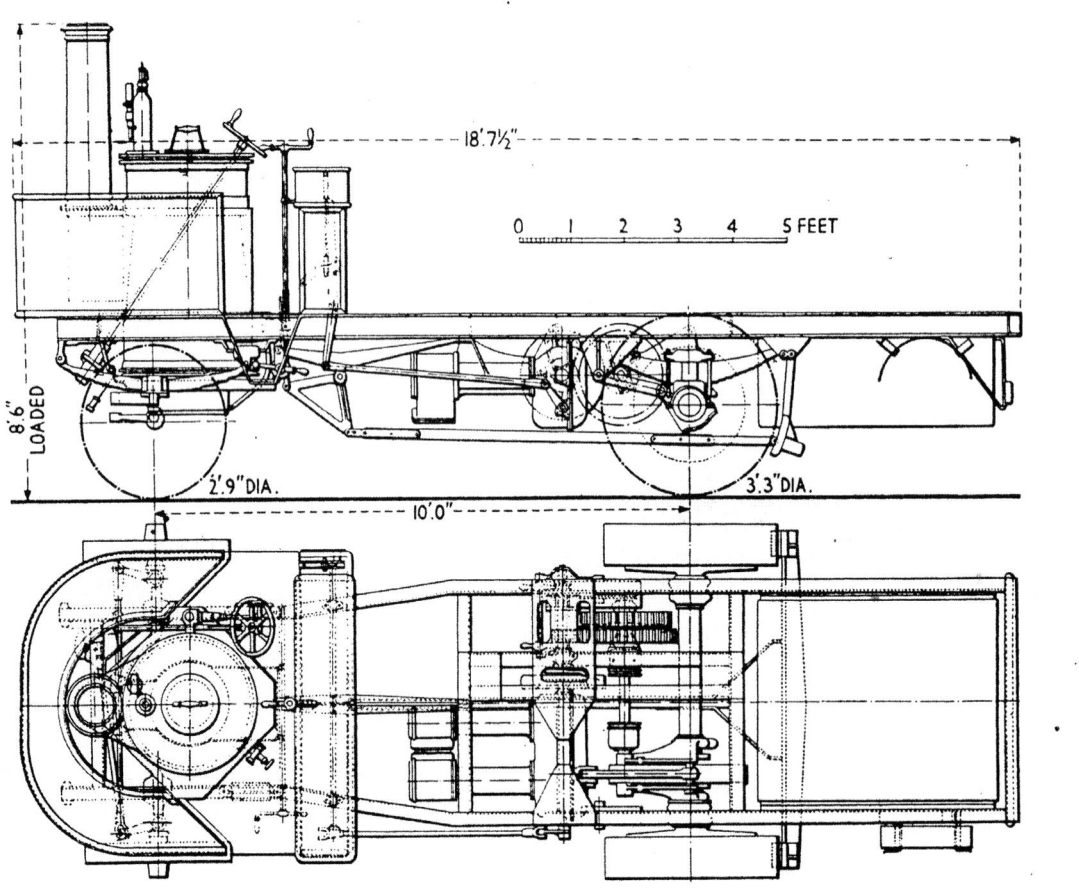

Standard 4-ton steam wagon of the Thornycroft Steam Wagon Co. Ltd., traced from a drawing dated March 20 1903

A second steam wagon came into use after Alfred Baldwin (Chairman of the GWR) commented in a speech in 1904 on work done by the Agricultural Organisation Society (a national non-profit-making body founded in 1901 that aimed to give advice on forming agricultural co-operatives). It had arranged with the North Eastern Rly for a motor service from Tollerton station to Brandsby in Yorkshire to get produce to the railway. Acting on this, farmers from the Teme Valley branch of the Agricultural Organisation Society in Worcestershire made a case to the GW to provide a goods road service from Henwick station to Stanford Bridge at the head of the valley (a distance of some 10 miles) which, it was argued, was likely to be financially successful. The valley was difficult to reach, horse transport was slow and goods transport needed to be increased in capacity and speed. After some negotiation, the GW agreed to purchase a 3-ton steam wagon in 1905 from the Yorkshire Steam Motor Company of Leeds to institute the service (the engine was a variant of the overtype where its boiler was mounted transversely across the front of the vehicle). The vehicle was assigned fleet number 81. The bulk of the freight carried from Henwick into the valley consisted of coal, oats, feeding meal for cattle, artificial manures for hop growing,

Right: **Cover of the Transactions of the Swindon Engineering Society, 1910-11.**

[Pamphlet No. 104]

G.W.R. Mechanics' Institution.

SWINDON ENGINEERING SOCIETY.

"The G.W.R. Road Motor Car Department,"

BY

F. C. A. COVENTRY (Member).

EXCERPT OF TRANSACTIONS, 1910-11.

Published by the Society:
G.W.R. LOCOMOTIVE AND CARRIAGE DEPT., SWINDON.
1911.

ALL RIGHTS OF PUBLICATION ARE RESERVED.

GW steam lorry (Yorkshire Patent Steam Wagon Co, Hunslet, Leeds), fleet 81 (not 'S1') number plate U308, of 1905. Worked between Henwick Station (Worcs) and Stanford Bridge at the head of the Teme Valley at a maximum speed of 5mph. On side of coal bunker is 'Great Western Railway/G K Mills/Secretary/Paddington Station/No 81'. Under the transverse boiler is "Great Western Railway Paddington/UW 4 Tons 16 cwts/Axle weight 3 Tons 10 cwts/8' 0". The 4-plank trailer has the load and 'G K Mills Secretary Paddington Station' painted on. Crude wooden brake blocks attached to cross beam of wood push on rear wheels of trailer, controlled through a handwheel by the man riding on trailer. Baskets piled at rear of trailer are marked AEF on the sides and M on ends. *Author's collection*

and general stores and provisions. During the fruit season, from July to the end of October, four to five tons per day were carried by the wagon out of the valley for onwards conveyance from Henwick. As part of the winter work, road stone was transported for the Worcestershire County Council. It was said that the costs of cartage were less than horse-drawn vehicles, and horse transport also took longer than the three hours allowed for the steam lorry (including loading and unloading on the way, and stops for watering from streams). These services anticipated what the 'Country Lorry Service' did in later years. However, because of the rules at the time, the steam wagon could carry no goods that were not destined for further carriage by rail, or had arrived by rail, at Henwick; purely local carriage of goods from the Teme Valley to Worcester had to be done by horse wagons. These factors eventually led to the demise of the service. (This steamer is almost certainly the one that later worked at Birkenhead before being sold in 1913.)

Even so, steam-driven vehicles had the advantage of being able to haul heavy loads, and at the same time as the Henwick trial, two Wallis & Steevens steam tractors were bought from the makers at Basingstoke for use in the Black Country with its foundries and steelworks. One was 4½-tons with fleet number 54, (later re-numbered S4, then later to S1) based at Hockley; it was sold in 1924. The other was 3-tons given fleet 55 (re-numbered S5, and later S2) based at Bilston goods depot. According to the Road Wagon Department accounts the total cost of these two traction engines, including 4 'lorries' (i.e. trailers), was £1,054. A 3-ton Aveling & Porter steam traction engine, chassis 5613, was bought at the end of 1904 for use in London according to lot 608 of the Road Wagon Department accounts, but was soon sold to Messrs Parry of Bilston in 1906.

Three Clarkson steam-propelled buses, fleet 34-6, opened the service between Wolverhampton and Bridgnorth in November 1904, but they gave considerable boiler trouble. They were tried later at Cheddar, but the GW's inability to find really experienced men to drive and maintain them eventually led to their being sold in 1907 (34/5 to the Torquay Road Car Co; 36 to Death & Young of Lechlade).

Unsprung Foden 10-ton steam wagon fitted with three-way tipping body (fleet S20, UL4364) alongside 3-plank open with round ends. Man surveying load of (gravel?). Cover over chimney? A ¾ view of S20 may be found in Kelley, p 93. *STEAM Swindon*

S20 Foden steam three-way tipping lorry of 1929, photographed on 6/10/31. Fleet S20, UL4364. 'GREAT WESTERN RAILWAY/FREDAVIS SECRETARY/PADDINGTON'. Single electric headlamp below smokebox. Shaded GWR lettering on body and cab. Below S-20 is the maker's plate "By Royal Letters Patent/....13278/Fodens Ltd /Sandbach England". Below that is 'UW 10-7-3-0/SPEED 16 M.P.H.', and below the G on the cabside is 'GREAT WESTERN RAILWAY/FREDAVIS SECRETARY/PADDINGTON'. No rear mudguards owing to side-tipping action. Scuff marks from climbing up over rear wheels.
GWR/P J Kelley collection

Foden 6-wheel unsprung steam lorry loaded with sacks of grain at Exeter on 6/12/29. LG 4362. Fleet number S-18 on cab and left-hand end of body. "F R E Davis Secretary Paddington" below 'G.W.R', and 'UW 10 tons/FAW 4 Tons/MAW 7 Tons 10 Cwts/RAW 7tons 10cwts' below maker's plate on cabside, all in script lettering. Single headlight below smokebox. A broadside view of the vehicle is on p 93 in Kelley. *GWR/D J Hyde collection*

To complete the story of steam road haulage, it was suggested in 1920 that the GW should have their own steam wagons for hauling stone in connection with road repairs, but it was not until February/March 1929 that four Foden steam wagons were bought and put to use: two 9-tonners (Nos S17/18, Greater London road number plates UL4361/2) and two 10-tonners (S19/20, UL4363/4). S17 was a tractor with winch at the rear and was put to work initially at Swansea with a trailer hauling tinplate traffic and on C&D; S18 was a lorry used initially at Paddington and Theale, and later at Exeter. S19 and S20 were both tippers, the former employed at Theale on gravel extraction and the latter at first at Exeter for sand, ashes and building materials and general goods work, and then at Shrewsbury. Heavy taxation on road vehicles having high axle loadings were penalised under the Road Traffic Acts of the early 1930s, and steam wagons as load-carrying vehicles were almost eliminated from contention since their unsprung weight was high compared with the gross weight permitted. Even so, S17-20 remained on the GW books into WW2.

[As explained in the fleet list, Appendix 1, the intermediate S numbers up to S16 probably related to the GW's fleet of steam road rollers.]

Electric propulsion

The second sort of 'mechanically-propelled' goods vehicle to be tried in place of horse-drawn C&D lorries was a lightweight electric vehicle introduced in 1906 having Fleet Number 82. It was purchased from the Anglo-American Motor Co and an improved version was built in 1908 at the Motor Car Department workshops at Slough and allocated Fleet 95. The first vehicle operated in Slough itself and the other in London. Both had slatted sides and a flat roof, with rolled-up canvas side sheets. The vehicles, fitted with 4ins solid rubber tyres, were driven from 40-cell batteries that gave them a range of about 30 miles on one charge. Overnight battery charging typically took 6 to 7 hours, with the possibility of a supplementary charge for one-hour at midday. Performance graphs of fleet 82 were generated by the *Road Motor Department* workshops.

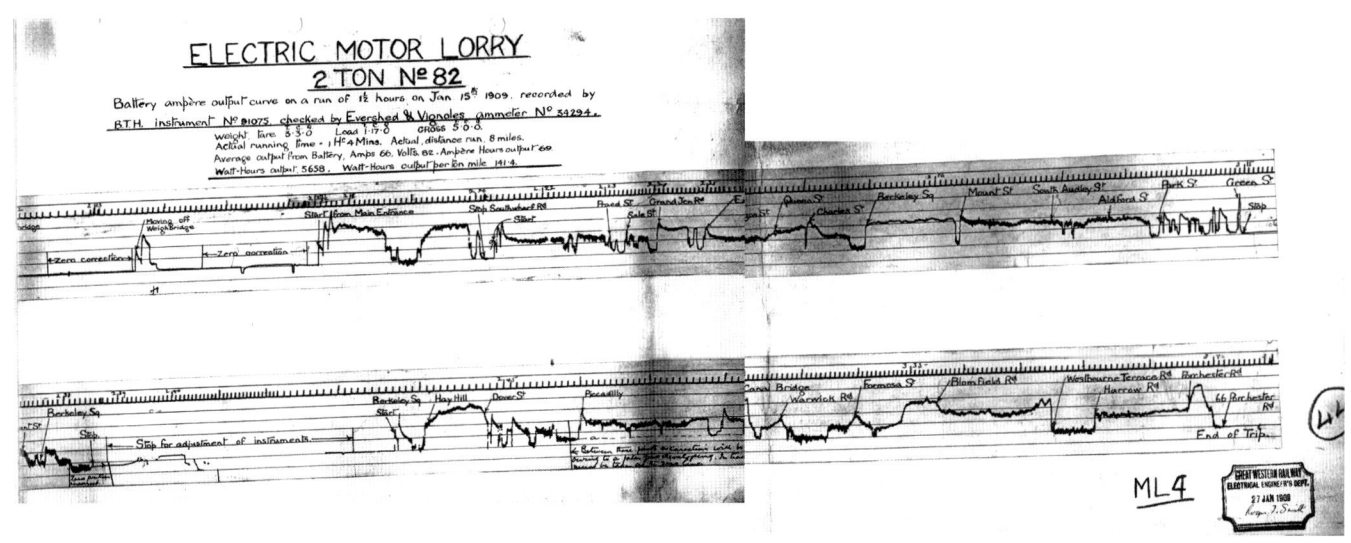

The first electric C&D vehicle on the GW, fleet 82, LC 4338. Bought from the USA in 1906, it operated around Slough where the accompanying performance graphs were obtained by the *Road Motor Department* workshops. It had slatted sides, hidden here by the canvas side sheet (for related pictures, see Kelley, pp38/90).

'MECHANICALLY-PROPELLED' GOODS VEHICLES BEFORE 1920: PARCELS TRAFFIC

It was not until after WW1 that more electric cartage vehicles were put into service by the GW. In 1919 eleven were introduced comprising (a) four 5-ton goods lorries with flatbed bodies manufactured in the British shops of the USA General Electric Co and allocated to Birkenhead, having Birkenhead CM number plates; and (b) five parcels vans from Ransomes, Sims & Jeffries of Ipswich, two of 3½-ton capacity, four of 2½-ton and one 1½-ton, allocated to Paddington, all with DX Ipswich plates. The principal difference between the two designs was that the back wheels of the USA vehicles were driven by chain from a centrally-mounted motor, whereas the motor was integral with the front axle in the Ransomes vehicles — indeed the front axle weight of a 2½-ton Ransome was the same as its maximum load.

Above: **General Electric 5-ton flatbed lorry, fleet E5, CM1770, of 1919. Tare 4-10-2. Renumbered 2/2/22 to fleet 185 (original fleet list has wrong E number). Speed 9mph on chassis. Chain-driven back wheels. Allocated to Birkenhead.** *GWR/P J Kelley collection*

Left: **Ransomes Orwell DX-1985 2½-ton van. The electric motor is integral with the front axle whose weight is about equal to the load! On body at left 'load not to exceed 2-10-0'. On body at right 'Great Western Railway/E A Bolter Secretary/ Paddington'. Cab has fleet E11 just below roofline and GW coat of arms below side window. Shaded GWR below windscreen. Chassis 1058 (cast in oval plaque bottom front of cab) with FAW 2-13-0 below that. "Ironclad Exide" on battery box in Gothic lettering. Photo 24/7/19.** *GWR/P J Kelley collection*

E13 Ransomes electric vehicle being charged at Westbourne Park/Alfred Rd depot. Man checking specific gravity of battery acid. The 'load not to exceed 2-10-0'. Notice on wall in front of van is to say what drivers will take out what cars: Herbert E1; Shelvey E?; Smith E12; Denman E10; Watson E9; 'E11 not to go'. *GWR/P J Kelley collection*

The 1919 vehicles all joined the cartage fleet at a time when the fleet numbering of some vehicles was prefixed by a letter (in this case E for electric, see Chapter 8), but on the formation of the *Road Transport Department* in 1922, they were given 'normal' sequential numbering. So the four 5-ton vehicles numbered E5-8 became fleet 182-5; the two 3½-tonners numbered E9/10 became 186/7; the four 2½-tonners originally given E11-14 became 188-91; and the single 1½-tonner, E15, was fleet 192. (Since the 1919 vehicles start at E5, it is likely that the two pre-WW1 electric vehicles were also re-numbered, but that would mean that two vehicles are 'missing' for which it seems there is no explanation.) The range of different capacities for the Ransomes vehicles was chosen in order to get data on the performance of electric vehicles in general. The USA lorries had 4-inch solid rubber tyres and could run about 30 miles on one charge of the 40-cell battery.

Cabs on all these vehicles were identical, having been designed by the GW *Road Motor Car Department* to give the driver reasonable protection against the weather while not obstructing his vision; they were fixed to the chassis, the load-carrying body being easily removed for repairs. Owing to the weight of the batteries, the maximum speeds of electric lorries were 9-14mph depending on capacity and road gradients. They were not competitive with petrol or steam road vehicles for long runs at high speeds, but were suitable for C&D routes involving many stops per mile (where their rapid acceleration was valuable) and the fact that no motive power was used when at rest. They were also suited to non-stop runs through city traffic on fixed daily mileages which were within the capacity of their batteries, such as transfer trips between stations of different railway companies in the same city.

Despite the advantages of simple equipment and smaller vehicle length than other motor vehicles of the same capacity (thus giving easier manoeuvrability), the disadvantages of low speeds and dependence on battery charging caused the abandonment of electric C&D vehicles by the GW in the mid-1920s. While petrol-driven platform trolleys at Paddington were replaced by electric trolleys in 1937, it was not until 1947 that the GW once more dickered with electric vehicles for road work, this time taking delivery of two 2-ton electric vans, E2800/1, for express parcels at Temple Meads made by Douglas (Kingswood) Ltd, and fleet E2802, a 25/30-cwt van supplied by Brush (see section on Parcels traffic below).

Internal combustion propulsion

It is wellknown that in May 1903, Sir George Newnes had put on a feeder motor bus service between Ilfracombe and Lynton for the Lynton & Barnstaple Rly, but owing to great opposition from proprietors of horse vehicles in the Lynmouth district together

One of two 2-ton electric C&D vans delivered by Messrs Douglas (Kingswood) in 1947 and used in the Bristol area (fleet E2800/1). For these vehicles, the E prefix for electric vehicles in fleet numbering was reintroduced, last used in the 1919/20 period. *Author's collection*

'MECHANICALLY-PROPELLED' GOODS VEHICLES BEFORE 1920: PARCELS TRAFFIC

Above: As early as 1897 the GW had issued a note on charges for motor cars and motor cycles to be carried by train. *GWR/D J Hyde collection*

Below: Milnes-Daimler 20hp bus, fleet number 8, registration A 4260, of April 1904 at Helston station in 1905/6 showing the front compartment that could be used either for goods or, by means of tip-up seats, for passengers wishing to smoke. In both cases, above the conductor is a destination board saying 'The Lizard, Mullion and Helston' in shaded gold lettering (as is the fleet number below window on cabside). Notice that the swing door to the front compartment has an upper part in the goods picture which is absent in the smokers' picture. The number of planks of the middle swing door is greater in the smokers' photo, suggesting that the upper part of the door shown in the goods picture may have hinged up in two parts from the middle swing door. Transmission brake. 'GREAT WESTERN RAILWAY/G K MILLS SECRETARY/ PADDINGTON /STATION' on cast plaque on cabside below driver. Tare 3 tons. Oil sidelamps but acetylene headlight at roof. A bus chassis of this type was used for the first GW goods lorry. *GWR/P J Kelley collection*

with police proceedings against him for exceeding the speed limit of 12mph, he was fed up and decided to sell the vehicles. The two buses (16hp Milnes-Daimler wagonettes) were bought second hand by the GW with which to inaugurate a service on 17 August 1903 between Helston and the Lizard where a scheme for a light railway had been promoted but not proceeded with. Despite Grant's reminiscence that on the first trip with the Mayor and other invited guests on board, the bus "......made such slow progress that a costermonger in a donkey cart headed the procession, beckoning with his hand and inviting the motor driver to overtake......", the service was so successful that an additional bus was required within days of the opening and in December 1903 the GW decided to purchase an additional 25 buses. Within a year, a dozen or so other country bus services were in operation across GW territory. While the intention of the bus services was to act as feeders for passenger trains, the buses often carried mails, parcels and light goods up to 1cwt per package. (Further details of early bus operations will be found in the September 1910 *GW Magazine*.)

It is no surprise therefore that the third experiment for C&D cartage related to the purchase of two petrol-engined goods motor lorries, both 5-ton Milnes-Daimlers fitted with 35-horsepower 4-cylinder engines. (From 1902, G F Milnes & Co of London imported Daimler chassis and engines from Germany which they sold across the British Empire until WW1.) The first lorry for the

The first GW goods lorry was a Milnes-Daimler 20hp 5-tonner of October 1904, with chassis based on the contemporary Lizard buses having a low radiator. Its registration was A7645 and fleet number 37 (but was not marked on, even though this photograph dates from a few years later; for its condition as-received from the makers see Kelley, p35, and notice there the original peculiar 'tangential-spoke' front wheels). Shaded GWR on sides of body of externally-framed wood. No front brake. Rear brake is externally-acting pushing on outside of rear solid rubber tyre (and is different from original brake). Chassis corresponds now with the 2nd Milnes-Daimler lorry. Framework to hold fish boxes on the run between Billingsgate Market and Paddington. *GWR/P J Kelley collection*

The second goods motor lorry bought by the GW photographed on station platform with Siphon milk churn van behind. Unlike the first lorry, this has a high radiator. The Plymouth registration of this Milnes-Daimler 5-ton flatbed lorry was CO 112 of February 1905; the fleet number was 44. Braking was achieved by an externally-contracting shoe only on the solid rubber tyres of the rear wheels. *P Kelley*

GW was delivered in October 1904 and was registered in London A7645 (fleet 37); the second in February 1905, registered in Plymouth CO112 (fleet 44). The first lorry retained the old low-slung radiator of the early Milnes-Daimler buses, but the second had what became the usual sort of high radiator arrangement. Instead of employing the lorries on multiple-delivery 'smalls' work in the way that the Thornycroft steamer had been used in Birmingham, they were allocated to take fish from Paddington to Billingsgate Market (returning with empty boxes) and also to carry traffic between Paddington and the GW Victoria & Albert depot in the London docks. These lorries typically averaged three trips daily totalling 52 miles and moving 15 tons in total. They were long-distance cartage trips for their time and the route was later used to try out the reliability of new types and makes of motor lorries. For example, two 5-ton Maudslay vehicles (fleet 175/6) were fully loaded in each direction for long periods in 1913. Long routes reduced 'idle time' and better suited the motor vehicles of the period.

The first GW motor lorry driver was Charles Willis who had been in charge of a pair-horse team at Paddington. An article in the 1936 *GW Magazine*, at the time of Mr Willis's retirement after 50 years' service, highlighted the 'primitive features' of the GW's first motor lorry — oil lamps, low radiator and iron-rimmed wheels which 'rattled like thunder over the cobbled streets'. In favourable circumstances ('which were rare') 20mph could be achieved. Upkeep of the early lorries was expensive, but improvements in solid rubber tyres allowed the iron-rimmed wheels to be replaced and made it economic to employ heavy goods lorries. (As supplied, the wheel spokes of the first Milnes-Daimler lorry were strangely curved which may have had to do with contemporary ideas on so-called 'tangent spokes' which did not run radially from the hub.)

It is worth remarking that the usual practice at that time was for makers to supply chassis, complete with engines and running gear, which would be completed by separate body builders (sometimes, in the late 1920s, the chassis might come with the maker's own cab as well, see Chapter 5). This was the norm until mass-production became widespread in the mid-late 1930s after which the GW sometimes bought complete vehicles — but not always, still preferring that the Swindon Road Wagon shop build goods bodies and cabs on bought-in chassis. The one early exception concerned Ford vehicles added to the fleet in 1921, and in later years, that came complete with bodies and cabs (Chapter 5).

```
ISSUED 28-12-35.          SUPPLIED LNA.


   BRITAIN'S FIRST MOTOR LORRY DRIVER.
   RETIRES AFTER FIFTY YEARS' SERVICE.

   A man who claims to be the first motor
lorry driver in Great Britain, is retiring
today (Saturday).

   He is Mr. CHARLES WILLIS of Bathurst
Gardens, Kensal Rise, who has served the
Great Western Railway for the past fifty
years, and during practically the whole
of that time, has driven goods from Paddington
station to the Royal Albert and Victoria Docks.
He had been driving horses for some years, when
he was informed that he would have to drive a
motor vehicle, a lumbering contraption, which
carried six tons of goods.

   O.P.S.  CHARLES WILLIS on the first lorry he
drove.
```

The GW purchased three Wolseley vehicles in 1905. This is parcel van fleet 40, LC-1083, photographed alongside the triangle at the end of Sussex Gardens, near Paddington Station. Chain drive. Method of braking not obvious; perhaps a transmission brake. Note the use of 'parcel' (singular): it soon became 'parcels' on subsequent vans. *GWR/P J Kelley collection*

Wolseley 2-ton lorry with fixed canvas tilt. "G K Mills/Secretary/Paddington Station" painted on side of lorry near driver, but no fleet number. The vehicle was fleet 39 and in 1907 was re-registered as AF 280 in Cornwall; the original number plate is unknown. Chain driven to middle shaft. Chain again to rear wheels (metal guards covering sprockets). Engine under seat (radiator on side). Is really a 'forward control' arrangement. Method of braking unclear; possibly transmission braking. "Diver's helmet" front and rear lamps. The original photograph is rubber-stamped 'The Wolseley Tool & Motor Car Coy Ltd' and dated 11/1/06. *P Kelley*

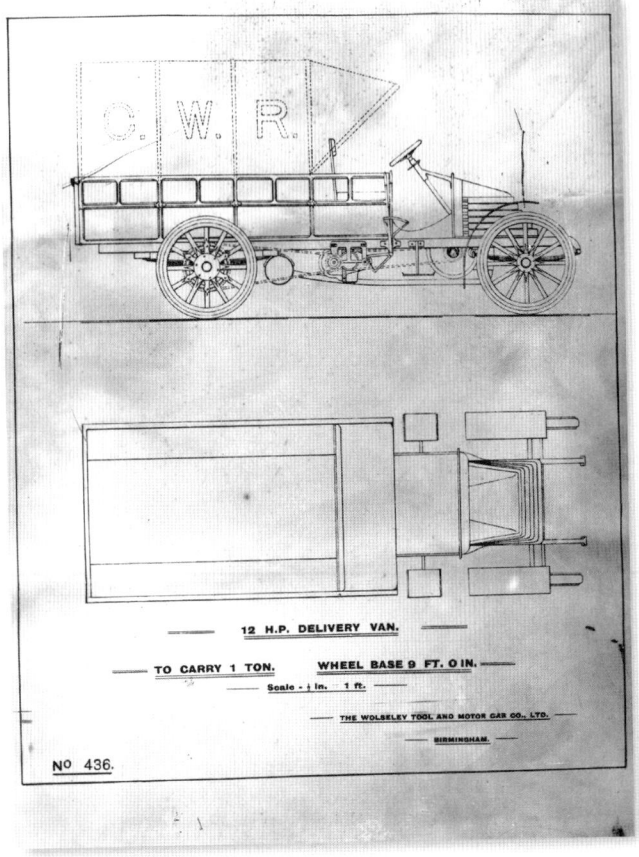

In 1905 the GW purchased a 12hp Wolseley van for parcels, fleet 40 (Wolseley Tool and Motor Car Co of Adderley Park, Birmingham, then part of the Vickers Armaments group). At about the same time a 2-ton Wolseley lorry with tilt was bought, followed in 1909 by 6 Straker & Squire 15-cwt chassis that had chains for transmission to rear wheels and leather-lined cone clutches. The firm was based in Fishponds, Bristol, (in Edmonton, London, after 1919) and made a large proportion of London motor buses before WW1. The Straker-Squires were faster than the pony and horse vans then used for express parcels traffic and they were bodied at Swindon as parcel vans to operate in Birkenhead, Birmingham and Cardiff with fleet numbers 106-111. These new vehicles enabled earlier and more frequent collections and deliveries to be made, and widened the areas in which traffic could be dealt with. In 1910, three Goodchild Auto-Carrier cyclecars (motorised tricycles, fleet 119-121) were bought to aid in this work. Designed by Messrs Goodchild of London, they were manufactured by Laycock Engineering in Sheffield. One was employed at Paddington on express parcels; another carried advertising materials around London; and the third worked on parcel work around Acton. The Auto-Carrier firm of Edmonton in London later morphed into the AC car company that among other vehicles made racing cars. [Regarding motorcycles, in 1923 a Douglas machine came into the GW fleet (number 397); in 1926 five Carette motorcycle carriers were experimentally introduced for rapid delivery of urgent perishable consignments; and about 1930 a Raleigh motorcycle (fleet 1684) was added to the stock.]

'MECHANICALLY-PROPELLED' GOODS VEHICLES BEFORE 1920: PARCELS TRAFFIC

The larger firms of GW cartage agents also introduced mechanically-propelled vehicles, Bantocks in the West Midlands having a Fowler and a Garrett steam tractor in Edwardian times. Its first petrol vehicles were Model T Ford lorries acquired in 1910. Four Foden steam wagons were put in service in 1916, and at the end of WW1 Bantocks operated eleven.

Goods motor lorries used bus chassis but parcels vans had lighter chassis. In 1911 the GW directors authorised the purchase of ten 3½-ton and one 5-ton chassis for C&D use in London, and one 3½-ton lorry for transfer work traffic between Poplar and Paddington. The makers included Commercial Cars of Luton ('Commer' vehicles founded in 1905), who delivered five chassis in 1911 (fleet 163-167) to be bodied at Swindon. The engines had 4 cylinders with 100 mm bore x 110mm stroke, rated at 25 horsepower (see Appendix 4), and a 3-speed gear box. The lorries were able to travel at 12mph with the rated load of 3½ tons.

Above: **Goodchild Autocarrier LD-7190** (number plate attached to rails around top of body on this side; there does not seem to be a corresponding plate on the other). Fleet 119 of 1910, the first of three assigned fleet 119-121. These 'cyclecars' were designed by Messrs Goodchild, and manufactured by Laycock Engineering in Sheffield. The Auto-Carrier firm of Edmonton in London later morphed into the AC car company that among other vehicles made racing cars – but not for the GWR! *GWR/P J Kelley collection*

Right and below right: **Milnes-Daimler 5-ton lorry, LC3636 of 1911,** fleet 48 painted on chassis and in white on brown plaque on cabside (2nd use of fleet 48; first was a Liversidge-bodied Durkopp bus DA100 of 1905). Transmission brake. Stronger and longer chassis compared with contemporary Milnes-Daimler parcels van fleet 53, and has heavy-duty rear wheels with large drum brakes. Swindon-built flat body is high off the chassis. The same vehicle loaded with goods, and now having 'SPEED 12MPH' on chassis (not on the other official photograph). Headlamps are alongside driver at the scuttle rather than at radiator in the case of the parcels van. Spare wheel at rear under floor. Wagon tarpaulin (before days of tarpaulins given lorry fleet number). *GWR/D J Hyde collection*

Left: Milnes-Daimler 30cwt parcels van of 1911. Second use of fleet number 53 (1st was a Maudslay bus in 1905). Liverpool registration K1564. Unladen weight (UW) 2-6-3 to right of '53' on chassis at bulkhead. GW body number G42 on lowest body plank beneath '53'. Unlike Milnes-Daimler lorry fleet 48, the headlamps are at the radiator and the rear wheels are lighter-duty. Drum brakes on rear wheels with linkage to driver's lever. 'GREAT WESTERN RAILWAY/AEBOLTER/SECRETARY/PADDINGTON/STATION' on side below driver's seat. Between 1914-20 was a bus for the GW Tregenna Castle Hotel at St Ives. *GWR/D J Hyde collection*

Below: One of five 3½-ton Commer vehicles delivered to the GW in 1911, fleet 163-167. Photographed in muddied road condition with tailboard down. Registration LE9658 and fleet 166 painted in white on chassis at bulkhead; in shaded gold on top plank of body. Half tilt body with brackets for storage of four hoops (not present) at end of tilt. Three hoops would be put into brackets along the body to support a tarpaulin. Three radiator header tank holding down bolts each side characterise these Commers. Roof and top storey of old derelict Paddington goods building. *GWR/D J Hyde collection*

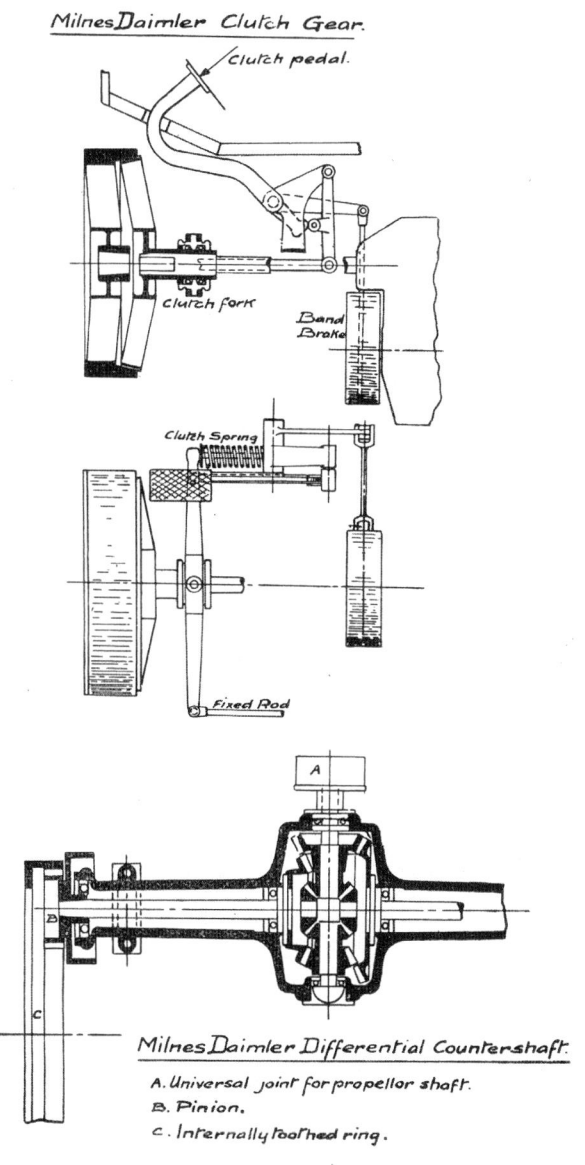

Above: **Milnes-Daimler drawings clutch and differential.**

By 1911, there were 23 centres at which GW buses operated, and eight centres from which goods and parcel vans operated. These included:

Birkenhead:	1 steam wagon (probably the Teme Valley vehicle) and 3 petrol parcel vans
Birmingham:	5 petrol parcels vans
Bilston Goods:	2 steam tractors
Cardiff:	2 petrol parcel vans
Paddington Goods:	2 petrol lorries, 2 electric lorries and 5 motor parcel vans
Slough Goods:	1 petrol lorry
Saltash and Callington:	1 petrol lorry

[The circumstance of the last entry is of interest. The GW had opened a bus service from Saltash to Albaston (Gunnislake) via Callington in 1904, and there were plans for a GW branch railway. However, Callington in 1908 became the terminus of the Bere Alston & Calstock Light Rly (Plymouth, Devonport and South Western Jct Rly) and so did not become part of GW territory.]

The 15 parcels vans were made up of the early Wolseley, Straker & Squire 15cwt vehicles, and Milnes-Daimler 4-cylinder 22hp vans, one of which was based at Birkenhead/Liverpool. Twenty-four more Straker & Squire parcel vans were on order for London, Birkenhead and Liverpool but, as the June 1911 *GW Magazine* warned, 'owing to the present pressure on all makers of commercial vehicles, consequent upon the boom in commercial motor traction, delivery is likely to be somewhat delayed'; they eventually arrived in 1914.

By 1913 there were some 67 motor lorries and in that year '...... experiments have been made upon a more extensive scale with the latest design of motors, with the object of ascertaining whether motor traction is more economical than horse power for the collection and delivery of rail-borne traffic............' But delivery of new lorries ordered for the end of 1914 was delayed owing to the onset of WW1. Ten 24hp Thornycroft vans were ordered for parcels work in 1915; there were several other vehicles on order, but delivery could not be completed until 1919. (J I Thornycroft,

Right: **One of two 5-ton Maudslay lorries trialled on the long Paddington-Billingsgate-V&A Docks route.** Photographed on 5/3/13 before going into service, and before fleet number 175 has been painted on the plaque on the cabside, although 'speed 12 mph' is on chassis. Registration LC5034. No brake blocks, so it must have a transmission brake. *GWR/P J Kelley collection*

One of ten Dennis parcels vans (fleet 153-162) brought into service between May and August 1911. AF705, fleet 155, has brown livery with white lettering. Photographed in Bishopston, Bristol. 'A E Bolter, Secretary, etc' painted on curved panel between driver's seat and back of body, to left of bulb horn. Wicker basket on driver Stewart's left; guard/van-boy Phillips. *Author's collection*

One of the first batch of ten Thornycroft 30cwt vans ordered in 1914, but not all delivered until after WW1. Registration LH 9236. Original fleet number C6 painted in white on black chassis below bulkhead and in shaded gold on plaque on permanent tilt below 'S' in 'Services'. Photographed after change to 'chocolate and cream' livery in 1923. Poster about costs of luggage in advance which is priced at 1/3d that is less expensive than the figure of 3/- on the comparable vehicle (fleet C1) illustrated in the section below on Parcels. Side brackets for lamps at bulkhead. C1-10 renumbered in sequence to fleet 501-10. *STEAM Swindon*

originally of Chiswick and later Basingstoke, manufactured steam wagons, motor cars and commercial road vehicles from 1895.) During the period before the *Road Transport Department* was set up in 1922, some C&D vehicles were given letter-prefixed fleet numbers, and these Thornycrofts were C1-C10, later numbered fleet 501-510 (see Chapter 8).

Charges by the Swindon Road Wagon shop for the construction of cartage bodies just around WW1 are indicated by: seven bodies for 5-ton Maudslay chassis cost £210 or £30 each in 1913; twenty-one bodies for 1½-ton Thornycroft chassis totalled £625 or again about £30 each (this order was not completed until 1919). In contrast, inflation by the end of the war increased the cost of lorry bodies to £65 each in 1919 (for ex-army AEC chassis), as discussed in Chapter 5.

During WW1, over a third of the staff of the GW's *Road Motor Car Department* had enlisted, many of whom joined the Mechanical Transport Branch of the Army Service Corps. Nevertheless, all twenty-three regular passenger and mail road bus services were kept going (albeit with a reduced timetable).

Transport of government stores and munitions increased the tonnage of goods and parcels traffic on the GW, resulting by 1916 in a doubling of the number of road cartage motor vehicles just at Paddington alone and led to increased road mileage.

Of the three types of 'mechanical propulsion', petrol motors seemed more suited to C&D work and, of course, were the driving force in all the GW buses operating at the time. An American Knox petrol tractor was purchased in 1918 from the importers Rudds of Poplar (see Chapter 6). Nevertheless, in comparison with the more than 3,000 horses employed on C&D work on the GW at the turn of the 19th/20th centuries, the number of self-propelled vehicles used for railway goods work before WW1 was very few indeed. Matters would change however after WW1 when the versatility of petrol-engined vehicles made them popular; price and running costs were low and only wear was a problem. Of the different makes of motors purchased by the GW before WW1, no further Milnes-Daimler and Straker-Squire vehicles were bought after the war.

The question of alternative fuels came up during the final years of WW1 since petrol had to be imported by sea, and was subject to submarine attack. Coal gas, readily available from gasworks, was a candidate fuel. It had to be carried on the moving road motor and either it could be held (i) compressed in steel cylinders (which were expensive and difficult to obtain owing to the war); or (ii) at gas-holder or mains pressure in flexible containers made of balloon fabric carried in high-sided trays on the roofs of vehicles. The GW employed the second idea (invented by T H Barton of Beeston, Notts) in 1917 on some buses and parcel vans (see Parcels section below). About 700 cu ft was the typical capacity of a 45-seater bus, but the height of GW standard garage doors played its part. The bags experienced wear and tear in the wind as they deflated. Anchoring the bags to the trays caused problems initially, instances occurring where rubber cords snapped off in high winds and drivers had to chase the containers over adjoining fields! Output of engines fuelled by a mixture of coal gas and air was slightly less than by petrol alone, but the vehicles were popular with drivers as they started easily.

Parker producer gas apparatus fitted to 3½-ton AEC ex-army lorry in 1921, LU9869. Note the painting style used just before the *Road Transport Department* came into being: the fleet number 633 is in shaded gold/yellow on a brown plaque on the cabside below the tax disc, lamp irons and 'Speed 12 MPH'. 'SOUTH LAMBETH' is painted at the right on the bottom plank of the body, the stanchions of which correspond with the cross beams sitting on the chassis. Towing hooks at rear. T & W Farmiloe Ltd of Cringle Street, Wandsworth, were paint manufacturers. *H W Bamber*

Latil tractor fitted with producer gas apparatus in 1939, the anthracite coal for which was obtained from Powell Duffryn's Ystrad Mynach pit connected to the old Rhymney Rly. This producer gas-driven vehicle is running on south wales fuel' is inscribed in brown on cream at the rear window and in cream around the large cylinder. Fleet S419, FGT471. Yellow encircled GWR shirtbutton on door and tool boxes; brown on cream at cab roof. Transition from brown to cream is at usual height on door, but is very low over engine owing to cream-painted bonnet. *Author's collection*

An alternative was to manufacture 'producer gas' on the vehicle itself from anthracite or coke and, as shown in the photograph, experiments along this line were under way in 1921, even though the war was over. Producer gas was obtained by converting carbon through various stages into carbon monoxide which was combustible in a petrol engine when mixed with further oxygen made by adding steam to the primary air, resulting in the formation of hydrogen and more carbon monoxide. In order to start the plant, it was necessary to fill the furnace with a suitable fuel (anthracite coal). The fire was started by means of a small torch and suction was produced by a hand-blower until the engine fired, after which the necessary suction was created by the stroke of the pistons.

Parcels Traffic

Parcels traffic, conveyed by passenger train at higher rates than ordinary C&D traffic, was an important earner for the railway. Parcels were smaller than heavy goods and could be quickly collected and delivered using light 'express parcels vans' — originally horse-drawn and later by motors. Prompt delivery was essential for its success. As much money could be made conveying higher-charged parcels as heavy lower-charged goods. In rural areas, even though parcels had to be carried by C&D vehicles (often Country Lorries, Chapter 10), the parcels service was better than the ordinary C&D service.

The subject is relevant to a number of chapters in this book, but is placed here between horse-drawn vehicles/early motors and 'modern' later motor vehicles for convenience, even though by so doing it does anticipate material in Chapter 5 and elsewhere. After the formation of the *Road Transport Department* in 1922, while the wording 'Express Parcels' was retained on horse-drawn parcels vans, on motor vans it was usually changed to 'Express Cartage'.

The parcels classification, perhaps surprisingly, permitted items up to 2cwt in weight. It was not until the Rates & Charges Act of 1891 that railways were obliged to carry parcels and light goods by passenger train, although they had done so for many years before. The 1891 statutory obligation was limited to butter, soft cheese, eggs, fish, fruit and vegetables (including 'hot-house' produce and flowers), dead game, ice, fresh meat, dead poultry and dead rabbits.

'MECHANICALLY-PROPELLED' GOODS VEHICLES BEFORE 1920: PARCELS TRAFFIC

Above: Pony parcel van to Diagram D1 (footrest for driver is a curved continuation of the floor, unlike other vans which are straight and hinged). Brakeshoes on rear wheels, lever for which is inside the van (shaft passes through to right of fleet 243). Cream on brown livery with yellow 'Henley etc'. Grocer's plural for "parcel's".
GWR/P J Kelley collection

Above: Two-horse tilt van with dickey for passenger train parcels to Diagram D10. Cream on brown livery but with 'GREAT WESTERN RAILWAY PARCEL VAN' and '161.P. PADDINGTON STATION' in yellow. Letter 'P' after fleet number is unusual (see similar vehicle harnessed to a pair of greys in Chapter 2). *GWR/P J Kelley collection*

Above: One-horse tilt van with a fixed head (i.e. fixed 'tarpaulin over' with side windows) to Diagram D2, fleet 287, photographed in 1909. Based at the GW Receiving Office at 170B Strand. The tilt has painted on (all in white on brown) the services that the driver could provide. Brake shoes on rear wheels operated by driver's foot pedal.
GWR/P J Kelley collection

Above: This is a fixed-head parcels van but without side windows based at Bristol, fleet 232. *GWR/P J Kelley collection*

Above: One-horse tilt van with a fixed head (i.e. fixed 'tarpaulin over' with side windows) to Diagram D2, fleet 68, photographed in 1933. White-on-brown lettering now simplified from before and tilt has space for commercial advertisements (but in this case telling about the railway parcel services). 'PADDINGTON STATION' and fleet number in yellow. Whip in driver's right hand; his right foot is on the brake pedal.
GWR/P J Kelley collection

One of the first group of Straker-Squire 15cwt parcels van delivered to the GWR in 1909. This is fleet 110 and was one of three that operated in Birmingham, hence the local registration O 4505. The other three (fleet 106-108) operated in Birkenhead and had local CM number plates. Fleet 110 was later sold to Messrs Mahoney in Newport. Four-plank body with permanent tilt. Arch over rear wheels does not extend to a full mudguard. Other views may be found in Kelley on p 41. *P Kelley*

'MECHANICALLY-PROPELLED' GOODS VEHICLES BEFORE 1920: PARCELS TRAFFIC

In the "Instructions for the Guidance of the Company's Representatives engaged in Canvassing" issued in September 1910 under James Inglis's general managership, it was stated that it was the duty of parcel carmen to call the attention of station masters to any decrease in the number of parcels handed to them to be forwarded by the GWR, and for enquiries to be made. It was said that "…..the constant aim is to provide and maintain an efficient and economical service in order to secure the maximum traffic to the railway."

Apart from the two goods motor lorries based on the same type of chassis as used for buses, the majority of the first motor vehicles purchased by the GW were vans for parcel traffic, again emphasising the importance of speed. As described and illustrated earlier in this chapter, the first purchases of motors from the following makers were all parcels vans: Wolseley, Straker & Squire, Dennis and Thornycroft.

The GW Receiving Office at 17 Commercial Road, London EC, in 1911. *GWR/A G Atkins collection*

Another fixed head parcels van with side windows to Diagram D2, fleet 305, operating from Addison Road station. Photographed in 1908, the lettering leaves space for GW (not commercial) advertisements. *GWR/P J Kelley collection*

In 1915, the very first Thornycroft vehicle was bought by the GW and is illustrated here. Original fleet number C1 painted on chassis below cab door and on plaque on planked body side just behind driver (changed to fleet 501 after formation of the *Road Transport Department* in 1922). Greater London registration LH9237. The 30cwt parcels van with drum brakes on rear wheels was photographed in 1921 in all-over brown livery with black chassis, and white/cream lettering ('parcels services' seems older and dirty; 'parcels' is in block capitals, but seriffed letters for 'express' and 'services'). Name of company secretary, etc, low down on curved back to driver's seat. Still with extended canopy over driver — compare the much smaller hood over the driver on parcels van C6 illustrated earlier. *STEAM Swindon*

Ransomes electric express parcels van of 1919, in crimson lake livery, with Ipswich DX1986 registration and fleet E14 (renumbered fleet 191 on the formation of the *Road Transport Department* in 1922). Contemporary lettering of 'load not to exceed 2-10-0' at left of bottom plank of body with 'great western railway/aebolter secretary/paddington' at right, with fleet E-14 immediately above (and above window). 'FAW 2-13-0' in script on chassis at front wheel, above which is maker's plate. GWR garter coat of arms below cab window and 'GWR' in shaded gold lettering at front of vehicle. *GWR/D J Hyde collection*

Before WW1 in the London area, parcels arriving at Paddington on long-distance passenger trains would be taken by local passenger services to the relevant station for delivery by horse vans — and vice-versa for outgoing parcels. But after the introduction of large numbers of motor parcels vans that could cover a wider area than horse-drawn vehicles, delivery and collection could be performed directly from Paddington, with no requirement for parcels vehicles to be based at many local stations (this was true of course in most of the large towns served by the GW).

Parcels at Paddington used to be dealt with on the 'Lawn' (the area between the buffers of the passenger tracks and the GWR Royal Hotel), but operations there became congested as the number of parcels handled all over the GW increased inexorably (in 1924, 16 million parcels were carried; by 1930, it was 22 million;

'MECHANICALLY-PROPELLED' GOODS VEHICLES BEFORE 1920: PARCELS TRAFFIC

Above: Some parcels vans operating in Cardiff, Manchester and Penzance were converted to run on coal gas in 1917. The gas was held in flexible containers on the roof. Since forward motion drove the gas to the rear of the flexible bag, pipework to the engine was connected from the back, and gas was drawn in by the suction of the engine. The photo shows Straker-Squire 15cwt van of February 1912, fleet number 142, with Cornish registration AF 781, posed outside the 'Edwardian baroque style' City Hall in Cardiff which was built in 1906. *GWR/D J Hyde collection*

and in 1934, nearly 27 million). Consequently, when the Paddington terminus was rebuilt to incorporate Bishops Road station in 1933, opportunity was taken to move parcels handling to the old excursion and milk platform (Platform 1A built in 1908 as an extension to Platform 1) — with much greater working area than the Lawn — to which all platforms of the main station had trolley access either though subway or by bridge. A new parcels depot with offices was built above, with entrance on Bishops Road and exit into Orsett Terrace at the end of Westbourne Bridge (see vol 2A of *GWR Goods Services*). When the General station at Cardiff was rebuilt to incorporate the Riverside station in 1934, a new parcels depot was opened in the triangle of land between the two.

Children watching the 'Dunkley' pedal tricycle introduced at Ealing Broadway station in 1923. Although it says 'parcels service' it does not say 'express parcels service'! Dunkley's main business was pram manufacture at Jamaica Row in Birmingham. *GWR/D J Hyde collection*

Five Carette motorcycle carriers (made by the Chater Lea company of Letchworth and given fleet 1155-60) were experimentally introduced in 1926 for rapid delivery of urgent perishable consignments at locations where the traffic did not justify the use of full-size motors. This example has shaded gold lettering and a single tax disc attached to vertical part of steering handle. Wagons at back left. *STEAM Swindon*

GREAT WESTERN RAILWAY.

The Great Western Railway Company will open a

NEW
BOOKING AND GENERAL RECEIVING
OFFICE
AT
5, HOLBORN VIADUCT, E.C.1
(with a rear entrance in GREEN ARBOUR COURT),
ON
OCTOBER 12th, 1925.

ORDINARY, TOURIST and EXCURSION TICKETS
will be issued, and, if desired, dated in advance.

Seats can be booked in the Company's principal Express trains, and Picnic and Pleasure Parties arranged for.

PASSENGER TRAIN PARCELS and GENERAL MERCHANDISE

will be received at the Green Arbour Court entrance,

for conveyance to All Parts of the United Kingdom.

THE COMPANY'S VANS COLLECT

Parcels and Merchandise from Premises in the neighbourhood and all orders for collection will receive prompt attention.

The Booking and General Receiving Office at 23, Newgate Street, E.C.1, will be CLOSED when the business has been transferred to the new Office at 5, Holborn Viaduct, E.C.1.

Information regarding Fares, Rates, and other arrangements can be obtained on application at the Office (Telephone City 6172), or from Mr. H. R. CAMPFIELD, Divisional Superintendent, Paddington Station (respecting Passenger and Parcels business), and Mr. J. W. LOVEJOY, District Goods Manager, 23, Newgate Street, E.C. (respecting Merchandise Traffic).

FELIX J. C. POLE,
General Manager.

PADDINGTON STATION,
September, 1925.

Morris Commercial 1-ton van YU 5011 of 1/9/28, originally fleet 1105. Photographed in February 1941 in blackout regulations (mask to nearside headlamp; no offside headlamp; white edges to what appear to be different pattern mudguards). Renumbered to A1006 in 1935 (as a van, supposed to have been prefixed 'B', see Chapter 8). Size and positioning of advertising board squeezes shirtbutton and 'express cartage services' to left of body side. Advert is for Solidox toothpaste, introduced into the UK from Norway in 1939 and manufactured by John Knight of Wapping, London. *GWR/D J Hyde collection*

'MECHANICALLY-PROPELLED' GOODS VEHICLES BEFORE 1920: PARCELS TRAFFIC

Two 8hp Ford 5cwt vans purchased in 1933 for express parcels work in London. One was employed on urgent consignments of cream, fish and other perishable traffic. Most cartage motors were labelled 'express cartage services' by this time, but these vans retain the older inscription.
A G Atkins collection

Fleet 2839 (but no registration number plate yet), a Morris Commercial 2-tonner of November 1934 with van body and newly-introduced shirtbutton in encircled brown on cream above 'Express Cartage Services' on side. Instructions on front axle (about jacking?). 'gwr paddington station' on bottom plank of body.
GWR/P J Kelley collection

Fleet E2802, a 25/30cwt electric van delivered to the GW in 1947 from the Brush company in Loughborough. No registration plate yet. Shirtbutton is painted in encircled brown on cream body side, and on circular cream patch on brown front of vehicle. *Ian Allan Library*

6-ton Scammell trailer having a lightened body (coded Dyak J) fitted up for tranship traffic in London. Photographed 1/2/37 with fleet number T-520. Shirtbutton is brown-encircled GWR on cream fixed tilt, and cream-encircled GWR on metal panel on planked sides.
GWR/P J Kelley collection

Despite the increased capacity at Paddington, parcels traffic for the districts of Hammersmith, Shepherds Bush, Chelsea and Fulham in the south-west of London was served separately from Kensington (Addison Rd) joint station rather than Paddington. Overall some 60 square miles were covered by the two depots. Business in London continued to increase through the 1930s: in 1930 just under 7 million parcels were handled by 112 staff; in 1937, over 10 million parcels by 136 vanmen. The cartage wages bill in 1938 was £700/week. There were 132 regular rounds at Paddington Parcels of which 123 were operated by motor vans and the remaining 9 by horse. Typically 37,000 parcels per day were carted, for which 96 motors (with capacities of 1 ton to 8 tons) were provided. About half of them were involved in double shifts and they covered a total of 3,400 miles every working day. Fifty vans left between 8.0am and 10.30am clearing some 2,000 packages for all parts of London. This continued throughout the day, and incoming perishable traffic including fish and poultry for the markets was sent out up to 5pm. Returning vans had either collected outgoing traffic from GW Receiving Offices and parcels agencies, or had performed collection rounds for the Receiving Offices; it would be evening before these vehicles returned to Paddington. At busy times extra vehicles were brought in, especially at Christmas when about 80 extra vans were employed, a dozen of which were reserved for poultry sent from Ireland (it was not unusual for 180 tons of turkeys to arrive within a 24-hour period in the 1930s).

There was a heavy traffic of through parcels (7,500 packages daily) from all over the GW system intended for destinations on other main line companies. For this there were some 80 transfer trips daily, spread over day and night, to 10 other main line London stations from Paddington. After dropping off packages at another company's terminal, GW vehicles picked up return loads intended for destinations on its territory. Similar transfer trips were performed to Paddington by the LMS, LNER and SR; on return, they too took away some goods from Paddington for their systems. Kensington received its incoming parcels for distribution by similar road transfer trips from Paddington.

On the collection side, 17 of the GW's London parcels Receiving Offices (see *GWR Goods Services*) had their own vans collecting locally from the public. On returning to the Receiving Office, parcels from different rounds were bulked and sent at frequent intervals in other vans to Paddington for dispatch. Collections were made from 10.0am and lasted as late as 10.0pm in the East End. Parcels were also picked up from 20 receiving offices belonging to other railways, and from 13 agencies with which the GW had arrangements. Each vanman had a daily schedule of duties that included a list of regular calls. Outwards traffic from Kensington (Addison Rd) included cake and ice cream from J Lyons & Co for all over the GW system. It could exceed 1,000 tons a month in the summer peak period and was carted by road motors to Paddington Parcels. Road transport also conveyed extensive traffic from Messrs Kearley & Tongue in Southall, and Walls in Acton, to Paddington Parcels (see Chapter 13).

CHAPTER FIVE

COLLECTION & DELIVERY MOTOR VEHICLES AFTER WW1

THE demand by the armed forces for motor vehicles during WW1 stimulated manufacturers both to increase the rates of production of vehicles, and to improve technical specifications. Motor lorries became cheaper and more reliable than before the war. Buses made by the Associated Equipment Company (AEC) of Walthamstow (London), and later Southall, had proved very reliable, and had been ordered in great quantity by the government for army use. Following the Armistice, the War Disposals Committee sold off these vehicles at low prices from the army repair depot that subsequently became the Slough Trading Estate. Between 1919 and 1927 the GW purchased 130 ex-army AEC 3½-ton 45hp ('Y-type') lorries from the Slough Trading Co, from the Disposals Board and from a few agents. The first ex-army lorry was Fleet 184, registration LT9897. The chassis of these lorries were used to expand the fleet of both buses and goods vehicles. At the time, this included the practice of using interchangeable bodies which permitted winter lorries to become buses and char-a-bancs for summer holiday traffic. Exchange of bodies was relatively easily done on vehicles with simple, straight-sided chassis. After the GW ceased operating buses in the late 1920s/early 1930s, the idea of interchangeable bodies fell out of favour, but in later years fixed bodies were designed to be adaptable by having detachable sides, removable hoop sticks for tilts and so on.

New cartage makes bought by the GW after WW1 were Ford and Burford. [Complete Model T cars and lorries were first imported into Britain in 1908, and from 1911 were assembled from component parts at the Trafford Park industrial estate in

A photograph of one of the first ex-army AEC 3½-ton 45hp lorries bought by the GW in 1919. Registration LT 9939 is on scuttle and fleet 187 is on a plaque near the driver's seat. The picture is significant because the vehicle's numbering was changed to fleet 408 in 1920, after which the second user of fleet 187 was one of the Ransome, Sims & Jeffries electric cartage vehicles, originally fleet E11. The lorry has drum brakes on the rear wheels only and is equipped with a three-plank body and five-hoop canvas tilt. All-over brown livery. Typical of the time just before the *Road Transport Department* was formed, 'Load not to exceed 3-10-0' is in large lettering on bottom plank. On the chassis below the cab fleet number plaque is the unladen weight and front and back axle weights. *Alan Lambert*

GWR GOODS CARTAGE VOLUME 1

Above: Witney in September 1923 where blankets from the local factory have been brought to a special train carrying them to Maples of Tottenham Court Road under the watchful eye of the station master. The ex-army AEC lorry fleet 484, XO3935, had only come into service in June 1923 and has the 'new' brown and cream livery. It has a cab with side windows rather than the driver's awning of the first ex-army lorries. The railway van is one of the few metal-roofed examples of a Mink A to diagram V16 and was itself new in 1923. *GWR/D J Hyde collection*

AEC ex-army 3½-tonner fleet 264 (registration XL1792) of May 1922, now with proper cab and painted in chocolate and cream livery. About 1926. *GWR/D J Hyde collection*

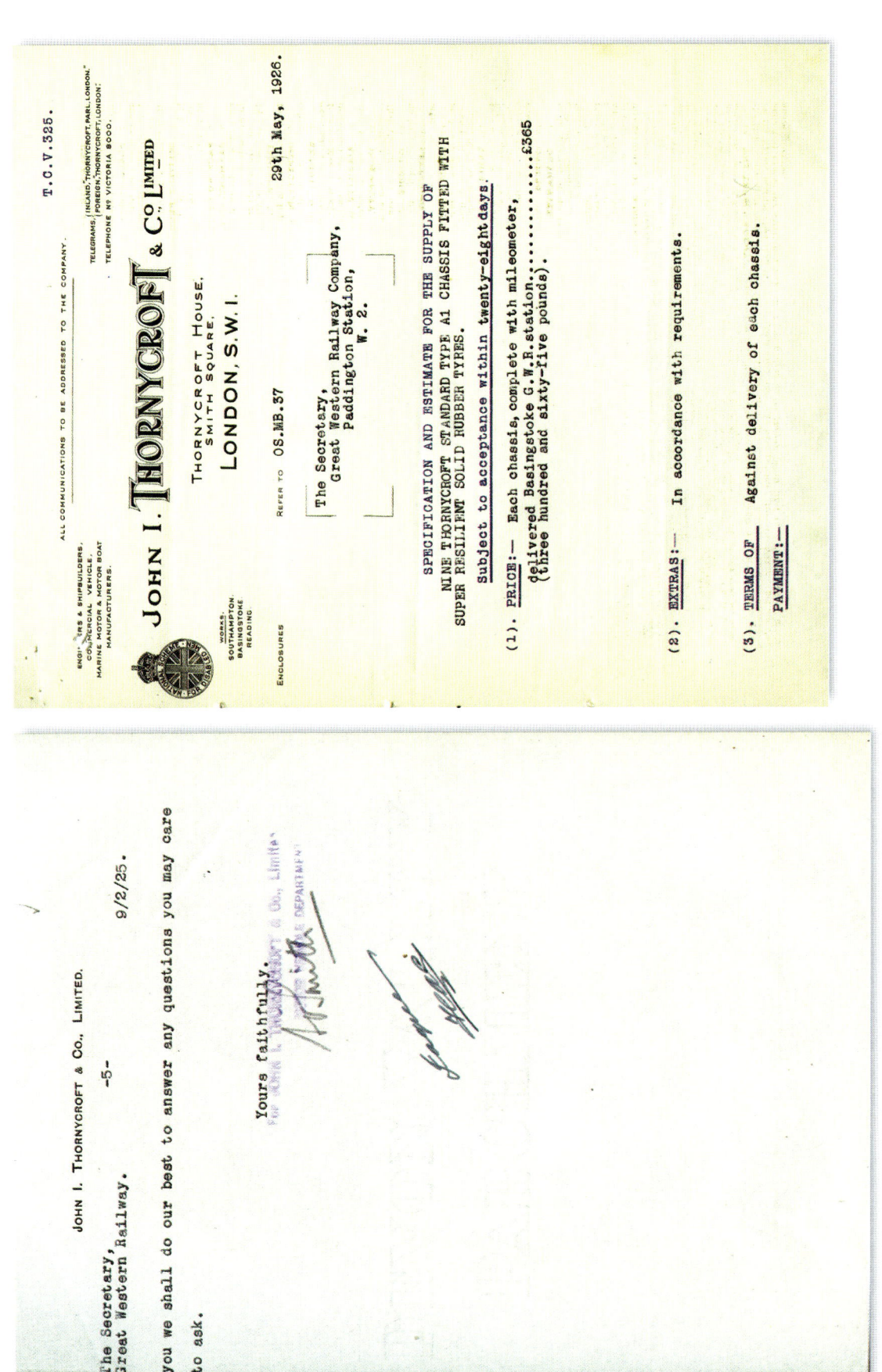

Above: Loading of C&D vehicles was easier when the body was open; this could be readily achieved in tarpaulin-covered lorries simply by rolling back the tilt, but was not possible in permanently-roofed vans. To provide easier access to the insides of vans, the GW tried out the sliding tilt design of the Portsmouth Motor Co on two vehicles. The tilt was constructed in two sections: when the rear section was slid forward on roller bearings, three-quarters of the loading space became open (the moveable tilt came over and alongside the forward-control cab); moving it back to clear the cab left half the loading space exposed; and fully back exposed the front covered portion at which point the vehicle was ready for the road with driver at the wheel. Here the design is fitted to Thornycroft 'PB' fleet 1351, YU9358 (but no number plate), of November 1927. Speed 12mph in script on chassis to right of fleet number that is also in brown on cream plaque on planked lower body. The Portsmouth company appear to have painted this vehicle since the G, W and R on the cream mid-side plank are in a non-GW style. This van was based at Tyseley. The other vehicle equipped in this way was a forward control 4/5-ton Thornycroft fleet 1334 of March 1927, that was based at Park Royal, shown in Kelley, p61. *Ian Allan Library*

Above: An unusual body (Swindon number G 531) on a 30cwt Thornycroft A1 chassis, fleet 1404, UC5329, photographed on 30/3/28. Jointly owned by the GW and GC (LNER), it was intended for chair traffic at High Wycombe. Since chairs were light, but bulky, they were carried roped on the extended cab roof as well as behind the cab. Ladder to extended cab roof, with 'kicking patches' on cabside behind rungs of ladder, and bars over cab side window behind ladder. Cream raves with arch over rear wheel having brown 'g.w.r.'. Narrow pneumatic tyres. Later vehicles for chair traffic would use tall wire-netted frameworks around ordinary lorry bodies. *GWR/P J Kelley collection*

Above: Burford forward-control 30cwt 2-plank lorry fleet 875, YK3805, photographed on 26/2/30. Formerly Buckingham-bodied bus of 24/6/25. Detachable sides with provision for 5 hoopsticks. Owing to spacing of supports, 'railway' is condensed to 'great western raily ' on cream panel along rave. 'speed 20mph' on chassis. Transitional design of Burford cab: instead of no windscreen at all and two vertical rods to support roof, there is only one rod on passenger/near side, since driver has a half-windscreen. One licence disc (on cabside). Pneumatic tyres (single on rear) with spare wheel under chassis this side. *GWR /P J Kelley collection*

Left: **Morris Commercial (Morris '21') Express Cartage Services van, fleet 1122, YX5026 of July 1928.** 'Services' is in seriffed lettering. 'great western railway/ f r e davis (secY)/ paddington' at bottom of cab. Normal control. Electric lights all round. Pressed-steel artillery-style wheels with pneumatic tyres. Is the roof a different colour? *GWR/P J Kelley collection*

Below: **Thornycroft 4-ton 'PB' forward-control chassis fitted with a rigid tilt slotting into six brackets along the three-plank side.** Bottom of inserts on tilt painted cream to match central cream plank. Fleet 1361, YV1122 of March 1928. Good view into cab showing dashboard, with hand brake and pedals passing through floor, etc. No windscreen, tarpaulin to protect driver rolled up in front of steering column. Tailboard held up by chain on far side of van, since chain this side is slack. Body curves up over rear wheel with no mudguard. Horse-drawn vehicle, fleet 374 to Diagram D4/8 in right background. *GWR/P J Kelley collection*

many old GW goods vehicles including two Straker-Squire 15cwt parcel vans (fleet 110/123) dating from 1908; and one of the Goodchild Autocarriers (fleet 120). A curious entry in the road motor register is that a German Adler car (the fourth user of fleet number 180, originally registered LL987, but subsequently unlicensed) was used in the salvage department at Paddington, and had been "taken in lieu of unpaid fees" in the early 1920s. It was later sold on to Mahoney. A Ford 1-tonner AF4311, fleet 1054 that had come to the GW in February 1929 from Agent Lean in Truro, was sold after only 18 months in August 1930 to Messrs Rees in South Farnborough, and a 1926 Scammell 6-wheel permanently-articulated lorry, fleet 1171, was sold on to Messrs Dell of Porthcawl.

In 1928, second-hand chassis from redundant GWR buses were returned to the makers for reconditioning and were fitted with suitable new bodies for cartage work. Ten 3-ton and thirty 30cwt C&D vehicles were obtained by this means. A couple of years later a number of Maudslay ML3 buses not passed on to the national bus companies were also converted to lorries (Maudslay was based in Coventry and had been building chassis since 1905). For example, fleet 1512 (YV8570) — originally a Strachan-bodied bus (body C32FR) of 6/6/28 — received lorry body G1699 for chair traffic from High Wycombe; fleet 1550 (YV5431) was a new Vickers-bodied bus delivered in May 1928 that later became a lorry at an unknown date.

A new make of lorry came into the fleet in 1929, namely the 'Associated Daimler'. In 1926 the Associated Equipment Co (AEC) had separated from the London General Omnibus Company and with Daimler (by then part of the Birmingham Small Arms Co, BSA) formed the Associated Daimler Co with new works at Southall to produce commercial vehicles. Between February and July 1929 the GW took delivery of 94 ADC '428' forward-control 4/5-ton flatbed lorries that were assigned fleet numbers 1900-93. However, the joint venture was short-lived, Daimler concentrating on design and manufacture of cars and AEC on lorries and buses, and the GW had no more.

Condemned vehicles of all makes had to be replaced to keep the cartage fleet up to strength. By the early 1930s many of the WW1 AEC chassis had been withdrawn, and money for 'renewals' began to appear in the motor cartage fleet accounts from 1931. In

Above: Forward control AssociatedDaimler '428', 4/5 ton lorry, registration UL9494 new on 27/2/29, photographed 15/3/29 in Birmingham having original solid tyres (double at rear). Number plate is at top of radiator (plate below near starting handle is blank). Fleet 1928 in black on cream plaque placed over brown cabside, below which in white is 'f r e davis (secY) gwr paddington' in line with bottom of door. Painted in white on black chassis is fleet number and 'u.w. 4-0-0/f.a.w. 3-0-0/b.a.w. 6-0-0'. Petrol tank filler cap is above number plaque. No windscreen, single tax disc on front of scuttle. Lamp irons either side. Large towing hook to right of radiator (also at rear). Body number is G1016 on extreme left of cream panel on side rave. Loaded with flat wooden packing cases. *GWR/P J Kelley collection*

Left: Fleet 1923, Associated Daimler '428' forward control van, UU5002, of 1/9/29. 'great western railway/f r e davis secretary/paddington' at bottom right hand of side. Vehicle bashed a bit at driver's door, rear mudguard, etc. Half-round bumper to protect radiator. Filler cap above fleet number on cabside. Head- and side-lamp irons. Pneumatic tyres (double at rear). Poster advertises for 'South Wales......Atlantic breezes......Golden Sands'. *GWR/D J Hyde collection*

that year 65 replacement vehicles were purchased — separate from the 148 additional new vehicles brought into service. The GW had been buying an increasing number of motor vehicle chassis (50 or so every year in the early l920s, 200s/year in the late 1920s and 300s/year in the 1930s — these figures include not only chassis for C&D vehicles, but purchase of special heavy duty vehicles and trailers which are discussed in Chapter 12). From over 1500 vehicles in the early 1930s, by WW2 there were some 2500 motor vehicles and some 2000 trailers. As shown in the Fleet List, there were also some cartage vehicles jointly-owned with one or more of the other main line companies — but the numbers were not great. Examples were Thornycroft A1 lorries for chair traffic from High Wycombe (GW & GC); Burford lorries and Morris vans for the GW/West London Joint Committee; and Morris 22 and Thornycroft vans jointly with the LMS.

The GW tended to buy new vehicles of the latest design from a limited number of manufacturers, often 'local' such as Thornycroft and AEC. As part of their contracts, these firms would deliver chassis to the nearest railway station, i.e. Basingstoke and Southall respectively, for onwards delivery by rail usually to Swindon where bodies would be fitted. Only for special vehicles might they use other makes. Before WW1 it was believed that lorries fitted with (solid) rubber tyres and taking a load of 3½-tons were best for general cartage work, but ideas changed as pneumatic tyres became common. Capacities of different vehicles in the cartage fleet were later influenced by regulations in the various Road Traffic Acts of the early 1930s (Appendix 5). In 1930 there were three types of parcels motor vans in use on the GW, of 30cwt, 4-ton and 6-ton capacity. About 50% of the total number of open lorries employed on GW cartage services at that time were of 4-ton capacity. Later 6-ton vehicles (fitted with hinged, detachable sides) displaced some of the 4-ton four-wheel vehicles owing to the growth of container traffic, while at the same time the 2-tonner was found to be generally more useful for C&D work. The 2-tonner with a two-wheeled trailer was more economical than the single 4-ton lorry. The 6-ton lorry carried the largest legal load allowed on four-wheeled rigid-chassis vehicles at that time. Yet heavier cartage loads were conveyed in permanently-articulated vehicles. The vehicle that would revolutionise C&D operations was the non-permanently-articulated mechanical horse that became widespread after the early 1930s, and which is described in Chapter 6.

Traditional motors had so-called 'normal control' where the driver was positioned behind the engine, with a long bonnet in front and the load-carrying space behind him. In 'forward control' lorries the driving position was alongside the engine and the radiator more-or-less flush with the front of the cab. Such an arrangement gave two improved features over the traditional layout. Either the capacity of the vehicle was increased when the overall length was retained (this was the case with the first GW forward control vehicles introduced in late 1923 which were 30cwt Burford light cartage lorries, that gave maximum body space and good weight distribution); or, for the same capacity vehicle, the overall length was reduced so giving easier manoeuvrability in the restricted areas of goods yards and trading places. This second arrangement was employed in 1926 for the fifty 4/5-ton forward control Thornycrofts delivered between December that year and March 1927.

Another innovation for the GW cartage fleet was the introduction on trial of diesel-engined lorries. The compression-ignition engine was invented in 1890 and was originally used as a more efficient replacement for stationary steam engines in factories and ships,

Fleet 2106, GC9667. Thornycroft type 'PB' forward control 4/5 ton lorry with full cab, photographed in the early 1930s. Three-plank detachable sides and five hoopsticks of which only one has been moved along body with tarpaulin spread over. Scalloped hand-grips in planks to allow driver/assistant to climb up from rear wheels. Electric headlamps. Pneumatic tyres. Fleet 2106 in black painted directly on to upper cream cabside below which in white on brown is 'f r e davis (secY) gwr paddington'. Painted in white on black chassis is fleet number and 'u.w. 4-0-0/f.a.w. 3-0-0/b.a.w. 6-0-0'. Offside front mudguard badly damaged. *GWR/D J Hyde collection*

Left: Tilt van body fitted to 1-ton Morris Commercial chassis of March 1929, fleet 1062, registration UL9940. Four hoopsticks with tarpaulin over that has white area for advertisements. Electric head- and side-lights. Single tax disc on cabside. Photographed in 1932. *GWR/P J Kelley collection*

Below: Large capacity 6-wheeled forward control type-JC Thornycroft van. Fleet 1075, registration GH4100 of 1931, used on the Portal contract. *STEAM Swindon*

Thornycroft 'JJ' of 1930, fleet 2223, GK 6123, body G1823. Hinged sides in two parts with 3 hinge straps each and central stanchion. Split windscreen with a single wiper at driver's side. For this type of chassis fitted with a livestock body, see Kelley p102. *GWR/D J Hyde collection*

COLLECTION AND DELIVERY MOTOR VEHICLES AFTER WW1

where weight was not of concern. However, weight prevented its application to road vehicles until the late 1920s. In 1930 the GW ordered two 'heavy oil' Thornycroft JJ-type 'Taurus' lorries for experiments to compare their performance with petrol engines for haulage. Both came into service in 1933 with fleet numbers 2285/6. £600 was spent in 1934 on the conversion of another 10-ton vehicle and fitting it with a crude oil (diesel) engine. While the operating costs of the thermally-more-efficient diesel-powered vehicles were lower, the capital cost (owing to the need for robust high-stress design) and standing charges were higher than for petrol. It was argued at the time that unless diesel vehicles ran more than 20,000 miles/annum, they could not compete with petrol. In 1930 the *Railway Gazette* averred that "owing to the 'creeping characteristic of mineral oil that causes it to spread over the engine, chassis and bodywork, its objectionable odour to passengers, and unpleasant exhaust fumes' it will probably be some time before the Diesel engine progresses very far in road passenger service, though the same arguments are not of such importance where goods transport is concerned."

There was GW cartage in the Channel Islands. In 1928 one type-PB Thornycroft, fleet 1400, and one type-A1, fleet 1415, were sent to Jersey; two type-A1, fleet 1406 and 1413, to Guernsey. All four were returned to the mainland fleet in 1931 when their Channel Islands registrations were replaced by Greater

One of two Thornycroft 6/8-ton 'Taurus' lorries fitted with a diesel engine ordered by the GW in 1932. Extended bumper owing to weight of engine. As shown here, fleet 2285, GX 3365 was fitted with a drop-side open body in two halves (3 hoop sticks in each) in January 1933. In February 1933 the sides were removed in order to carry containers (Chapter 13), but in March 1933 was fitted with a van body (Chapter 6). The over-written fleet number relates to the 1935 fleet renumbering scheme (Chapter 8). *GWR/D J Hyde collection*

```
[6.]  IMPROVEMENTS TO
      ROAD MOTOR VEHICLES.

      Vote required:-
                £17,220

        On 25th May, 1933, the Directors
      authorised an expenditure of £15,331 on
      alterations to road motor vehicles in
      order to reduce the licence duties
      payable and comply with certain
      provisions of the Road Traffic Act,
      1930.  This work is nearly complete,
      and will result in an annual saving of
      about £6,100.
        In order that further economies,
      estimated to amount to £6,600 per annum,
      may be realised, it is recommended that
      the following expenditure be incurred:-

      Conversion of 176
        vehicles from solid           £
        to pneumatic tyres       14,400
      Rebuilding bodies of
        six 12-ton tipping
        lorries ...   ...           720
      Alterations to vehicles
        to reduce weight            500
      Conversion of horse-
        drawn vehicles from
        iron to rubber tyres
        for use as trailers       1,000
      Conversion of one 10-ton
        vehicle and fitting
        with crude oil engine       600
                                _____
                                 £17,220
```

London plates. A possible reason for the return was that the 1930 Road Traffic Act imposed width limits for vehicles in the Channel Islands. Other vehicles were sent as replacements and the Road Wagon shop was asked in 1936 to provide a flat body for a 2-ton Morris forward control chassis for work on Guernsey on Lot A620 under the renewal account.

The GWR took as much pride in its modern motor lorries as in its horse-drawn vehicles and regularly exhibited at the biennial Commercial Motor Show at Olympia (having, for example, nine vehicles on display in 1927 including buses, goods lorries and trailers). At the 10th show in 1931, a GW express parcels van was displayed on the Thornycroft stand. This vehicle was of the latest

Burford 15cwt flat petrol lorry used on Jersey (fleet 346, mainland registration XU 6914), one of three (fleet 344-6) purchased on 28/8/24. Photo July 1925. Air-cooled engine. Solid rubber tyres on pressed steel wheels. Brackets for oil lamps. Cream panel with 'G.W.R.' painted on black chassis. 'Load not to exceed 0-15-0' in italics at left of cream panel. 'Bolter secretary etc' below driver's seat. Deck of lorry is longitudinally-planked. *GWR/P J Kelley collection*

Dennis 2-ton forward control vehicle of 1931, photographed in March 1939 after 1935 fleet number pre-fixing (2647 happened to be the original number). Hinged sides but also tilt: brackets for 5 hoopsticks in between hinges, but only 4 in use. 'Tarpaulin over' held down by a series of short ropes. Body number is G 1647. Guard rail between wheels. Bashed rear mudguard. *GWR/D J Hyde collection*

Parcel van fitted to 2-ton Morris forward-control chassis in 1932. Registration GX3314, fleet 2804 (altered to 2361, see Chapter 8). Single tax disc on outside of cab. Front bumper and electric lights and electric horn. Is the circular cover missing from inspection hole bonnet side? *GWR/P J Kelley collection*

Above: The only Dennis 4-tonner in the GW fleet, ex-Wilts Cooperative Society of early 1930s, with Wiltshire registration MW 7994. Furniture removal employing a K-type container at Maidenhead on 27/11/35. In the 1935 renumbering scheme, the original fleet number 2341 has just been prefixed, but B was supposed to indicate a van (not a lorry which was A) and a 4-digit number starting with 2 was supposed to mean a 2-ton vehicle! Shirtbutton on cab door is a yellow-encircled yellow 'GWR'. *Author's collection*

Left and above: Renewals for 1934, showing what vehicles were to be condemned and what were to be their replacements, viz: 50 ex-army AECs/ 26 six-ton lorries; one Foden steam wagon/25 mechanical horse tractors and 50 six-ton trailers; 31 Burfords, five Fords, 1 low deck lorry and 1 Thornycroft 'J'-type vehicle/38 two-ton vehicles; 20 Fordson tractors/15 Fordson tractors and 5 special vehicles; and 4 officers' cars/4 Austin saloons. Data shows the lives of older vehicles being condemned.

| 6. | PURCHASE OF ROAD VEHICLES FROM L. W. BRYANT (QUARRIES), LTD.

Vote required:—
£820 | 26-4-34

Difficulties have been experienced in providing suitable vehicles for the conveyance of roadstone and similar traffic, and authority is desired for the acquisition from L. W. Bryant (Quarries), Ltd., of five second-hand lorries and one tractor with trailer. |

| 6. | PURCHASE OF ROAD MOTOR VEHICLES.

Vote required:—
£415.2s.6d. | 31-5-34

Authority is desired for the purchase of the undermentioned vehicles:—

Two 8 h.p. Ford saloon cars at a cost of £222 for use by the Company's representatives at Worcester and Thame. (R. Pratt, Ltd.'s tender of £111 for one car).

One industrial Fordson tractor on renewals account at a cost of £193.2s.6d. from R. Pratt, Ltd., for use in connection with Show traffic. |

design, the front axle having been moved back to enable a load of 6 to 6½ tons to be carried without exceeding the new legal weights (Appendix 5). Mr Coventry, chief of GW Road Transport, led discussions among manufacturers and users of motor vehicles at the show, pointing out that improvements were still required on automatic control of engine temperatures and extra lubrication when starting cold. Data given in his talk showed that at that time the LMS fleet of road motors was 1,864 strong; GW 1,486; LNE 1,000; and SR 387.

The increasing importance of motor vehicles in the cartage fleet is reflected in the changed contents of the Rule Book for those engaged in cartage activities. In 1915 it was entitled *Instructions to Foremen, Carmen, Van-Guards, Checkers, Loaders & Others employed in the Cartage Department*. In 1925 the title was *Instructions to Foremen, Motordrivers, Carters, Van-Guards, Checkers, Loaders & Others employed in the Cartage Department*; and in 1933 had become *Instructions to Foremen, Motordrivers, Carters, Van-Guards, Checkers, Loaders & Others associated with Cartage Operations*.

An unusual New Work Order in July 1932 was to construct two Post Office vans for 1½/2-ton Morris forward control chassis (Morris Motors of Oxford). To improve delivery times in London, May 1933 saw the purchase of two 8hp, 5cwt Ford vans. Even though the vans had to return more frequently to the depot owing to their small capacity, earlier delivery was achieved than by greater-capacity short-distance 1-horse teams. This was particularly helpful for urgent consignments of cream, fish and other perishable traffic.

The largest-ever order for cartage motors (£156,514) was placed by the GW in 1934 when 396 vehicles in all were bought comprising 190 three- and six-ton mechanical horses, and 206 other motor vehicles. There were 100 renewals in the same year, as well as replacement trailers. Some of the new vehicles ordered in 1934

Six-ton AEC forward-control 'Monarch' chassis (fleet 3406, BLB 506) photographed new in October 1934. Fitted with flat body and removable hinged sides in two halves with 3 hinges each and middle stanchion. Starting handle held by leather strap. 'u.w. 4-7-0/speed 20 m.p.h./gwr/Paddington station/london' on cab door that opens by sliding forwards. *GWR/D J Hyde collection*

Morris Commercial forward-control lorry fitted with hinged sides. Photographed on 21/2/36 with letter-prefixed fleet number A3800, subsequently altered to 2638 to reflect 2-ton capacity (see Chapter 8). Front bumper with electric horn above, but has bulb horn as well at cab front. 'gwr paddington station london' at bottom of nearside door. Used in Guernsey. *GWR/P J Kelley collection*

A line-up of nine Morris Commercial 4-ton vans outside the Swindon Carriage manager's office in December 1935. *A G Atkins collection*

were to cope with the increasing C&D business and also special contract work (e.g. 3 Latil tractors), but others were to replace horses under the plan to completely motorise various goods depots across the GW. South Lambeth in London had been the first goods depot to have an all-motor fleet (authorised in 1928 that became effective in August 1930). The first goods district to eliminate horses altogether from its delivery fleet across its whole region was Exeter Goods District. One consequence of the policy was that old weighbridges, suitable for the lighter loads of horse-drawn vehicles, had to be replaced with heavier-capacity machines.

Not all cabs/bodies newly-constructed at the Road Wagon shop in the Carriage Works at Swindon went directly on to new chassis; some went into stock as spares. NWO 1091 of 1933 was to build two bodies to replace bodies taken from stock and used for two Guy chassis (Guy Motors of Wolverhampton). The new bodies were to be suitable for 2-ton Thornycrofts. In August 1937 there was a spurt of orders for spare bodies and cabs that were kept in store for emergencies. These orders included flat bodies with detachable sides for Thornycrofts (one for a 6/8-ton chassis; five for 4-tonners; and four for the 2-ton BE chassis) and one for an Associated Daimler (ADC) chassis; cabs for Thornycrofts (one 6/8-ton; four for 2-ton A1 chassis; and two for the BE chassis with doors hinged at the front rather than at the rear as then normal); cabs for Scammell mechanical horses (two for 6-tonners; two 3-tonners); and two cabs for 3-ton Karrier Cob articulated vehicles. The Garner Motor Co of Tyseley, Birmingham, made lorries in the 1930s and, in 1938, the Road Wagon shop was asked to alter Garner body No G2440 and fit it to a Fordson Sussex chassis No 3194 and to provide a cab.

Co-ordination on C&D transfer traffic in London between the Big Four companies was improved in the mid-1930s. There were 36 articulated lorries and 120 trailers involved, and similar arrangements for parcels were being prepared. The expenditure on new cartage vehicles in 1936 was £75,405 and an additional £44,765 was allotted to renewals. At the end of that year the fleet consisted of 2,326 mechanical units and 1,589 trailers, with the number of horses falling to 1,773. There were the following number of petrol C&D vehicles: 877 Thornycroft; 318 AEC; 205 Scammell; 176 Morris Commercial; 132 Ford; 111 Dennis; and 30 Karrier. In addition, there were 59 4-wheel tractors (the makers of which included Fordson, Latil, and Leyland) and a few steam and diesel vehicles, all of which are discussed elsewhere in this book.

In seeking an idea of what, if any, new vehicles would be required in 1936, Mr Challenger (District Goods Manager at Exeter) reminded stations in his area that the standard vehicles were: light vans; 2-ton vans; 2-ton flats with or without sides and hoopsticks; 3-ton, and 6-ton, articulated lorries and trailers; Fordson or Latil tractors; and flat or pole trailers. He also pointed out that carriers' licences for any vehicles proposed for

Left: Fleet A3205 is a 2-ton Thornycroft BE chassis fitted with hinged sides, photographed on 14/5/36. Registration CLM 787, it has 'gwr paddington station london' below the sliding cab door. Subsequently renumbered A2642 to indicate a 2-ton vehicle. *GWR/D J Hyde collection*

Below: Fordson 6-wheel 'Sussex' chassis of 1936 fitted with 14ft long flat body having hinged sides in two halves, and a metal-framed bolster behind the cab to take long loads. (For a similar body on a later Sussex chassis with different radiator, see Kelley p126-7.) Below the fleet number on the cabside are the unloaded weight (uw 2-19-3); speed 20mph; and 'gwr/paddington station/london'. For an explanation of the change in fleet number from S3184 to (S)4604, see Chapter 8. *GWR/D J Hyde collection*

throughout-road work, such as cattle haulage, would likely be opposed by private carriers under the 1933 Road and Rail Traffic Act. The illustration from the 1939 Telegraph code book lists the recognised principal types of cartage vehicle body by that time together with appropriate suffixes

From 1 January 1937 windscreens had by law to be fitted with safety glass and in that year also vehicles had to have speedometers. Following the *Finance Act* of 1933 (Appendix 5), special plates were to be displayed on vehicles limited to a legal speed of 20mph, and also on trailers. Powers were given to Police to inspect and test brakes, silencers and steering gear of any motor vehicle or trailer at any time, even in a garage. Further regulations came into force in 1936 whereby sand and ballast conveyed by road could be carried either by weight or by volume, requiring wagons to be calibrated both ways; maximum tyre sizes were to be indicated on heavy vehicles; and mudguards had to be fitted on trailers (except timber carriages). In some cases, rubber was used for 'mudwings' on GW vehicles to minimise the constant damage to the orthodox type of metal mudguard; again, the bodies of side and tail lamps were often rubber. Since solid rubber tyres were to be outlawed from 1940, money was spent on fitting pneumatic tyres to motors and trailers: £4,525 in 1937 and £2,500 in 1938. All these regulations gave rise to different information at different times having to be painted and displayed on vehicles (Chapter 8).

COLLECTION AND DELIVERY MOTOR VEHICLES AFTER WW1

Easy driver access van manufactured by Trojan of Croydon at Alfred Rd garage on 22/4/1936. Fleet A1637, CLR875. Two licence discs on windscreen, single wiper blade. 'gwr paddington station london' on body near bottom step. Electric lighting and horn, the latter in the shape of an old bulb horn. The dark-coloured roof is of double-deck /canvas tacked in place all round. *GWR/D J Hyde collection*

73

Subject.	Interpretation.	Code.
Missing and Tracing	Advise me by wire before 9.0 a.m. if traffic is not received.	Morn *Serf*
Motor-cars	Covered truck conveying Motor Car, accompanied by passengers.	Adca
,,	Covered truck conveying Motor Car, unaccompanied by passengers.	Unca
,,	Wire immediately whether following consignment can be accepted by Consignee by Road Motor and unloaded immediately on arrival.	Roadmo
,,	Road Motors left at time shown below with the following consignments. Arrange return load and wire when leaving and particulars of load.	Backmo
,,	Expect Road Motors with goods for......	Exmo
,,	Send on all speed 1 in. copper stay, 6 in. long (unless otherwise stated), and taps and tools to suit. (If more than one stay is required, number to be quoted.)	Stay A
,,	do. 1 1/16 in. copper stay, etc.	Stay B
,,	do. 1 1/8 in. ,, ,,	Stay C
,,	do. 1 3/16 in. ,, ,,	Stay D
,,	do. 1 1/4 in. ,, ,,	Stay F
,,	do. 1 5/16 in. ,, ,,	Stay G
,,	do. 1 3/8 in. ,, ,,	Stay H

74

Subject.	Interpretation.	Code.
Motor-Cars	Connecting rod complete with big end bearing, inside diameter.	Connie
,,	Big end bearing, inside diameter.	Bigend
,,	Water circulating pump.	Circ
,,	Provide truck load........'s (owner's name) car through Tunnel, on........ (train)........(date).	Carsev
,,	Cartage Motor Vehicle 1/1½ tons carrying capacity.	Toner
,,	Cartage Motor Vehicle 2 tons carrying capacity.	Tooton
,,	Cartage Motor Vehicle 4/5 tons carrying capacity.	Forton
,,	Cartage Motor Vehicle 6/8 tons carrying capacity.	Sixate
,,	Cartage Motor Vehicle 10 tons carrying capacity.	Dixton
,,	The undermentioned Suffixes are available for use in connection with all capacities shown above:— A. Standard Flat body. B. Standard Flat body with detachable sides. C. Standard Box Van with tail curtains. D. Cattle Lorry. M. Movable Floor Lorry. T. Tipping Lorry. X. Morris 6-wheeler.	

While traffic had increased year by year between the wars — 200,000 tons more goods were carted by the GW than before in 1930, and 1.2 million more parcels — there was a depression in trade in 1938, so that no additional cartage equipment was purchased. Instead a vote was obtained for 74 cartage vehicles and 14 trailers to replace old and discarded stock, among which were twelve 16-ft bodies and cabs for Thornycroft PE chassis. Furthermore 29 vehicles purchased as additional new stock in 1937 were considered in the accounts as renewals for 1938. The authorised stock at the end of 1938 was 2,393 GW motors and 23 jointly owned; 1,865 GW trailers and 12 jointly owned. There were 1,500 horses on the books. In the case of jointly-owned motors, two van bodies and cabs were constructed in 1938 for Morris 30cwt forward control chassis for stations at Ruislip, Gerrards Cross and Denham (GW & LNE joint — but still called in the paperwork GW & GC joint).

The international crisis in the years before WW2 again brought to the fore the question of alternative fuels. France had been experimenting with producer gas but its use was not popular in England. Nevertheless, the GW purchased in 1938 a heavy duty Latil tractor fitted to run on the different fuel. Power produced was less than for petrol, and engines having 40% greater capacity were required to do the same work. Furthermore, the Road Traffic Acts deemed that the weight of all the additional equipment was taxable within the unladen weight, as it would be for other alternative fuels.

The quest for cheap vehicles for lightweight work continued through the 1930s: in 1935 a Trojan chassis having a 2-stroke low-speed engine with epicyclic gearbox and special differential was tried out in the expectation that it would be inexpensive to maintain. One feature desirable in C&D work was that the driver should have easy entrance and exit on *both* sides of the vehicle. The problem was common to all the main-line railways and in 1938 they jointly requested Scammell to design an experimental 30cwt 4-wheel lorry chassis propelled by a 10hp twin-cylinder air-cooled engine situated *beneath* the body, thus permitting the cab to be arranged to give the desired either-side entrance and exit. The GW vehicle was fleet S4600, having registration EGT297.

An improved cab for road motors was designed at Swindon in 1939 which occupied the full width of the vehicle, thus enabling an unrestricted view when reversing. It also had sliding doors. Thornycroft 'Nippy' chassis were fitted with these cabs and high-sided lorry bodies.

With all the government activity in 1939 in anticipation of war, 25 additional motor lorries and 50 new trailers were bought and

Above: Experimental Scammell lorry with 10hp, twin-cylinder air-cooled engine beneath the body so as to free up cab floor area for driver to get in and out easily on both sides during deliveries. Starting handle still at front and collapses when on the road. As a 'special' vehicle was given Fleet S4600. Registration EGT297, body number G2501. Photographed 28/1/38. *GWR/P J Kelley collection*

Thornycroft forward-control 'Trusty' S2939 DLX 146 with sliding door to cab. UW not painted in. 'speed 20 m.p.h.' 'gwr paddington station london'. Double split sided hinged sides, having yellow shirtbutton painted directly on brown body sides, as well as GREAT WESTERN RAILWAY in cream on brown panels within bigger cream panels on raves. Starting handle held up by leather strap to cross rod on which headlights are mounted. Photographed in 1937. *GWR/D J Hyde collection*

Above: **New Swindon safety cab in which the cab extends the full width of the vehicle on the right hand side thus providing the best possible view for reversing. In one illustration, the cab is fitted to a 3-ton Ford in August 1939. 'gwr paddington station london' on cab door below fleet number A3014. Door slides on runners extending on bottom outside the raves as far as the end of the cream panel. Small shirtbutton on cab front is brown encircled GWR on cream disc that is same size as outside circle. On 26/8/46 the safety cab is shown on a Karrier Bantam D3804 with Scammell hitch. When the safety cab was fitted to a Thornycroft 'Nippy' chassis (fleet A3339, HLY 775) in 1947, it necessitated the body to be cut away behind the cab. This particular Nippy was uprated from 3-ton to 6-ton by fitting larger brakes and larger carburettor jets, but the fleet number did not become an A6xxx and remained in A3XXX.** *Author's collection*

Above: **Fleet A3065, a 3-ton Fordson van photographed on 30/11/1940. It has a sliding door that requires the body of the van immediately behind the cab to be recessed and looks very fiddly to make. Turned out in chocolate and cream, but with blackout regulation white-edged mudguards, front bumper, cab steps and masked offside headlight. 'gwr paddington station london' along bottom of body (above unprefixed fleet number on chassis). Shirtbuttons in various locations, including in what appears to be yellow-encircled GWR on brown front of body and small ones either side of radiator. There were 20 of this type of vehicle in all (3063-68 on Lot 762; 3069-79 on Lot 761; and 3051-53 on Lot 763).**
GWR/P J Kelley collection

3-ton Fordson fitted with flat body and chain surrounds for milk churn traffic. Photographed new in Dec 1939 in grey livery with white lettering and back chassis (but this was not general: there were vehicles finished in brown & cream during the war). White edges to mudguards and running boards, and front bumper is white. But no masks on headlights. 'gwr paddington station london' on cabside, with fleet A3047 above (no A-prefix for fleet number on chassis). *GWR/P J Kelley collection*

there was also a considerable number of renewals — 182 condemned motors and 10 condemned trailers were replaced. The Road Wagon shop at Swindon built 102 van bodies and cabs, and 230 were repaired. Three bodies and cabs were built for 15cwt Commer chassis. Attached to NWO5319 of August 1939 to build 4 bodies and cabs for Fordson Sussex chassis, was that the bodies for two to be provided with bolsters ('high sides not required but necessary holes [for brackets] to be drilled').

The headquarters of the GW Road Transport Department was moved to the countryside away from London to Beenham Grange near Reading during WW2 (GW postal address Aldermaston).

The activities of the department during WW2 rose to levels exceeding the already much-increased loadings of the 1930s. At first, in 1940, many fire engines and ambulances had to be made available for works around the system as described in the September 1940 *GW Magazine*. Joint pooling of resources of the cartage fleets of all the main line companies was in force at more than 100 places in 1941 and led to efficiencies. For many years it had been the practice around the GW to borrow lorries from large depots when extra transport was required at places not so well supplied and this was fine-tuned during WW2 in a scheme managed by a *Cartage Controller* in the Chief Goods Manager's Office at Paddington. It aimed at better balancing traffic requirements and road vehicle stock allocation, and at giving greater flexibility to meet peak demands. For example, large amounts of traffic conveyed to wartime sites could have caused congestion at stations local to the delivery point; the controller could spread the delivery over a number of stations so as not to interfere with delivery of essential commodities to the principal station. A section of the road motor fleet was established for relief purposes and was strategically dispersed to cope with emergencies such as unexpected arrivals of ships under the convoy system. There were GWR Home Guard units that used GW cartage equipment. It was agreed between the Minister of War Transport and the War Office that the Battalion Commander paid 10d per mile for all journeys and supplied petrol coupons to cover the replenishment of GW stocks.

When the Railway Clearing House (RCH) set up an Emergency Headquarters Despatch Service at Amersham in WW2, the GW as a matter of convenience purchased on its behalf one 10cwt and four 5cwt Fordson vans from Pratts of Sutton and registered them in the GW's name. Costs were £144/17/6 and £422/5/0 respectively and were debited to the RCH for division between the main line companies 'in the usual way'. New vehicles were hard to obtain during the war; some Bedford-Scammell 4-wheeled articulated tractors joined the GW fleet in 'army-guise' (Chapter 6).

The 24 million tons of goods carted in 1943 surpassed any previous GW tonnage: it was 44% above pre-war levels and 90% of it was war-related. Despite this increased tonnage, the cartage control scheme produced a 7% reduction in miles run by cartage vehicles and a reduction in use of well over 200 motor lorries (this, in turn, meant that the railway had to hire fewer outside lorries to get the job done). In the peak months before D-Day in May/June 1944, 27,000 tons were carted per day. Such was the effort applied to getting the work completed that daily 'leave-over' (i.e. cartage left unfinished at the end of the day) was cut by half, and the entire year's work was accomplished with approximately one million fewer running miles which gave a significant saving in petrol and rubber. These trends continued into 1945, the fleet of 1,700 motors and 1,000 horses moving 6¼ million tons in the year (at times 23,000 tons/day), and the mileage was reduced yet again by 200,000 miles compared with 1944. How cartage vehicles were serviced and kept on the road in difficult times, when new motor lorries were almost impossible to obtain, is described in Chapter 7. There were fewer staff too, and supplementary allowances were paid to drivers and carters working without van-guards; this had been a question during WW1 as well.

After WW2 ended, the aim was to restore domestic cartage activities back to pre-war standards as soon as possible. During the war, cartage to outer London districts direct from the GW's central goods depots had been abandoned resulting in extra handling of goods with consequent delay in transit; with the

G.W.R., Chief Goods Manager's Office,
Paddington Station, London, W.2.

1st February, 1941.

Please quote this reference:—
G.D.22600/18.

Telegrams:
ASST. PADDINGTON STATION, LONDON.

Telephone:
PADDINGTON 7000. Extn.

Your reference:—

Dear Sir,

Application from Motor Drivers and Carters at Paddington to be paid an allowance when working without a Vanguard.

An application has been submitted by the accredited representatives of the men at Paddington Goods for an allowance of 3s.0d per day to be paid to Motor Drivers and Carters who are called upon to work without a Vanguard.

These representations have arisen from the fact that for some time past difficulty has been experienced in obtaining the services of Vanguards and as a result it became necessary to send out motors and teams without boys. This created a position to which the men took strong objection but, nevertheless, an agreement was reached with the Committee for approximately 40 Motor Drivers and Carters to work without a lad.

Since the agreement referred to above was reached the situation has become worse and the attached statement indicates the extent to which the men have been required to work as single units during the seven weeks ended 11th ultimo.

Upon the subject being referred to Mr. Hoskins he took the view that, having regard to what has taken place in the past as between the Company and the men's representatives on this question of the employment of Vanguards, the application should be declined and the Paddington Goods Agent was notified accordingly on 17th January. Since that date the position at Paddington has become even more acute and at the present time the deficiency of Vanguards is in the region of 100 and although a commencement has been made with the employment of women Mr. Hoskins fears that it will not be possible effectively to make up the shortage from that source as the shed requirements should take precedence if the women available are of the requisite physique. It may be possible to recruit women for Vanguard's

- 2 -

duties from the wives of the Motor Drivers and Carters, husband and wife to work together; it being understood that a number of women who would not otherwise offer their services would thereby be made available. It has been ascertained that the Committee at Paddington expect the adult women's rate to be paid to all women of 20 years of age and upwards filling Vanguard's posts irrespective of whether or not these are wives of the Motor Drivers and Carters.

Meanwhile, however, and so long as the present conditions prevail I am of the opinion that some special steps must be taken to deal with the position. As you may be aware, during the last war, an amount of 1s.0d per day was paid to men working without Vanguards and I am given to understand that this payment is made in the Parcels Department, Paddington, today in consequence of the situation created by the war. I have given the matter very careful consideration and in all the circumstances am prepared to recommend that the sum of 1s.6d per man per day be paid to each Motor Driver and Carter who cannot be provided with a Vanguard, the whole position to be reviewed on return to normal conditions.

Will you kindly give the matter your consideration and favour me with your instructions.

I am informed that the Motor Drivers at South Lambeth are also likely to raise the question of payment in similar circumstances. The shortage of boys at this station and at Smithfield at the present time amounts to 15 and 6 respectively.

In conclusion it may be mentioned, incidentally, that the earnings of the cartage staff under the existing war conditions have resulted in the men suffering considerable losses in tonnage bonus and overtime.

Yours truly,

Sir James Milne.

GREAT WESTERN RAILWAY.

Telegrams:
TRANSIT, PADDINGTON STATION, LONDON.
Telephone:
PADDINGTON 7000: EXTN........ BM.

CHIEF GOODS MANAGER'S OFFICE,
PADDINGTON STATION, LONDON, W.2.

13/1/44.

Please quote this reference:—
GD.22,600/88/B.

[Stamp: ESTABLISHMENT OFFICE 18 JAN 1944 G.W.R.]

Your reference:—
SW/38,174 (6d) (B).

H. Adams Clarke, Esq.

Employment of Vanguards.

With reference to your letter of the 15th ultimo and telephone conversation between our representatives, statements are attached showing the numbers of staff employed in this Department in the grades mentioned for the years 1939 and 1943. It should be mentioned that the staff shown under the heading "Road Motor Attendants" are actually units paid at the Porter's rate of pay whose main function is to assist with the loading and unloading of the vehicles on which they are employed. They do not undertake the full duties and responsibilities of a Road Motor Attendant.

Generally speaking, no difficulty has been experienced in securing the services of lads to act as Vanguards. In some cases delays have taken place but it has usually been necessary to wait only for the conclusion of the current school term for the required candidates to become available. The exception to this is in the London area where sufficient lads cannot be recruited to fill the vacancies arising and where most of the Vanguards posts are filled by adult women. When the shortage arose early in 1941 owing to lads leaving the service for more attractive employment, it was impossible to obtain lads and it was decided to engage women for the work, it being considered by the District Goods Manager that the duties required women of good physique and somewhat stronger than girls. The recruitment of adult women for this work has ceased for some time, however, owing to a reduction in strength and a small number of juniors (lads) now being obtained.

So far as the general question of the employment of Vanguards is concerned I should like to refer you to my letter dated 1/2/41 regarding an application submitted by the Paddington Goods staff for an allowance of 3/- per day to be paid to Motor Drivers and Carters when called upon to work without Vanguards, and also to my letter dated 23/3/42 under your reference SW/1573/8 (A).

P.T.O.

- 2 -

Vanguards working in the London area are not essential from the Company's point of view, their employment being due to the attitude adopted by the Motor Drivers and Carters. Similarly, at Birkenhead the attitude of the Unions is responsible for the employment of adult attendants on vehicles dealing with traffic to and from the docks.

The position elsewhere in the Provinces is quite different inasmuch as Vanguards are only employed where required by the Company. These units assist the Motor Drivers or Carters in the loading and unloading of their vehicles, giving direction when manoeuvring into or out of restricted premises; while in the case of certain valuable traffic they are essential for the proper protection of the goods. You will, of course, be aware that the employment of a small number is necessitated by the requirements of the Road Traffic Act.

For F. W. Hampill,
Assistant.

Above: **Rear view of Fordson V8 4/6-ton flat with hinged sides in two halves with 3 strap hinges each separated by central stanchion. Registration GYH 81, fleet A4645, photographed on 16/4/46. The fleet number is not repeated on the chassis as in pre-war years, nor 'GWR Paddington' etc. Ford cab and chassis but GW body (number G3125 given in extreme right cream panel). Cream encircled shirtbutton on brown sides and on brown back of cab. A front view (not shown here) shows that there are small shirtbuttons either side of the radiator and that 'Fordson' is painted on the front of the body just above door handle on the driver's side.** *STEAM Swindon*

Above: **Two-ton Karrier Bantam van fleet A2813, GXY 181 photographed on 16/2/1945 at Swindon in brown and cream livery. Shirtbutton is encircled brown when painted on cream part of body, and encircled cream when on brown parts. Blackout details (white-edged mudguards, masked single headlamp at nearside, white bumper). There's no 'gwr paddington station' etc painted on cab.** *Author's collection*

agreement of customers, some town cartage routes were altered in 1940 to save on petrol. In November 1946 the pre-war cartage arrangements were re-established thus restoring to traders the same service as before. The major post-war development across the GW system was, however, 'Zonal C&D' aimed to give next-day delivery everywhere to all traffic passing in less than truck loads. This involved new ways of loading/unloading vehicles (Chapter 10). Various new implements aimed at simplifying handling and reducing costs were demonstrated in 1947 at St Irvans Rd yard (Portobello), such as new portable cranes, a Bedford-Scammell articulated hydraulic tipper and a 25-ton trailer for use with Foden motor tractors.

Construction at the Road Wagon shop picked up after the war with, for example, 5 van bodies for Fordson 3-ton chassis in 1945, and bodies and cabs for various Karrier 'Bantam' 2-ton chassis numbered in the A28xx series. That work went over into 1946, along with four van bodies for Austin 2-ton chassis (but not cabs as they came with the chassis). The existing flat bodies on two Thornycroft 'Sturdy' chassis, Nos 5034/5 in 1945/6, were removed in 1946 and replaced by newly-built livestock bodies. The flat bodies were retained as spares. Spare cabs/bodies were built into nationalisation for various vehicles, including 15cwt Commer, 3-ton Ford Thames, 3-ton Thornycroft Nippy, and 6/8-ton Thornycrofts.

Other GW Users of Road Vehicles

The CME's Dept used motor vehicles both within the factory at Swindon and on the public highway. Two 1-ton Straker-Squire parcels vans of 1914 were allotted to the works' fire brigade in 1915 (fleet 315, Y2643 from Somerset, and London-registered LL7901, fleet 304). Fleet 315 was later stationed at Ebbw Junction, Newport. The replacement for 315 was fleet 1707 of February 1929, a Thornycroft 'PB'. Many lorries or buses (for train crews) were noted in the register as being at Ebbw Jct as at various times, such as three Devon-registered Maudslay ex-buses from 1914 (registrations T4420/2/44). Various ex-army AEC 45hp lorries fleet 439/685/88/90 were at Ebbw Jct immediately after WW1 and into the early 1920s. Further ex-buses at Newport were Thornycroft A1 YK3824 fleet 914 of 1925 in 1928; and XY7375 fleet 930 in 1930. Burford 30cwt YK3801 of 1925 was at Ebbw Jct in 1926/7 and another, YK3803 of 1925 in 1925-26. Two Albion (Albion Motors of Glasgow) single-decker buses were purchased second-hand in 1937 from Oxford Motor Services, to replace the Thornycroft buses. At the end of 1939, a cab and body for 3-ton Fordson chassis Fleet No A3034 (FYL183) was built to replace Thornycroft lorry fleet 1497 that had been a stores lorry since 1930. In 1940 Albion buses Nos 118/9 were replaced by two second-hand Leyland and AEC buses purchased by the Road Transport Department from City of Oxford Motor Services.

In 1927 the GWR in Bristol bought a road sweeper, fleet 1108, from Karriers of Huddersfield. it was replaced in 1932 by a sweeper from Guy Motors in Wolverhampton, fleet 1647. In 1932 also, Mr E T J Evans, manager of the Road Wagon shop, was asked to provide a body for a 2-ton Ford chassis to replace the K-type Burford 15cwt lorry fleet 357 of 1925 used at Swindon works; the cost was to be covered by 'Sundry and Suspense' accounts, the authority for the expenditure coming from the Traffic Committee. The stores department at Wolverhampton were allotted a Morris 35/40cwt van fleet 2572 with an ex-Burford body at the same time.

Right and below: **The Guy normal control Road Sweeper bought on 28/10/32. Fleet 1647, GX3371. Brushes mounted below near-side door under covers with large brush at rear. Pipe of what may be a gulley-emptier held on side of vehicle. Pneumatic tyres. No rear mudguard. Livery is brown with white lettering.** *GWR/P J Kelley collection*

Cars were purchased for senior staff and company salesmen. For example, in 1928 there was added to the fleet one Morris Cowley car, and on 31/5/34 two 8HP Ford saloon cars at £111 each from Pratts in Sutton for GW representatives at Worcester and Thame.

The Signal Dept had a few vehicles such as the Thornycroft A1 van of February 1926 (fleet 962), and in 1938 the Road Wagon shop was asked to provide a van body and cab for a Morris 2-ton 'Equi-Load' van, fleet No A4055, for the Signal Department at Neath (see Chapter 8). In 1938 also, one flat body for a 3-ton Tasker articulated

Above and left: The October 1925 ledger entry for the purchase of a van for transport of men and materials to outlying stations in the Neath District. The total cost of £600 was split between Signals (£400) and Telegraphs (£200). The Swindon-built body was mounted on a Thornycroft 'A1' normal control chassis. Fleet number is 962 on plaque above side window and on black chassis beneath door; the registration was YM 7735 of 28/1/26, although there is no number plate. 'speed 12 mph' on chassis. Pressed steel disc wheels with solid tyres. Brackets for lamps but none fitted. Livery is brown. Loriot low down at left behind guard chains. *GWR/P J Kelley collection*

drop-frame trailer was made for the Stores Department at Cardiff Docks. The civil engineers had a number of tipping lorries.

In addition to fleet numbers, vehicles employed by the CME were given 3-digit numbers prefixed by the letter 'L' (see Chapter 8), including the many small 'platform trolley' tractors and full-size tractors that came to be used at Swindon. For example, in 1928 a Bramco (Mercury) tractor [the firm was in Coventry and later Gloucester] was purchased by the Road Transport Department for

Above: Trailer painted in departmental-vehicle grey photographed outside Slough station in 1937. Tipping achieved by rotating handle at end of side which moves the floor (patent of Principality Wagon Company in Cardiff whose name is cast on the '< plate' but is painted over). The rubber floor can be free or locked (below '<'). Tipping is also possible at the front end. The 4-plank body has two hinged sections. Plates indicating 5cu yds required by the Sand and Ballast regulations of 1937. Trailer number T1611 altered to T7950 (see Chapter 8). The tractor is a Morris Commercial 'Leader' fleet 4020, DXX271, having 3 tax discs on windscreen. Spare wheel immediately behind cab this side. *GWR/P J Kelley collection*

Four-ton Morris Commercial 'Leader' with tipping body in November 1936, used by the GW civil engineers and painted in service grey (including tyre walls!) and black underframe. Fleet A4003 on door and (without prefix) on cylindrical petrol tank. 'gwr paddington station london' along bottom of cab door. Blank number plate. New regulations permitted sand and gravel to be carried by weight or by the cubic yard. If the latter, load plates had to be attached to lorries (the black plaques at the top plank indicate 3cu yds) and it was the responsibility of the GW to have vehicles calibrated and certificates obtained. If carried by the ton, there was no need for calibration. *GWR/P J Kelley collection*

Left: Van body constructed in 1942 on Fordson 'Thames' chassis for conveyance of train crews between Bristol and Stoke Gifford. Blackout regulations require white-edged mudguards, etc. Offside headlight masked but nearside is plain. *GWR/D J Hyde collection*

Below left: Two-ton Fordson lorry used by the CME department, registration FGT 500, used in the factory and on outside roads. Ford cab and chassis but Swindon body. Painting date (sn 25.1.39) at rear of black chassis. Fleet A2788 on cab door and (without A-prefix) on cylindrical petrol tank, where works L337 is painted — a Swindon loco factory number. Cream half-circular-ended panel on side raves having three brown rectangular panels containing great, western and railway, to left of which body number G2779 is painted and, further left again, incised. Rear rave is cream. Cream shirtbutton on back of cab which is painted brown above waist. On this nearside, there is a bracket at the headboard (leather holding strap at cab) and a double one sticking up near the rear perhaps to carry long loads. *GWR/P J Kelley collection*

the loco factory. It was given fleet 1110, but subsequent works tractors do not appear in the fleet list and are known only by their L-numbers. The reason was that vehicles confined to works at Swindon, Wolverhampton, Caerphilly and Newton Abbot did not run on the public highway and had no need to be licensed. In 1936 four 'No 8' 14.9hp Mercury tractors costing £247/10/- each were purchased to replace numbers L255/7/74/5 in the loco factory; four more in 1937 to replace tractor numbers L251/2/63/76; six 'No 9' and one 'No 9A' in 1938 to replace L256/8/9/60/1/2/73. In 1939 two 'No 24F' Mercury tractors were purchased on behalf of the loco factory to replace tractors L266/7; similar purchases continued in later years, for example new Mercury tractors were ordered in 1943 to replace L271/2. In 1937, a Fordson shunting tractor was bought from Messrs R Pratt Ltd of Sutton, Surrey, to replace L265 at Swindon.

New Works Order 7642/82/84 of December 1940 (signed by the Principal Assistant to Collett, Hawksworth, who became the new CME in 1941) recorded the transfer of a 4/5-ton lorry and Ford Utility Car No 226 from the Road Transport Department to the Loco Works at Swindon. In 1942, a van body was constructed and mounted on a Fordson 3-ton 'Thames' chassis No 3053 for conveyance of train crews between Bristol and Stoke Gifford, and similar bodies were mounted on two 25cwt Commer chassis for train crews at other depots. Two trailers (T426 at Shrewsbury and T427 at Albrighton, valued at £25 each) were to be borrowed from the Road Transport Department for factory transport at Swindon works in 1946, but the order was cancelled. In January 1946, an Austin 2-ton lorry was purchased for £450 from Vincent's of Reading for the conveyance of locomotive parts between Cardiff General Station, Caerphilly Works and locomotive depots in the district. These CME vehicles operating on the public highway had to be taxed, and so had number plates and fleet numbers as well as L-numbers.

Right: Fordson road tractor (with Muir-Hill sprung rear wheels) fleet 199 (on side beams) shunting at Cardiff docks in April 1931. No awning for driver. Use of shunting tractors was possible where the roadway was built up to the level of the rails. *STEAM Swindon*

Below: Muir Hill shunting tractor at Central Boiler House, Swindon Works. Eight-ton 3-plank open wagon 'For use at Loco Works only'. Cast plate on side-beam says 'Muir Hill Old Trafford Manchester……….' *GWR/D J Hyde collection*

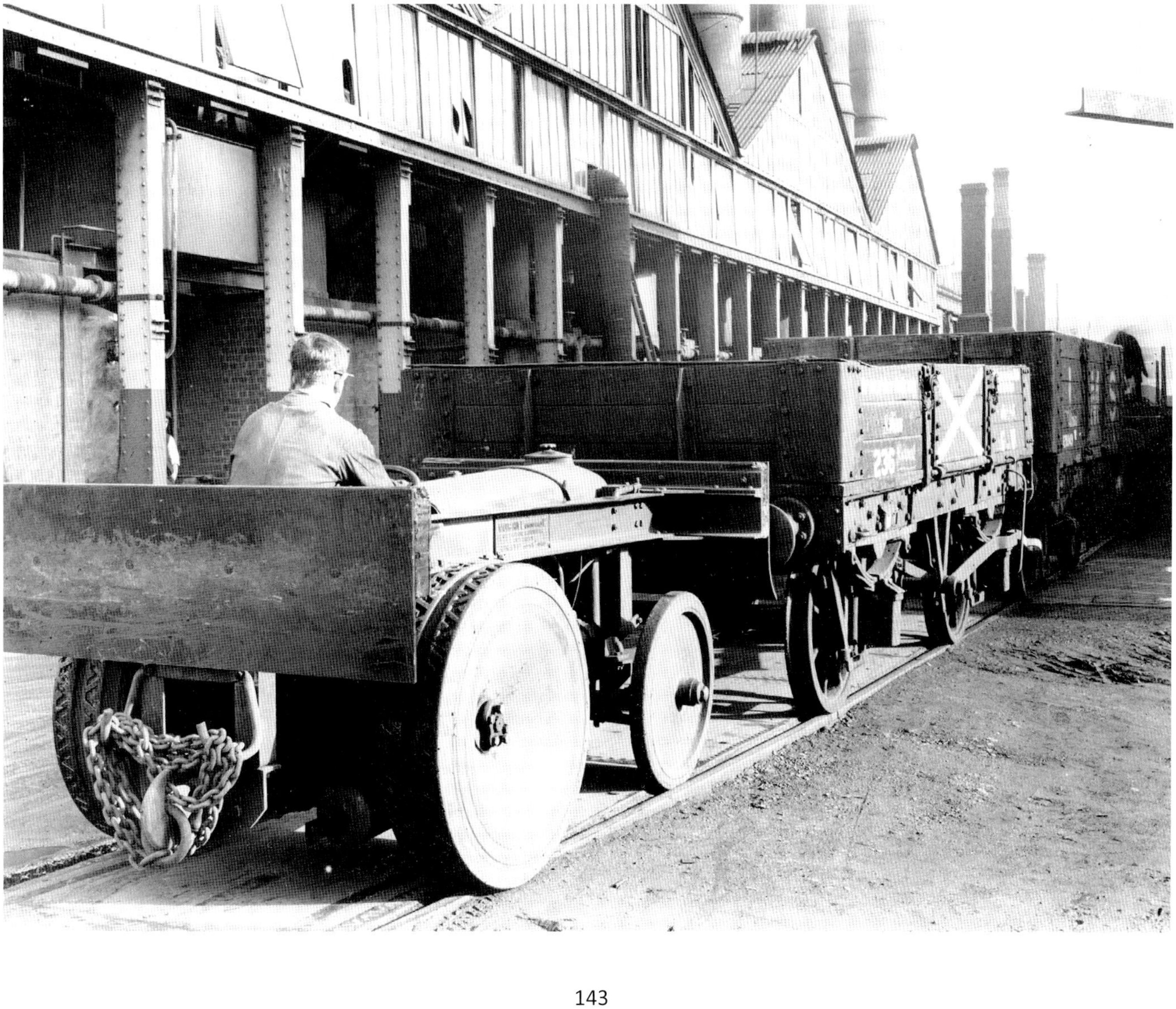

Above: Fordson shunting tractor (with Muir Hill rear wheels) fleet 384 of 1925 (and originally with number plate YL 6505) now fitted with experimental snow plough. Man sitting in vee of plough controls the screw to raise and lower the plough. Behind him there are weights to keep the plough down. Electric headlight at the front of the plough and a raised headlight on the tractor. As with this particular Fordson design, the awning is quite low over the driver. *STEAM Swindon*

Left: Trailer for carrying parts around Swindon works. Would be hauled by 'platform trolley' tractors. Number 437 on front end. Unladen weight has not been painted in after script 'Tare'. *STEAM Swindon*

COLLECTION AND DELIVERY MOTOR VEHICLES AFTER WW1

Left: Fordson 3-ton van for use of Loco Dept at Ebbw Junction photographed on 19/4/40. Fleet A3034 (just 3034 on chassis), registration FYL 183. Brown and cream but in blackout guise with white-edged mudguards. Front of body above cab is brown. Shirtbuttons are encircled GWR, either brown on cream or vice versa depending on background. *Author's collection*

Below: Tractor pulling a weed-killer spraying tank over sidings at Laycock in the Bristol Division. Sleepers for the sidings are made from concrete blocks and occasional tiebars, typical of WW2. *STEAM Swindon*

CHAPTER SIX

DEMOUNTABLE BODIES: TRACTORS & TRAILERS; THE MECHANICAL HORSE

Initial costs of road motors were more expensive than those of horses and carts, and to offset this the GW tried different ways of best using motors particularly to avoid their standing around not doing work while cargo was being loaded and unloaded ('idle time' during which the large capital outlay of motors was earning nothing). Towards the end of WW1, a drawing issued from the Motor Car Department at Slough sketched out various schemes for obtaining maximum daily mileage from 'mechanical road vehicles'. There were: (A) Demountable bodies hauled on and off the motor vehicle by existing hydraulic or electric capstans, which was utilised by various haulage contractors in the USA; (B) Demountable bodies lifted from above by existing gantry or high-lift jib crane, utilised by the L&YR for both horse and motor lorries at their Manchester goods depots, and by the GNR at their Leeds depot; (C) A variant of lifting on and off from above using hand or electric block and tackle, utilised by the Pennsylvania Railroad, USA; (D) Demountable bodies lifted from below by a power mechanism on the vehicle itself, the bodies standing on retractable wheeled legs, utilised by the Midland Rly at their Nottingham and Leeds depots; (E) Existing motor or steam lorries attached to 2-ton horse lorries acting as trailers, exemplified by *one GW experimental trailer working between Liverpool and Birkenhead*; (F) Petrol or steam tractor serving a number of two-wheeled semi-trailers. It was said that, "……These semi-trailers having only one pair of wheels are easy to haul, while their front ends being pivoted on to the rear end of the tractor, the latter can manoeuvre at right angles to the semi-trailers in awkward places, utilised by (a) haulage contractors very widely in the USA; (b) government services in Europe; (c) *one set is on order for the GWR* [the Knox tractor, see below]; (G) Steam or petrol tractors serving a number of 4-wheeled trailers which is especially suitable when it is desired to haul more than one trailer at a time, utilised by (a) *GWR steam tractors in the Bilston area*; (b) in South Africa; (c) various government departments; (d) various contractors; and (H) —

within goods depots — Electric platform trolleys hauling a number of 3- or 4-wheeled platform barrows…."

In the 1920s, the Superintendent of GW Road Transport and his staff attempted to solve the problem of idle time of motor lorries by two approaches: (a) the use of 'demountable bodies' on ordinary motor lorry chassis; and (b) the use of trailers, either drawn behind a conventional motor lorry already having its own load, or by a separate tractor.

DEMOUNTABLE BODIES
The demountable body system of working was thought of by the GW as 'the [railway] container principle applied to roads'. On arrival back at a goods depot after completing a round of C&D, the body (in practice, a flat tray like a pallet) was removed from the motor chassis and its load taken away for putting into railway wagons, and then the same demounted body was reloaded with incoming goods for local delivery. Long before this had been completed, there would be ready another previously-loaded body waiting to be transferred to the motor chassis so that a new round of C&D could be quickly commenced. Bodies were removed on rollers from the chassis of the motor lorry; similarly when placed on the vehicle. There were, confusingly, *two* versions of the demountable body concept on the GW depending on what happened to the removable bodies in the intermediate stage between unloading and loading.

The first application was a system patented by H T Rendell of the GW, in which flats were transferred from motor lorry in the yard to goods platform by means of old horse lorries. Order 326 of 6/11/19 was for '9 demountable flats, and convert for use in connection therewith 9 horse vehicles and 3 motor lorries'. Demountable bodies had grooved wheels fitted with ball bearings which ran lengthwise along T-iron rails fitted on the chassis of motor lorries, and on the decks of redundant horse-drawn flat lorries which were used as temporary go-betweens ('tenders') for

DEMOUNTABLE BODIES: TRACTORS & TRAILERS; THE MECHANICAL HORSE

On the approach road to Paddington Goods depot before its rebuilding, the Rendell (first) system of demountable flats being demonstrated on 19/11/1920. On left, the specially-adapted AEC ex-army lorry fleet 422, Warwickshire-registered AC 94 of 1919, is about to back up to the tender with its V-frame up in position. On engagement in the V-notch of the redundant horse lorry fleet 1910, the swivelling rails on both are automatically lined up. The load of goods on the roller-bearinged demountable flat on the lorry may then be pushed off on to the tender in minutes and vice versa. *Author's collection*

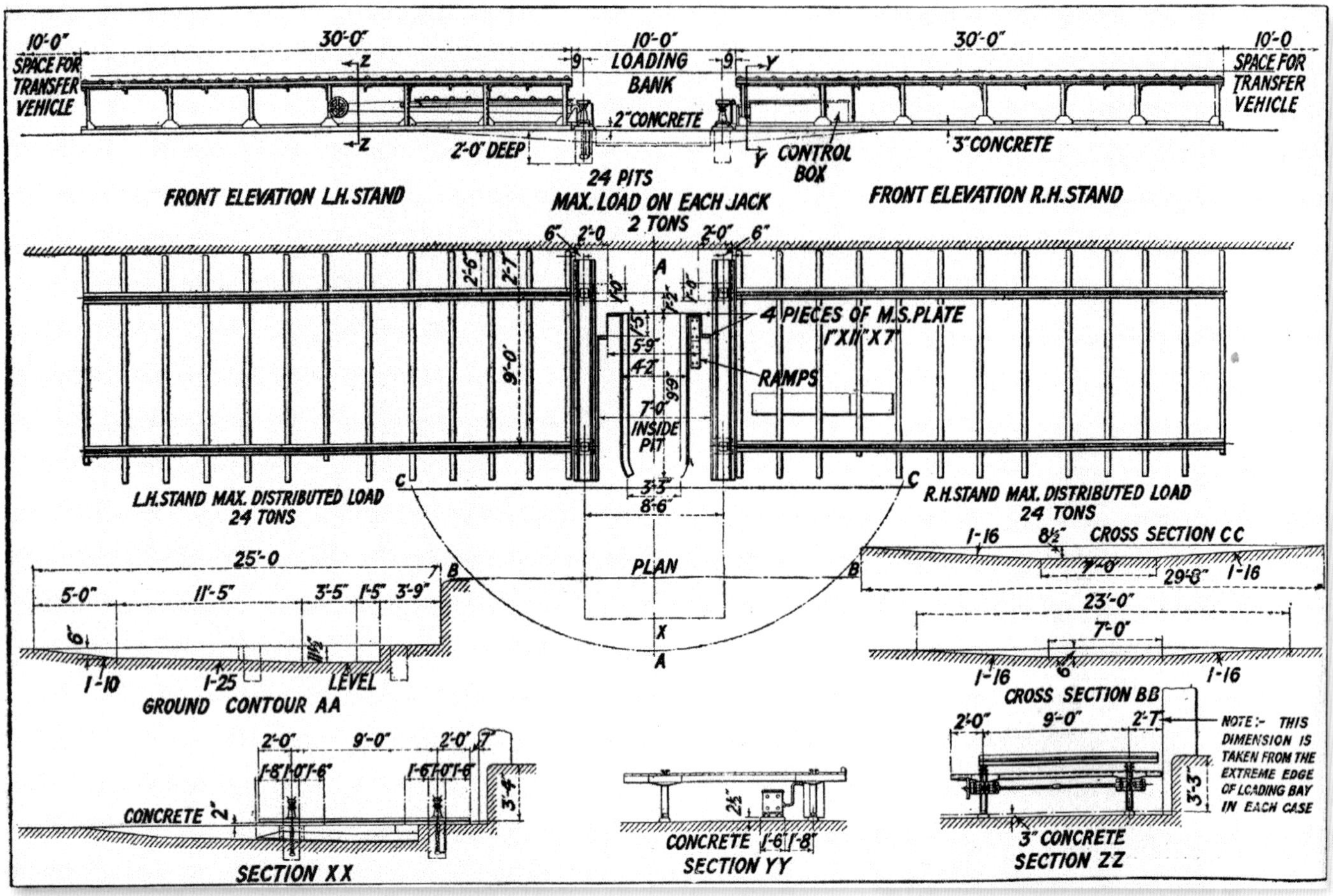

Early lash-up to test the second (Coventry) system of demountable flats at South Lambeth, photographed on 10/11/27. Rollers by which flats can be transferred sideways on/off lorries are held in the chassis of an early Maudslay of 1913 (fleet 201-3 ex-178-80); front wheel and spring dumb irons are to the right. A flat with hoopsticks is about to be unloaded from Burford 30cwt forward control lorry (fleet 828, registration AW4640, new in December 1924 and with disc wheels). The plan of the subsequent permanent installation is also given, photographs of which are in Kelley, p60. *GWR/D J Hyde collection*

the flats. Lorries and tenders had to be lined up properly before transfer of flats could take place and this was achieved by mounting the T-rails on the tender on a pivoted frame that could swivel. On slowly backing the vehicle against the braked tender, a triangular tailpiece on the rear of the motor lorry engaged in a triangular notch on the turntable frame of the tender, and when fully home not only gave alignment of the two sets of rails but also locked the two vehicles together. When backing, the driver had a range of 10 inches either side of the centre of the notch to aim for. Tenders had notches at both ends of the swivelling frame, so either end of the horse lorry tender could be used. After engagement, a loaded flat on an incoming motor could be rolled lengthwise by two men on to an empty tender, thus freeing the motor to back up against another tender carrying a flat ready-loaded for delivery which was transferred to the motor lorry. Both operations could be completed in 3-5 minutes, and a new round could begin. The tender having the incoming load would be moved to the depot for unloading. Demountable flats were also designed to fit into any common-user railway wagon and had side rings to enable them to be craned between rail wagon and motor vehicle in the case of transfer loads or bulk consignments.

The Rendell system was tried at a number of depots on the GWR including Paddington. There were some misgivings about the system in an article in the August 1922 *GW Magazine*. It was observed that unless the saving in time from not hanging around at terminals enabled the same number of motors to do more work, there was no point in having the system. The equipment required at depots was special and expensive; the tare weight of the trays reduced the carrying capacity of each vehicle (some trays weighed half-a-ton); and there was no quick turn-around advantage in peak periods of C&D such as first deliveries of the day. The demountable system was best for jobs between selected points with short journeys where the usual terminal delays, that formed a large proportion of the total time involved, were avoided. It was also best when the loads were not mixed (ie were for a few consignees only).

Despite these reservations, a new 'Coventry' demountable scheme was introduced in 1927 in which intermediate horse lorries were dispensed with. As part of the 1929 enlargement of South Lambeth Depot (see *GWR Goods Services*, volume 2A), £5000 was voted by the GWR Board for the installation of special equipment to move demountable flats to and from motor lorries. The flats were transferred *sideways* this time instead of axially as with the Rendell system. The scheme consisted of a 90ft long roller conveyor that could deal with eight flats, which was installed adjacent to the cartage road loading platform of the depot. Midway along the rollers was a bay, containing a hydraulic lifting rig, into which motor vehicles with demountable bodies could reverse. After the vehicle had backed into the bay, two roller-fitted lifting bars were 'shot' between the chassis and the body, after which the body was lifted hydraulically to the level of the rollers on either side and pushed by hand on to one of the stands to be dealt with by the shed staff. A loaded replacement body was then pushed into place over the central bay and lowered on to the lorry chassis, after which the lifting bars were retracted and the lorry sent on its way. The operation took just two minutes. Two hundred new motor lorries were purchased with this type of arrangement, the demountable bodies for which were built at Swindon. When Morpeth Docks goods depot at Birkenhead was improved in 1930, an extra-wide cartway faced the outwards platforms in anticipation of installation at a later date of the same equipment as at South Lambeth. However, it was never installed since demountable bodies on rigid chassis motors were not very manoeuvrable and fell out of favour after the 'mechanical horse' (see below) had been shown to be so versatile in the early 1930s.

TRACTORS & TRAILERS

For heavy loads (steel plates, rolls, boilers, etc) four-wheeled trailers on iron tyres hauled by small steam tractors became common after the *Heavy Motor-Car Act* of 1903 was passed. There were, however, severe speed restrictions based upon axle loading (5mph legal speed limit for tractors and four-wheeled trailers). The slow maximum speed meant that there was little commercial incentive to develop properly-designed trailers with solid rubber tyres at that time.

There are various ways of coupling a trailer to a towing vehicle: (i) by a triangular-shaped hinged tow bar on the forecarriage of a 4-wheeled trailer at the apex of which was a circular ring that dropped on to a pin on the rear of the tractor, and which could be placed on the ground or up in the air when parked; (ii) by a tow bar on 2-wheeled trailers which similarly hooked to the rear of a tractor, but which stuck out when parked. In all cases the ring at the front of a tow bar might be rigid and integral with the sides of the tow bar, or might be sprung-loaded to ease the start of towing. A third method (iii) did not involve tow bars where the front of the (usually 2-wheeled) trailer overhung the back of the towing vehicle at the coupling point (so-called 'superimposed trailers', what we now call an articulated lorry). Superimposed trailers might be permanently coupled to the tractor, or the trailer was detachable. The large-capacity GW Scammell lorries of the 1920s that were called '6-wheeled', meaning two axles on the towing part and one on the trailer, were examples of permanently-coupled vehicles; the later mechanical horses of the 1930s are examples of trailers detachable from the tractor. An important consideration for all trailers was what type of braking (if any) they possessed, and from where it was applied.

In 1918 a four-wheeled chain-driven Knox petrol tractor (made in Springfield, Massachussetts, USA) was bought by the GW for use in London from E W Rudd in Poplar (Rudds started out as agents for steam wagons and later became haulage contractors). Knox tractors had been used by the French army to haul guns in WW1. It had an electric starter and was unusual in that its rigid chassis ended at the chain-drive sprocket cross-shaft, the rear axle being attached to the chassis by 'reach rods' with the weight of the rear end of the chassis being taken by the ends of two long cantilever springs. A separate frame carrying a central spigot for receiving the semi-trailer pin was held by two half-elliptic springs anchored to the rear axle. This construction made the rear axle and wheels an entirely separate unit as far as carrying the load to be hauled was concerned. The front end of the trailer was thus carried only by the rear wheels of

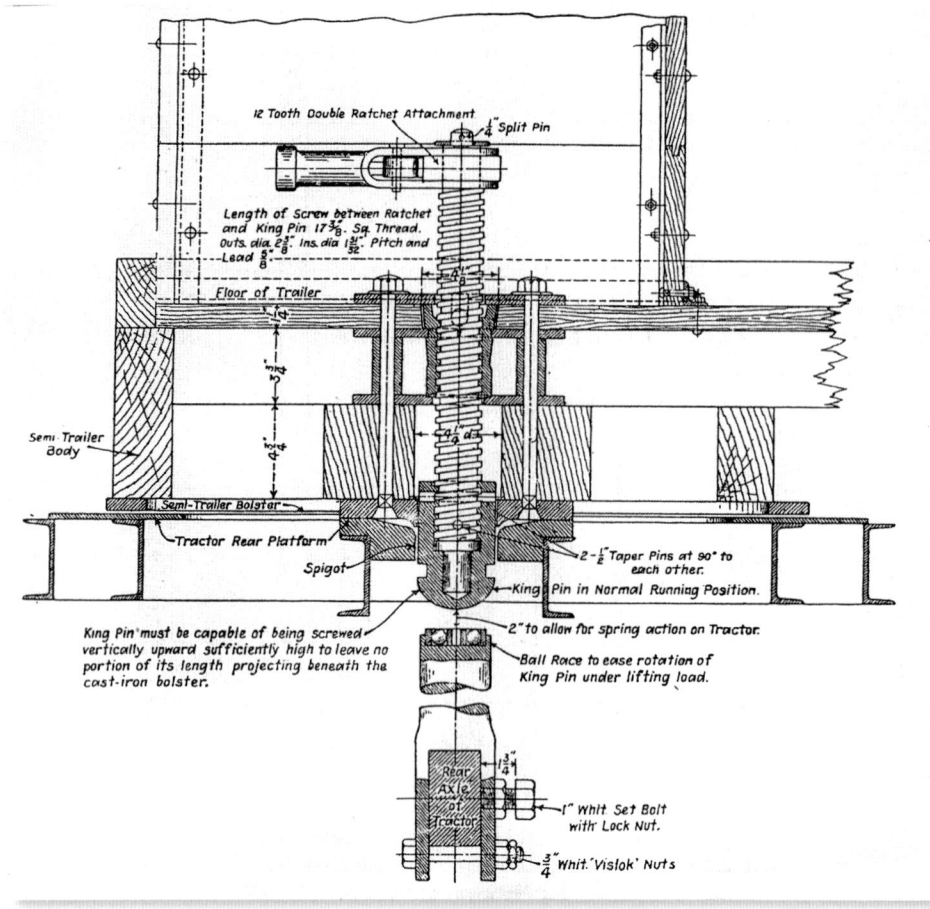

Drawing of patented jacking/kingpin system.

the tractor, the springing of the tractor chassis proper being unaffected by the load. This artifice permitted the 5mph legal speed limit for tractors and four-wheeled trailers to be raised to 12mph for the same tractor and a semi-trailer.

Three 2-wheel, flatbed trailers each having a 7-ton capacity were bought for the Knox from a British maker. (We note in passing that GW trailers for motors were numbered from the earliest days, the trailer number being prefixed by the letter 'T': see Chapter 8.) Retractable legs (to prop up trailers when parked) were fitted at the Slough workshops. The idea was the same as for horse vehicles, namely that one trailer would be unloading at the end of a route; another, laden, out on the road; and a third being loaded at the other end of the route. Both tractor and trailers were equipped with solid rubber tyres. The attachment to the tractor was via a kingpin which provided the necessary movement so that the tractor and semi-trailer could be easily manoeuvred in crowded spaces. The patented coupling was designed by the GW's Charles Bolton, supervisor of the Road Motor Garage at Paddington (biosketch in Chapter 7). Bulkeley pointed out that the disadvantage of a two-wheel trailer being immobile when the legs were down could be overcome by a 'jockey-wheel' arrangement (which later became common practice). He also reported the savings made by an independent haulage contractor who had substituted tractors and semi-trailers for horse-drawn transport.

Owing to problems when attaching and detaching the trailer (lining-up of vehicles, accurate location of attachment points, raising/lowering of trailer on to the turntable with jacks and so on), the use of detachable superimposed trailers fell out of fashion during the 1920s. Instead, trailers with towbars or, for high capacity vehicles, permanently-coupled articulated trailers were employed. (Detachable superimposed trailers became popular again after the invention of the Scammell automatic coupling, see below.)

In September 1922 a Fordson agricultural tractor (fleet 199) was bought from A & S Andrews Ltd of Ealing for experiments in road cartage using 4-wheel trailers. It was adapted for road use by fitting with solid rubber tyres. The trailers first used were existing one-horse lorries with their shafts removed and tow bars substituted. A three-day trial was run between Paddington and the GW depot at the Victoria & Albert Docks, a 14-mile route on which regular loads were available in both directions. Two return trips were made each day, with average loads of 4-tons 2cwt per single trip. It was concluded from the trial that even more terminal gains would be made on shorter trips. In the trials, there was a problem in braking the trailer because the joining of existing mechanical brake linkages from tractor to horse lorry was difficult. Someone had to sit in the old horse lorry driver's position to apply the brakes on the lorry to prevent over-run or jack-knifing, independent of the tractor driver! This arrangement was clearly unsatisfactory, and the use of old horse lorries as trailers in this way was abandoned (another reason was that they became unstable when towed faster than the 4mph or so of horse haulage, as became apparent in trials with Karrier Cob tractors described below).

In the meanwhile, the versatility from horse-drawn practice of being able to uncouple a dray for loading or unloading at a goods depot while the horse went off on another job was something worth aiming to keep, and in consequence trailer developments in C&D in the 1920s took place with ordinary motor lorries, as well as with agricultural tractors. C&D trailers used in the 1920s by the GW were mostly 4-wheel; *Carrimore* and *Eagle* were makes purchased. Two-wheel trailers could be employed when an extension of the underframe itself became the tow bar.

Purchase of tractors and trailers proceeded apace in the 1920s, so that by the end of the decade the GW owned 28 Fordson 6-ton tractors (at least one with pneumatic tyres); three

In the early 1920s there were trials to see whether Fordson tractors could successfully haul horse lorries. In the first picture, fleet 199, XM101, of September 1922 is seen leaving Paddington Goods below Bishops Bridge Road arches (the old entrance to the Broad Gauge station) en route to the Victoria & Albert Docks 14 miles away. The second picture, taken in July 1925, (??? Way Road) shows the same horse vehicle 2116 to Diagram D4 (still with old-pattern naves, but now in different livery) being towed by fleet 390 (on side of radiator), XP2166, of September 1923 that has a low roof over the driver. The unsprung towbar is shorter than before and now steeply angled. In both cases a brakeman sits in the dickey seat; the head of the tractor driver is below the feet of the brakeman. On the radiator header tank are painted BAW 17-1-10/UW 1-7-2-10/FAW 10-1-0, indicating how the total unladen weight of 1 ton-7cwts-2 quarters-10lbs was divided between the rear (17cwts-2qtrs) and front axles (10cwts-1qtr). The lettering on the old horse lorry is now on a cream panel and has 'load not to exceed 4-10-0' at the left. The tail board is down and loaded. On the side of its forecarriage is painted 'TARE 1-9-3' on the left, and (partly obscured by the front wheel) 'GWR A E Bolter SecY Paddington Station' on right. *Author's collection*

Above: A Burford 30cwt lorry and 2-wheel trailer with a load of 45 'pockets' of hops at Worcester in the early 1920s. The caption to this picture published in the *GWR Magazine* emphasises that a horse-drawn wagon would not take more than 25 pockets and would even then require a second horse over a part of the journey. *Author's collection*

Centre: Carrimore 2-wheeled 5-ton cattle float with 3 hoopsticks and tilt, photographed at Hockley Basin in 1934. Jockey wheel (on a block) and raising/lowering screw gear on chassis extension, at the front of which is the hitch coupling. Ramp at rear held up vertically by diagonal metal stays. There may be drum brakes on the solid-rubber-tyred wheels, but no evidence of brake lever. 'Tarpaulin over' has same number as trailer. Full stops between G, W and R on cream panel on side, but no full stops between white lettering on tilt. Would be later coded Nico A. *GWR/P J Kelley collection*

Right: Solid-tyred Carrimore 5-ton trailer at Hockley in 1934. Later to be coded Dido E. Unusually, there are drum brakes on the forecarriage wheels connected by wire to the lever on the long hitch that is pivoted on the front axle, along which slides the vehicle's original coupling. Maker's plate on lowest rail below T-71. *GWR/P J Kelley collection*

Fordson tractor fitted with Muir Hill internally-sprung rear wheels. Fleet 1195, YU5266, the last of a group of 18 tractors purchased from Messrs Pratt of Sutton, Surrey, in September 1927. *Author's collection*

Above: Aluminium cylindrical tank leaving the maker's premises in Bristol en route to Waltham Abbey (LNER) via Acton and Hackney Wick. Fordson tractor fleet 384, YL6505, of October 1925 hauling a horse timber carriage (C in the Diagram index). The tank was 34ft long with a 5ft 6ins diameter and rests on packed-up bolsters. *Author's collection*

Right: Cylinder on ex-horse timber carriage now fitted with old lorry wheels for tractor haulage. International Harvester tractor purchased by the GWR on 16/1/29, fleet 1049, UL 1775. *STEAM Swindon*

A Carrimore four-wheel solid-tyred 2-ton trailer having fixed sides, fleet T17, with towbar lashed vertically being lifted by rail-mounted crane from goods carriage truck coded Serpent C number 42132 built in 1907 (G21 in the Wagon Diagram Index). The Serpent number is seen just above the bonnet of the bus, which is a Guy 'FBB' chassis of 1927 with a Buckingham canvas-roofed 'all-weather' body. After 1937, the trailer would be renumbered and its code Dido G painted on. *GWR/P J Kelley collection*

Stern-first boat on trailer T-149 coupled to Associated Daimler lorry at Weymouth, possibly fleet 1970. Quay to the right hand side. Rail steam crane. *STEAM Swindon*

Carrimore 10-ton 3-way hydraulic tipping trailer (flexible hydraulic pipes linked to back of tractor that is an International Harvester fleet 1067, UW402 of September 1929). Trailer is numbered T-98 and will be coded Jason A in the 1935 renumbering scheme. *Ian Allan Library*

Eagle telescopic timber trailer at South Lambeth on 16 September 1931 (Eagle were based in Warwick), later to be coded Vibo C. Loaded with built-up girders placed on cross bearers over central pole (another load is on horse-drawn vehicle at extreme right). Bolsters on cross bearers with load roped to shackles. Solid-tyred wheels. Forecarriage has two heights to which unsprung towbar can be pinned. Distance between front and rear axles adjusted to suit length of load by mechanism at rear axle. Brake drums on rear wheels. South Lambeth's overhead gantry crane in distance at right centre. *Author's collection*

International Harvester 12-ton tractors, fleet 1049/67/8, that could haul up to 16 tons for specially-heavy consignments; and some 30 trailers for the cartage of cable drums, pipes and other special traffic (see Chapter 12). In addition there was an even more powerful GW tractor — fleet 1170, a McCormick-Deering (made by International Harvester). It was the only one of its type in the country on road cartage haulage. There is a photograph in the February 1927 *GW Magazine* of it hauling a 23-ton load in Birmingham. The first tractors had no suspension and solid rubber tyres offered little springing. However, in 1927 new GW Fordson tractors began to be fitted with springs within the rear wheels, via a Muir Hill (M-H) patent (Muir Hill of Old Trafford, Manchester). Originally the coil springs were visible, but later they were covered over. Note that these totals do not include tractors employed by the CME at the company's works (Chapters 5 and 8).

In 1930, 22 tractors and trailers were bought. The 1920s tractors had no weather protection for the driver but eventually had been

Left: Scammell tractor and permanently-articulated trailer. Fleet 1083, UV 686, of 9/7/29 (was referred to as a 'six-wheeled lorry' in company records). Loaded with steam-driven portable engines. *STEAM Swindon*

Below: A long built-up steel girder chained on to two separate horse timber carriages, and hauled by McCormick-Deering tractor at extreme left of photo. (McCormick-Deering was the tradename of tractors and farm machinery manufactured by the International Harvester Co in Illinois, USA.) The girder overhangs both trailers on the right-hand side viewed from the rear. Even going round a gentle curve, the forecarriage nearside wheel of the nearer trailer is lifted off the ground, as is the nearside back-axle wheel of the front pole-trailer. There is no coupling between the two trailers, continuity being provided by the girder itself. *STEAM Swindon*

given a very low roof. In contrast the 1930 tractors came with a proper cab and sides, access for the driver being from the rear. As explained in Chapter 12, a so-called 'roadless' Fordson tractor equipped with rubber crawler tracks was bought in 1931 for a special job up a mountain near Treorchy in the Rhondda Fawr; it was fleet 2316 and later appeared at many agricultural shows.

In 1932, two new 6-wheeled trailers were put into service and 2-wheel C&D trailers to go with 2-ton lorries were added to the fleet in 1933, being more economical than a single 4-tonner.

A 'new standard drawbar' for trailers was introduced in 1934 fitted to T274, a 15-ton timber carriage. While the new drawbars could be hinged up when parked, some did not reach the ground

DEMOUNTABLE BODIES: TRACTORS & TRAILERS; THE MECHANICAL HORSE

Queen's Head sidings at Handsworth & Smethwick in 1933, showing Fordson tractor fleet 2304 (GK6168) of 1930 coupled by means of a very low towbar to a Brockhouse pole trailer (later coded Vibo A). The tractor has a roof and is all-over brown (some were brown and cream); the driver gets in from the rear. Two long I-beams are being lowered in a sling from the Goliath crane on to the trailer. The men on the right are transferring barstock by hand between the AEC ex-army flatbed lorry (fleet 418, AC7353 of 1919 that had had a bus body in the summer of 1922) and the stack on the ground. See also GWR Goods Services, vol 2B. *GWR/D J Hyde collection*

At Bridgend goods yard in 1932. Ex-army AEC 3½-ton lorry with body removed acting as a tractor. Fleet 409, LT9968. A timber carriage is being used to support a long built-up assembly. *STEAM Swindon*

Rear view of trailer coupled to an A1-type Thornycroft at Paddington in 1934. *GWR/P J Kelley collection*

Above and left: **Two-wheel C&D trailer and special coupling. Fleet 2472, GX 3272 Thornycroft 'A1' lorry of 1931 outside 'GWR & LMS/GOODS & COAL DEPOT'. Trailer photographed with lorry is numbered T43, but trailer alone is unusually just numbered '40'. There appear to be no trailer brakes.** *STEAM Swindon*

DEMOUNTABLE BODIES: TRACTORS & TRAILERS; THE MECHANICAL HORSE

One of two Thornycroft 6/8-ton 'Taurus' lorries fitted with a diesel engine ordered by the GW in 1932. Fleet 2285, GX 3365 was originally fitted by Swindon with a drop-side open body in January 1933 (see Chapter 5), but in March 1933 was given this van body. Shown hauling a 4-ton, 4-wheel, Brockhouse trailer with Swindon van body (later coded Dido A). The unladen weight ('u.w.') has not been painted in on the cabside, although 'speed 20 m.p.h' and 'f r e davis (secy) g.w.r. paddington' has. Floor frame now lowered below the tops of the mudguards. *Author's collection*

Eagle six-wheeled 20-ton trailer T169 photographed at Paddington on 4/11/32. Sprung-loaded towbar. There is a dickey seat at the front nearside with lever to its left connected to internally-expanding brakes. Double solid tyres all round and heavy-duty rear suspension. Front wheels have 'Eagle Engineering Co Ltd' on boss (Eagle were based in Warwick). Side frame of channel-section steel with eight evenly-spaced brackets for lashing down load. At far left of underframe is 'Great Western Railway/F R E Davis Secretary/Paddington'. Six-wheel trailers were later given the telegraph code Mentor; this Eagle trailer was Mentor A (no load or code indicated on trailers until 1937). *GWR/P J Kelley collection*

In 1932 a consignment of boilers was taken by road from the manufacturers to Manchester GW goods depot for conveyance by rail to Abingdon. Three ex-army AEC lorries act as tractors and 'match trucks' for the overhanging trailers. The vehicle at the head of the procession is fleet 713, registration XP4951, purchased by the GW in October 1923, still with canvas cab door. Wooden bolster behind cab with folded tarpaulin on roof. *Daily Herald*

GWR depot at Manchester Dock (Salford) in June 1927. Quayside at left. An ex-army AEC 3½-ton lorry at centre left with original cab awning over driver (but now painted cream) and canvas doors. Another GW lorry to the rear is beneath the nearest of three loading bays having verandahs. A continuous verandah runs along the other wall where there are large sliding doors. There are two lorries with horses in the shafts, one at the left and one at the right. Neither has a headboard, nor dickey, so carter drives from the shafts. All loaded with sacks. *STEAM Swindon*

DEMOUNTABLE BODIES: TRACTORS & TRAILERS; THE MECHANICAL HORSE

Right and below right: **An Eagle 2-wheel trailer chassis with GW body and numbered T-340 at Lechlade in January 1935.** Sacks being loaded into O2/10 7-plank wagon with top doors, whose Dean-Churchward brake is off, even though the rear of the trailer is butted against the dropped door. ALN409 is the registration of the towing lorry (a Thornycroft 'A1'). Trailer hitch is at the left end and a single prop keeps the trailer level, but in the 'official' photograph of July 1934 it is seen that there are two jacks for use when necessary. *GWR/D J Hyde collection*

Thirty-foot-long pole trailer by Brockhouse of West Bromwich, photographed at Bilston on 2 November 1934. Fleet 319. Later coded Vibo B. Double pneumatic tyres all round. The dark-painted 'pole' is made of two steel channel sections and the wheelbase is adjustable using the device at the rear axle (the end of the pole is painted white to show up when overhanging). At the forecarriage end of the pole the tyre pressure is indicated as 65lbs (should be lbs/sq in). Mounted above the pole, on cross-bearers with bolsters and side-shackles positioned over the wheels, is a white painted platform related to the trailer's particular use in the Midlands 'to carry strips and flat plates only' (on the little plate in centre). At the back end of the platform is written 'Load not to exceed 6 ton/evenly distributed'. Unsprung towbar. *GWR/D J Hyde collection*

Horse-drawn 4½-ton glass wagon to Diagram E2 after conversion to tractor haulage by fitting with the 1934 standard drawbar, and numbering as T-280. Dickey seat and foot brake retained. On conversion, many horse-drawn vehicles had their wooden-spoke wheels replaced by solid-rubber-tyred wheels saved from old motor lorries, in this case the rear wheels from a Burford. Photographed 31/8/34. *GWR/P J Kelley collection*

Carrimore 10-ton trailer 'fitted with flat tipping body' according to annotations on the glossy print taken on 11/11/36. Tipping trailers were coded Jason, but this is coded Dido P, where Dido was the generic code for 4-wheeled trailers, and there does not seem to be any obvious mechanism for tipping. Original sequential fleet number T-99. Double solid tyres all round with rear brake drums linked by wire to lever to left of dickey seat. The triangular hitch is sprung at the towing eye. *GWR/P J Kelley collection*

when down, so that 'DANGER' was conspicuously painted on them in capital letters to warn people when in the down position. Older trailers were wearing out so in that year 38 flat bodies for Eagle 2-wheeled trailers appear in the renewals account. At that time, there were thirty-six 4-wheel 5-ton trailers and six all-steel tipping bodies suitable for 4/5-ton chassis and six for timber, all by the Eagle Engineering Co of Warwick; and twelve low loading, and two 10-ton tipping trailers by *Carrimore Six Wheelers Ltd* of North Finchley, London (this firm amalgamated with *G Scammell & Nephew* of Watford and Spitalfields in 1941). The tipping trailers would later be coded *Jason* with different letter suffixes. The February 1937 *GW Magazine* reported that the Road Wagon shop was converting a considerable number of redundant horse lorries into motor trailers by fitting them with towbars and pneumatic tyres; earlier conversions had used wheels with solid rubber tyres from old motor vehicles. Even after designs appeared for trailers not requiring a brakeman, some new trailers incorporating a dickey seat appeared, such as a Carrimore tipping trailer of 1936. By this time trailers, as well as motor lorries and tractors, had to carry licence discs.

Other makes of tractor included Rushton (built by AEC at their Walthamstow factory) and the French-designed Latil, that had

DEMOUNTABLE BODIES: TRACTORS & TRAILERS; THE MECHANICAL HORSE

Six-ton Tasker trailer chassis having double pneumatic tyres all round and equipped with the 1934 'standard coupling' on which 'danger' is conspicuously marked. The wiring running along the hitch is the connection for rear lights. There is no connection for brakes so there is a dickey seat for a brakeman with lever to his right. The body, with 4 slats above 2 wide planks, has hinged sides in two halves (stanchion up the middle to top of slats) and is for carrying sugar beet. Photographed in October 1935 with Numa D code painted on and original sequential number T-889. For subsequent renumbering to T-802, see Chapter 8. *GWR/P J Kelley collection*

Image Ch 6 032 - This former two-horse lorry has been converted to tractor haulage by fitting to its wide splinter bar on the forecarriage the new standard coupling of 1934 that here can rest on the ground. New double solid-tyred wheels all round with brakes at the rear operated by lever on offside of dickey seat. Later to be coded Dido F with a 6-ton capacity. *GWR/D J Hyde collection*

Although haulage of C&D horse vehicles by tractors had been given up, jobs requiring special vehicles to be drawn by tractor might still use horse special vehicles. Here the body of a withdrawn clerestory coach on a 10-ton horse pole (telescopic) trailer to which a special long towbar has been fitted for tractor haulage. At Canon's Marsh, Bristol, in 1934. *STEAM Swindon*

Morris Commercial 'Leader' normal control tractor, fleet C2533, CYP400, in 1937. Trailer number T1184 altered to T7957 (see Chapter 8). 'gwr paddington station london' along bottom of door below yellow shirtbutton. Trailer chassis is Tasker, coded DYAK X (not in 1939 telegraph code book). *Author's colllection*

108

Subject.	Interpretation.	Code.
Timber Loaders	Can you arrange to load………(Firm's name) timber on………(date)? (State whether fixed or travelling crane.)	*Apollo*
,,	Quantity of timber now lying at your station belonging to the following party requires loading at once. How many timber trucks do you require? Do you want travelling crane?	*Abase*
Time Tables	Return time table extracts to-day certain or must go to press without your particulars.	**Bat**
,,	Arrange for Time Bill Clerk come to ………(place)………(time)………(date) ………in connection with………Train Service.	*Ball*
Tracing	See **Missing and Tracing**.	
Trailers	CATTLE TRAILERS.	*Nico*
,,	Carrimore 2-wheeled Float—5 ton.	*Nico A*
,,	Eagle 4-wheeled Float—6 ton.	*Nico B*
,,	G.W.R. Converted 4-wheeled Horse Float—6 ton.	*Nico C*
,,	G.W.R. Converted 4-wheeled House Float—10 ton.	*Nico D*
,,	Harrow Industrial 4-wheeled Cattle Trailer—3 ton.	*Nico E*
,,	G.W.R. Cattle Float or Glass Lorry 4-wheel.	*Nico F*

109

Subject.	Interpretation.	Code.
Trailers	Tasker Articulated Trailer 2-wheel.	*Nico G*
,,	Brockhouse—15 ton (Flat).	*Titan A*
,,	Brockhouse—15 ton (Girder).	*Titan B*
,,	CONTAINER TRAILERS.	*Numa*
,,	A.E.C. (Hand-steering).	*Numa A*
,,	Dyson.	*Numa B*
,,	Dyson (Hand-steering).	*Numa C*
,,	Tasker or Carrimore 6-ton Low Loading.	*Numa D*
,,	FOUR-WHEELED TRAILERS.	*Dido*
,,	Brockhouse—4 ton.	*Dido A*
,,	Eagle—Carrimore—5 ton.	*Dido B*
,,	Eagle—10 ton.	*Dido C*
,,	Carrimore—2 ton (no sides).	*Dido D*
,,	Carrimore—5 ton.	*Dido E*
,,	G.W.R. Converted Horse Vehicle—6 ton.	*Dido F*
,,	Carrimore—2 ton (fixed sides).	*Dido G*
,,	Harrow Industrial Low Loader—6 ton.	*Dido H*
,,	G.W.R. Converted Horse Furniture Van—4 ton.	*Dido J*

110

Subject.	Interpretation.	Code.
Trailers	Wallis and Steevens—8 ton (Flat).	*Dido K*
,,	G.W.R.—6 ton (Bolster).	*Dido L*
,,	Atkinson Walker—2 ton.	*Dido M*
,,	PIPE TRAILERS.	*Lydus*
,,	Maudslay—4 ton.	*Lydus A*
,,	SIX-WHEELED TRAILERS.	*Mentor*
,,	Eagle—20 ton.	*Mentor A*
,,	TIMBER TRAILERS.	*Vibo*
,,	Brockhouse 16 ft. Pole Trailer.	*Vibo A*
,,	Brockhouse 30 ft. Pole Trailer } 6 ton. Tasker 30 ft. Pole Trailer	*Vibo B*
,,	Eagle Timber Trailer.	*Vibo C*
,,	G.W.R. Converted Horse Timber Trailer—4½ ton.	*Vibo D*
,,	G.W.R. Converted Horse Timber Trailer—10 ton.	*Vibo E*
,,	TIPPING TRAILERS.	*Jason*
,,	Carrimore Hydraulic 3-way Tipper—10 ton.	*Jason A*
,,	Eagle Hydraulic End Tipper—10 ton.	*Jason B*
,,	Eagle, 2-wheeled Hand Tipper—4 ton.	*Jason C*

111

Subject.	Interpretation.	Code.
Trailers	Eagle, 2-wheeled Hand Tipper—5 ton.	*Jason D*
,,	Eagle, 2-wheeled End Tipper—4 ton.	*Jason E*
,,	TWO-WHEELED TRAILERS.	*Dyak*
,,	Dyson—30 cwt.	*Dyak A*
,,	Dyson—2 ton.	*Dyak B*
,,	Eagle—2 ton.	*Dyak C*
,,	Karrier Cob—2 ton.	*Dyak D*
,,	Karrier Cob—(van body).	*Dyak E*
,,	Scammell A.L.—3 ton.	*Dyak F*
,,	Scammell A.L.—6 ton.	*Dyak G*
,,	Eagle—4 ton.	*Dyak H*
,,	Scammell A.L.—6 ton (lightened body).	*Dyak J*
,,	Scammell A.L.—3 ton (Country body).	*Dyak K*
,,	G.W.R. (Cob)—2 ton.	*Dyak L*
,,	Scammell A.L.—3 ton (Rubber floor).	*Dyak M*
,,	Scammell A.L.—6 ton (Drop frame).	*Dyak P*
,,	Scammell A.L.—6 ton (Winch fitter).	*Dyak R*
Trainmen	Provide Pilotman between points named for Driver of………	**Eger**

4-wheel steering, and Foden. Such heavy-duty tractors were often used in special contract work (Chapter 12).

As explained in Chapter 8, running numbers of motor-drawn trailers were always prefixed with the letter 'T'. In the renumbering scheme of 1935, their appropriate telegraph codes were painted on for the first time.

ARTICULATED VEHICLES: THE MECHANICAL HORSE

A significant development occurred in the early 1930s that was to have a long-lasting effect on railway cartage work. In the 1931 *GW Road Transport Department Report* it says that '……an experimental tractor is in use [introduced in September], the object of which is to replace horses. It is of simple design and intended to handle the existing horse vehicles after some small adaptation……'; and in 1932 '…..experiments are being pursued with tractors on hill work [at Hockley Goods Depot in Birmingham up Pitsford Street] in place of chain horses, and with tractors and trailers in substitution for horses and lorries for short distance C&D work. These tractors are small 3-wheeled machines, the motive power being supplied by a 9hp petrol engine……..' The tractors referred to were 'Karrier Cob' vehicles made by Karrier Motors of Huddersfield. They were powered by Jowett 2-cylinder horizontally-opposed water-cooled engines connected to the final drive by chain. The name Cob (meaning a small strong stout horse) was given to them by the manufacturer as they were based on 3-wheel Karrier Colt vehicles that were fitted up as municipal dustcarts (a colt being a young male horse less than four years old).

Karrier Cob tractors were trialled at South Lambeth goods depot using horse vehicles as trailers, modified with various different means of coupling between the forecarriage and tractor.

Left and below: **Trials of a Karrier Cob tractor at Hockley, Birmingham, in 1931 to assist horse-drawn vehicles along Pitsford Street. Painted brown and cream, and with 'AEBolter Secretary etc' at bottom of cab, the tractor has not been registered and is running on trade plates. On the left, taken at the bottom of the hill, the driver looks through the rear window as he backs to couple up to a loaded one-horse lorry, with lots of people including the law taking an interest. In the other shot, the tractor is on the hill pulling two lorries. Two chains, separated by a spreader bar, are employed attached to the top of a stout pillar on the back of the tractor. Chain horses walking on left of picture.** *Author's collection*

DEMOUNTABLE BODIES: TRACTORS & TRAILERS; THE MECHANICAL HORSE

A number of experiments were performed in 1931 to determine the best way of coupling newly-acquired Karrier Cob tractors to former horse-drawn vehicles and trailers (this was before the Scammell coupling was perfected). Three methods were tried and were photographed on 16/9/31 at South Lambeth with the tractors ready to back under and couple up to the trailers: (i) Fleet 2700 (GT 9495, but no number plate) and horse wagon fleet 370, that has older large naves on its forecarriage but new hubs on its back axle. The placing of the Shredded Wheat advert means that there is less space for the company name and 'load not to exceed 4-10-0' and tare weight at the left of the vehicle; (ii) Fleet 2702 (GT 4219, but no number plate) and horse wagon 2432 (Tare 1-2-3, load not to exceed 2-10-0), fitted with a jerry-rigged forecarriage, and whose wooden-spoke rear wheels have been replaced with solid rubber-tyred motor vehicle wheels; and (iii) Fleet 2700 before backing under a cross-bearered trailer converted from a redundant Burford lorry chassis (dismantled differential casing on back axle) having a different jerry-rigged forecarriage with jockey wheels. The number S24 indicates that the trailer is a special vehicle. The Shredded Wheat lorry is now behind the bonnet of the Cob and to its right is a man sitting on a timber trailer shading his eyes against the sun. In all three cases the idea was, by different devices, to lift the forecarriage up and over the back of the Cob to lift the front wheels clear of the ground and to articulate the vehicles. Pictures of the coupled vehicles are on pp 143/4 of Kelley. The two horse lorries retain their drivers' seats and brakes. Both Cobs have mascots on bonnet of laying-down horses. Semicircular bumpers protect radiator and starting handle. Although contemporaneous, their painting is different, particularly the positioning of fleet numbers and company secretary details; unlike 2700, 2702 does not have unladen weight and speed. On 2702 the bulb horn is mounted downwards on the outside of the cab; on 2700 it is horizontal and inside the cab. Overhead yard gantry crane in background. *Author's collection*

Scammell 6-ton mechanical horse (fleet 2737, ALN 367) with larger cab than the 3-tonner design. Before introduction of shirtbutton in 1934, brown 'GWR' was painted on cream rectangular panel (in this case with quarter-round corners). One licence disc on cabside. Tarpaulin has same number T228 as trailer. '12/33' indicates date when painted at sheet works. The sheeted load overhangs the trailer and tarpaulin, and rests on the tailboard. *Author's collection*

However, at speeds faster than the usual 4mph or so at which horse lorries operated, there were problems about vehicle stability. To overcome this difficulty and to make better use of the Cobs, the rear ends of old Burford chassis were adapted to become 'superimposed' trailers, ie articulated using a coupling designed at the GW road vehicle headquarters at Slough. Fleet numbers for these early Karrier Cobs were 2700-11 with registration numbers GT9495, GT4218-21 and GW9659-65 respectively

At the same time as the Karrier Cob vehicle was being tried out, a similar sort of light three-wheel tractor unit was being developed independently by the Napier Aeroengine Company using a more powerful 4-cylinder engine. After some initial work to prove the design concept, Napier sold the idea to Scammell Lorries (Watford) who registered the name 'mechanical horse'. By 1934 two capacities were available, 3-ton and 6-ton, driven by 10hp and 14hp motors respectively. The 6-ton design had a slightly bigger cab than the 3-ton. The front of the trailer used with the mechanical horse overhung the rear of the tractor to which it was joined, and the really important feature of the design was the Scammell patented coupling that overcame all the problems of previous forms of 'superimposed' turntable attachment such as those encountered by the GW with the 1918 Knox tractor. The coupling had two parallel ramps over the rear of the tractor chassis, and coupling hooks situated at the rear wheels. Underneath the front end of the trailer was a turntable (equivalent to the forecarriage of a dray) having a drop-down unit with two small (jockey) wheels that propped it up when parked. With the trailer handbrake on, the driver would back the tractor under the trailer to engage rollers on the turntable which ran up the tractor ramps. The front of the trailer was thereby lifted, and reversing continued until the securing hooks engaged with lugs on the trailer, attaching it securely. As the rollers ran up the tractor ramps, the jockey wheel suspension unit folded back after striking a plate below the ramps, which released a spring-loaded latch. During coupling, the trailer brake and trailer light connections were made automatically. All this was done without the driver having to leave his cab and the only task he had to do before setting off was to fix the appropriate registration plate to the rear of the trailer and release the hand brake. Reversing under the trailer could be done at an angle between the tractor and trailer, exactly as a horse would be backed into the shafts of a cart swung round from the line of direction of the cart. The turning circle of the Scammell mechanical horse was about the same as a horse vehicle (and was considerably less than that of even a short-wheelbase 'rigid-chassis' motor vehicle). Furthermore, the mechanical horse had both greater carrying capacity than a horse dray and was also faster. One problem with the Scammell mechanical horses seems to have been the petrol tank cap that had a copper segment locking device. Circular No 460 of March 1937 stated that the latest modified type of bayonet filler cap would be issued when repairs were required.

DEMOUNTABLE BODIES: TRACTORS & TRAILERS; THE MECHANICAL HORSE

Rear view of 6-ton mechanical horse showing Scammell coupling. Photographed on 28/1/40 with blackout regulation white edges to mudguards and to protruding parts of hitch. *Author's collection*

While many mechanical horse trailers were built to standard patterns, there were designs for particular depots, rather like the different sorts of horse-drawn vehicles described in Chapter 2. For example, in 1935 the Swindon Road Wagon shop was asked for 'one special Paddington-type tilt body, to Drawing D 844' and 'one country type of tilt body to Drawing D 845', both for 3-ton Scammell trailer chassis.

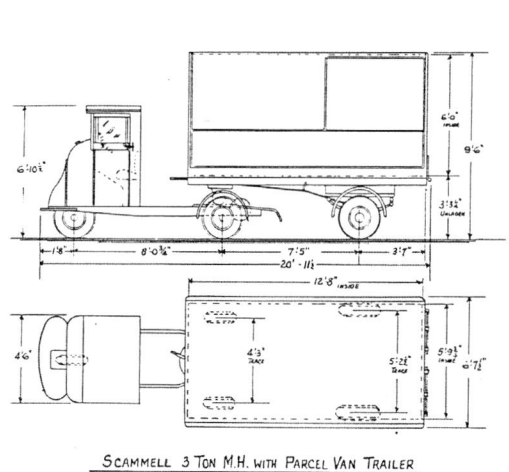

3 Ton MH Parcel Van Trailer

Tractors capable of coupling & drawing this trailer are:-
Scammell 3 Ton, Karrier, Wilson-Scammell Elec:

BODY	Std. Parcel Van Design, Drop Tailboard & Curtains
BRAKES	Operated from Tractor. Hand Parking Lever at Front
TYRES	8·25" x 10"
TURNING CIRCLE WITH TRAILER	24' 0"
WEIGHT OF TRAILER	1 Ton 5 Cwt 2 Qrs
TYPE OF COUPLING	Scammell
MISC: NOTE:	

Diagram No 445/37

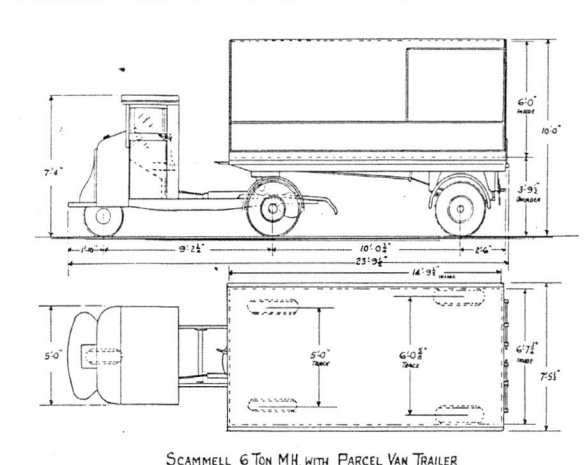

6 Ton MH Parcel Van Trailer

Tractors capable of coupling & drawing this trailer are:-
Scammell 6 Ton, Dennis 6 Ton MH, Bedford-Scammell M.H, Commer.

BODY	Std. Parcel Van Design, Drop Tailboard & Curtains
BRAKES	Operated from Tractor. Hand Parking Lever at Front
TYRES	10·50" x 13 LP
TURNING CIRCLE WITH TRACTOR	40' 0" app
WEIGHT OF TRAILER	1 Ton 17 Cwt 2 Qrs
TYPE OF COUPLING	Scammell
MISC. NOTE:	

Diagram No 445/38

3-ton Scammell AL flat trailer photographed on 14/5/36 with Dyak F coded painted on and original fleet number T-1059. Later altered to T-3304 to reflect actual 3-ton capacity (see Chapter 8). Notice difference in sizes of wheels on different Scammell trailers. *Author's collection*

Rear view of 6-ton Dyak G Scammell trailer, fleet T-1267, photographed on 15/4/37 before renumbering. *Author's collection*

Two-wheeled 6-ton timber trailer fitted with articulated Scammell coupling. Made by Taskers of Andover in 1937, the wheelbase was adjustable by winding a two-handled screw at the rear axle assembly that gave movement along the central pole made up from two channel sections. Cross-bearers with bolsters and shackles. Double pneumatic tyres. Fleet T1607 and coded Dyak Z (not in 1939 telegraph code book). *GWR/P J Kelley collection*

DEMOUNTABLE BODIES: TRACTORS & TRAILERS; THE MECHANICAL HORSE

One of a batch (fleet 4900-35) of half-tilt bodies on 3-ton Scammell trailers photographed on 26/8/46. Small wheels compared with some other mechanical horse trailers. Body similar to pre-war Dyak K ('country body'), but here coded Dyak AD (not in 1939 telegraph code book). *Author's collection*

Tasker articulated drop (step) frame trailer (with Scammell coupling) fitted for carrying glass. Risers over rear wheels. Photographed on 28/1/39 with sequential number T-1820 and code Dyak OL. Renumbering to T-4600 to conform to 1935 renumbering scheme.
GWR/P J Kelley collection

Six-ton Scammell AL flat trailer T-1780 photographed 15/9/38. War did not break out until 3/9/39 so cream rear with brown-encircled shirtbutton has nothing to do with blackout regulations. Provision for hoopsticks at front above panel giving fleet number and Dyak OG code. 20mph speed limit disc.
GWR/P J Kelley collection

The utility and versatility of the mechanical horse was so obvious that the Big Four railway companies came to an agreement with Scammell that they could both manufacture its patented coupling gear under royalty and also use the gear on vehicles that were not made by Scammell (the original Karrier coupling was incompatible). The reports in later years state that '……this type of vehicle had done all that was expected of it and seemed to have come as near to railway companies' requirements for deliveries within restricted areas as anything the manufacturers are likely to produce in the immediate future………… and will eventually form the nucleus of the cartage equipment for the ordinary C&D work at most goods depots……..' The trailer could be attached or detached at a moment's notice and, with the comparatively small expense of trailer bodies, one motor unit could deal with all sorts of traffic (general merchandise, cattle, tanks for liquids, and so on). Greater co-ordination of cartage activities between the Big Four railways, within London in particular, would not have been possible without the universal Scammell articulated coupling.

Mechanical horses were originally designed with three-wheeled tractor units and this limited use to comparatively flat districts; moreover, with a small engine it was uneconomical to use this tractor for deliveries remote from the starting point. It seemed clear that a more powerful four-wheeled tractor with the Scammell coupling would make a very useful articulated vehicle. To this end, in the mid-1930s, some GW lorries and vans had their bodies removed and their chassis were equipped with a heavy-duty Scammell coupling for use with bigger trailers. Four-wheeled tractors from other manufacturers which had the heavier Scammell coupling were also bought for the GW fleet. For example, cabs for Morris Leader normal-control tractor chassis were constructed at Swindon in 1936; other 4-wheel tractors were based on the Thornycroft Nippy, the Karrier Bantam, as well by Scammell itself. Four-wheeled tractors retained the ability to tow a trailer using a drawbar by means of a simple conversion.

Scammell mechanical horses and trailers were also bought by cartage agencies. Bantocks in the West Midlands had its first in 1935. By 1936, the GW fleet of articulated lorries and trailers for C&D work comprised:

Three-wheelers, 3-ton load   333
Three-wheelers, 6-ton load   194
Four-wheelers, 6-ton load   49

In the late 1930s, the Bedford lorry group of Luton marketed a tractor fitted with a heavy duty Scammell coupling that was widely used by the armed forces in WW2. In this design, the need to fold away the jockey-wheel unit on the trailer was avoided by omitting the rear cross-member of the tractor chassis. After the war, Bedford and Scammell jointly marketed the so-called OSS chassis that could take an 8-ton load (the radiator badge was *Bedford-Scammell*) and many were bought by the GWR.

The employment of articulated lorries, as distinct from ordinary rigid-chassis lorries hauling trailers by tow bar, became popular not only for C&D work but also for all sorts of jobs. A great variety of different designs for two- and four-wheel trailers became available; an articulated horse box was introduced to take horses from stables to adjacent railway stations for rail transit and special trailers for sheep and cattle were similarly introduced.

In March 1939, a 6-ton Scammell trailer body was built in the Road Wagon shop for Spiller's grain traffic and in August a body for a 3-ton drop-frame Tasker trailer for Kellogg's traffic. A great number of flatbed bodies for Scammell trailers were built in 1939 and 1940, most having the instruction 'all bodies to be drilled for bracket holes [to attach sides], but brackets and sides not to be provided at present'. Thus 10 bodies (T1828-1837), and 14 more (T1860-1873), all for 8-ton trailers; 35 (T1882-T1916) and 105 more for flat bodies (T1917-T2921) for 6-ton trailers in 1939. Twenty bodies for Scammell 3-ton AL trailer chassis (T2091-T2110) were ordered as renewals under Lot 753 from the Road Wagon shop in 1940 [under this order sides and brackets were exceptionally fitted to 6 vehicles (T2091-T2095)]; 16 flat bodies for 6-ton trailers (T2135-T2150); and 2 bodies for 10-ton trailers (T1826/7). More were built in 1942 along with other bodies and cabs for road motors. In 1944, 15 cabs were ordered for Scammell 6/8-ton chassis Nos 3683-3697 with the instruction that 'side doors to be left unglazed'.

As with all other motors, renewals appeared in the accounts to keep the fleet of mechanical horses up to strength when vehicles reached the end of their working lives. Hence in 1944 there was new construction of flat bodies for Scammell trailers (30 for 6-tonners T2464-2493; and 27 for 8-tonners T2498-2524); at the same time, 10 standard pattern cabs for 6-ton Scammell articulated units Nos 6434-6443 were constructed.

Three-ton Scammell Articulated Dyak AC T-4780 with metal bolster frame at front end. Cream-encircled shirtbutton directly on to brown body and similarly for lettering on side raves. Painting date SN14·8·46 below number on end, label clip alongside. 'tyre pressures/front rear/60 lbs' on front rave.
GWR/P J Kelley collection

DEMOUNTABLE BODIES: TRACTORS & TRAILERS; THE MECHANICAL HORSE

Above and left: WW2 Bedford-Scammell 6/8-ton tractor designed around the lorry version supplied to the army during WW2, with different bonnet, and radiator from the civilian version. At Hockley Basin in August 1944. All-brown livery and white mudguards for the blackout with nearside headlight mask. Fleet D8890, with simple cream encircled GWR shirtbutton. *Author's collection*

Index

Acts of Parliament
    Finance Act 1933 130
    Heavy Motor-Car Act 1903 .... 85, 149
    Light Railways Act 1896 85
    Locomotives on Highways Act 1896 85
    Railways Act 1921 11
    Road Transport Act 1928 .... 12, 13, 16
    Road Traffic Act 1930 126
    Road and Rail Traffic Act 1933 .... 14, 89, 123
    Transport Act 1947 16-17
    Transport Act 1953 17
AEC (Associated Equipment Co) 121, 123, 128, 129
    ex-army lorries 11, 40, 111, 112, 113, 114, 121, 127, 139, 147, 157, 160
Albion buses 139
Alexandra (Newport & South Wales)
    Dock & Railway 11, 114
Allen, Mr (Superintendent
    of the Horse Dept) 64, 66
Anglo-American Motor Co 89
'Artillery' wheels/hubs 39, 58, 59, 78, 79, 121
Associated Daimler lorries 12, 121, 122, 129, 154
Auld, J. 83
Austin vehicles 138
Aveling & Porter 87
Avonmouth 14
Ayres, C. & G. (agent)... 6, 7

Baldwin, Alfred (GWR Chairman) 86
Bantock (agent) 97, 172
Barton, T. H. 101
Bath 14, 58
Bedford lorries 172
Bedford-Scammell vehicles 17, 138, 172, 173
Bere Alston & Calstock Light Railway 99
'Big Four' railway companies 11, 12, 14, 129, 172
Bill, Mr (Hockley Goods Manager) 64
Billingsgate 71, 94
Bilston 14, 39, 58, 66, 87, 99, 113, 146, 161
Birkenhead 30, 66, 91, 96, 99, 104, 149
Birmingham 17, 30, 31, 78, 83, 96, 99, 104, 122
Birmingham, Wolverhampton & Dudley Railway... 7
Blaenavon 58
Blee, David (Chief Goods manager) 84

Boiler wagon 35
Bolton, Charles 150
Bradford 58
Brakes 38, 39, 58, 60-61, 62, 78, 103, 106
Bramco (Mercury) tractor........................... 141, 142
Bridgend 157
Bridgnorth 87
Bridgwater 81, 84
Bristol 12, 17, 31, 58, 61, 62, 73, 83, 84, 100, 103, 164
    Temple Meads 47, 92
    Tramways 13
Brixham 73, 75, 82
Brockhouse trailers 159, 161
Brooks, Bill (porter).. 78
Brush electric vehicles 109
Buckfastleigh 82
Bull & Mouth inn, stables 66
Burford vehicles 111, 113, 114, 115, 116, 120, 123, 126, 127, 139, 148, 152, 168
Buses and bus services,
    horse-drawn and motor............ 10, 13, 64, 83, 87, 92-93, 101, 116, 121, 139
    Lizard 10, 93

Caerphilly 142
Callington 99
Cambrian Railways 11
'Canvassing agents'.. 7, 9
Cardiff... 45, 96, 99, 107
    Docks 141, 143
    Newtown 12, 14, 17, 73, 83
Cardiff Railway 114
Carette motorcycle carrier.......................... 108, 116
Carmen and carters 78, 80-81, 83, 128, 136-37
Carrimore trailers 151, 152, 154, 155, 162
Cars for senior staff 140
Cartage and road motor fleets,
    size of 10, 11, 16, 50, 62, 63, 123, 128
Cartage staff, duties and working hours 73, 81
Carter, Paterson & Co 7
Chain ('trace') horses 84
Channel Islands..125-26
Chater Lea, Letchworth 108, 116
Cheddar 87
Cheltenham 14
Chester 12, 66, 82
Chippenham 47
Clarkson steam buses 87

Clevedon 58, 74
Collection and delivery (C&D) 7, 9, 11
Commercial Cars ('Commer'), Luton...... 97, 98, 116, 135, 138
'Common carrier' rules 16
Competition between railway companies 7, 9, 11, 14
'Concentration schemes'................................... 12, 16
Cork 14
Corris Railway 13
'Country Lorry Service' 87
Coventry, F. C. A. 85, 128, 148, 149
Crane wagons 35
Crosville bus company 13
Crumlin (LL) 73

Dean, William 61
Delivery rounds and drivers 78
Demountable bodies 146
Dennis vehicles 100, 105, 126, 127, 129
Devizes 62, 73, 74, 78, 83
Devon General bus company 13
Diagram numbers 29
    A4 30
    A7 .... 30, 31, 32
    A8 .... 30, 31
    A9 61
    A10 .... 30, 31, 32, 61
    A11 .... 30, 62
    A15 .... 30, 31, 32, 62, 78, 79
    B9 33
    B11 34
    B13 50
    B14 .... 35, 72
    B15 35
    C1 34
    C2 .... 36, 50, 72
    C3 37
    C4 37
    C5 37
    D1 103
    D2 .... 38, 59, 103, 104, 105
    D4 .... 30, 39, 121, 151
    D5 30
    D6 40
    D7 .... 30, 40
    D8 .... 30, 121
    D9 .... 40, 47
    D10 40
    D11 41
    D12 42
    D14 .... 43, 44
    E2 .... 30, 44

INDEX

E3 .... 30, 45
E4 30
G1 30
G21 154
Dickey seats 30, 31, 32, 33, 39, 47, 48, 103, 159, 163
Didcot Provender Store 77
Diesel engines for lorries 123, 125
Douglas (Kingswood) Ltd 92
Dowlais 14
Drewe, A. J. (carrier) 6
Droitwich 14
Dublin 58
Dudley 66
Dunkley pedal tricycle 107

Eagle trailers 151, 155, 159, 161, 162
Eaglesham, R. (veterinary surgeon) 76
Ealing Broadway 107
Ebbw Junction 138-39, 145
Ebbw Vale 58
Electric vehicles 10, 89-92
Evans, E. T. J. 139
Exeter 37, 83, 89, 129

Farriery 75
Floats 30, 63
 cattle 45
 glass 44, 61
 'windlass' 30
Foden steam wagons 88, 89, 127
Forbes, J. S. (carrier) 6
Ford vehicles 109, 111, 113, 116, 121, 127, 128, 129, 134, 138
Fordson tractors and lorries 113, 116, 127, 129, 130, 134, 135, 138, 139, 142, 143, 144, 145, 151, 153, 155, 156, 157
Forecarriage 50
'Forward control' of lorries 123
Frome 58
Furniture van 48
Futchels 50

Garner Motor Co, Tyseley 129
Gas as vehicle fuel
 coal gas 101, 107
 producer gas 102, 132
Gattie, A. W. 9
General Electric Co 91
Gloucester 83
Goodchild Auto-Carrier cyclecar ... 96, 97, 121
Goods agents 7, 12, 17, 18, 62
Great Bridge 66

Great Western & Great Central Joint Railway 132
Grierson, James 7, 29, 64, 66, 76, 77
Grouping of railways *see* 'Big Four'
Guy Motors vehicles 13, 129, 139, 154

Handsworth 74, 77, 157
Harnesses 50, 75
Haverfordwest 82
Henwick 86, 87
Hereford 14
High Wycombe 120, 121, 123
Hockley goods depot 7, 10, 12, 32, 42, 44, 58, 64-65, 71, 73, 75, 77, 82, 83, 84, 87, 166, 173
Horse Committee/Department 11, 64, 66, 77
Horse parades 81-82, 83
Horse-drawn vehicles, drawings/designs of 18-29
 costs of 61
Horses, costs of 66, 71
 feeding 66, 77
 veterinarian treatment of 75-76
 numbers employed 16, 66, 73, 83
 physical capacity of 10, 64, 71
 types employed 71
Hubs, design of 58

Ilminster 823
Ince, E. B. (veterinary surgeon) 76
Inglis, James 105
International Harvester tractors 151, 153, 155

Joint cartage fleets 14

Karrier 'Bantam' 134, 138, 172
 'Cob' 84, 129, 166, 167, 168, 172
Kennet & Avon Canal 62
Kensington (Addison Road) 105, 110
Kidderminster 66
Kingswear 58
Knox petrol tractor 101, 149, 150, 168

Lambert, Henry 66, 70
Latil tractors 129, 132, 162
Launceston 58
Laycock 145
Laycock Engineering, Sheffield 96, 97
Leamington 61
Lechlade 161
Leeds 58
Leney, S. & E. (horse contractor) 66, 67-69
Littleton & Badsey 73
Liverpool 58, 66, 83
Llanelly 12

London General bus company 13, 121
London Parcels Co 7
Lynton & Barnstaple Railway 92

McCormick-Deering tractor 155, 156
Maidenhead 6, 127
Malmesbury 82
Manchester 14, 58, 159, 160
Martock 74
Maudslay vehicles 13, 94, 101, 116, 121, 139, 148
Meat lorry 40
Midland Railway 6, 66, 84, 146
Midland Red bus company 13
Miles, Bert (carter) 78
Milne, Capt (Horse Superintendent) 76
Milnes, G. F. & Co 93
Milnes-Daimler vehicles 93, 94, 95, 97, 98, 99, 101, 113, 116
Mint stables, Paddington 7, 40, 41, 42, 66, 73, 75
Morris vehicles 71, 123, 126, 128, 132, 140, 172
 Commercial 108, 109, 121, 124, 128, 129, 141, 164
Motorcycles 96
Motorisation of goods fleet 62, 82, 83, 129
 disadvantages of 146
Muir-Hill wheels 143, 144, 153, 155

Napier Aeroengine Co 168
National Omnibus & Transport Co 13
Nationalisation 16
Neath 140
Newcombe, W. L. (Chief Goods Manager) ... 6, 7, 29
Newnes, Sir George 92
Newport 12, 14, 83, 139
Newton Abbot 142
'Normal control' of lorries 123
North London Railway 10, 66, 72

Oakengates 58
O'Neill, E. (veterinary surgeon) 76
Oswestry 58
Oxford 14, 58, 61, 74

Paddington goods depot 4, 12, 17, 31, 64, 66, 71, 72, 73, 89, 99, 132, 147, 151, 158, 159
 parcels traffic at 106-07, 110
 passenger station 15, 16, 95
 stables 73, 74, 76
 see also Mint stables
Parcels traffic 102
Penzance 82
Petrol-engined vehicles 10, 92, 101

Pickfords 7, 66
Plymouth 12, 58, 83, 94
Plymouth, Devonport & South Western Junction Railway 99
Pole wagons *see* Timber wagons
Poplar 73
Portsmouth Motor Co 120
Principality Wagon Co, Cardiff 141
Private road haulers 11

Ransomes, Sims & Jeffries vehicles 91, 92, 106, 111
Reading 6, 7, 135
Receiving offices 103, 105, 108, 110
Rendell, H. T. 146, 147, 149
Renewals of motor fleet 121, 123, 127, 128, 135, 172
Road Motor Department 11, 92, 101
Road sweeper 139
Road Transport Department ... 4, 11, 13, 29, 63, 76, 92, 101, 102, 111, 113, 114, 135
Road Wagon shop, Swindon .. 11, 13, 15, 29, 58, 60, 61, 62, 81, 83, 95, 101, 114, 126, 129, 138, 139, 140, 169, 172
Rushton tractor 162

St Austell 82
St Ives 82, 98
Scammell 'mechanical horse' 14, 16, 17, 43, 62, 75, 82, 127, 128, 129, 166-169, 172
  coupling 16, 150, 168-69, 172
  experimental full cab 132-33
  lorries 149, 156
  trailers ('Dyak') 15, 75, 110, 170-72
Shafts, drawings/designs of 50-55
Shrewsbury 58, 66, 82, 89
Shrewsbury & Hereford Railway 62, 66
Shunting horses 84
Signal Department 140
Simplex rail tractor 84
Skids 60
Slough 63, 89, 90, 99, 111, 114, 141, 146, 150

Small Heath 62
Smithfield 66, 71, 73, 75, 84
Snow plough 144
South Lambeth depot 16, 17, 61, 73, 82, 129, 148, 149, 155, 166, 167
Southern National bus company 13
Splinter bar 50
'Square Deal' campaign 16
Stables 73
  jobs at 77
  see also Mint stables
Staines 82
Stanford Bridge 86, 87
Stanier, W. H. 77
Steam wagons 10, 85-89
Stone lorries/wagons 34, 48
Straker & Squire vehicles 30, 96, 99, 101, 104, 105, 107, 116, 121, 138
Swan Village 66
Swansea 14, 40, 82, 83, 89
Swindon 59, 62, 129, 142, 143
  sawmill 59
Swindon safety cab 132, 134

Tasker trailers 163, 170, 172
Taunton 43
Tavistock 58
Telegraph codes 14, 73, 80-81, 130, 131, 165
Tenbury Wells 62
Thame 71, 140
Thames Valley Traction bus company 13
Theale 89
Thornycroft lorries 15, 99, 100, 101, 105, 106, 129
  A1 .... 12, 71, 116, 117-119, 120, 123, 139, 140, 158, 161
  A2 13
  BE 130
  J 127
  JC 124
  'Taurus' 124, 125, 159
  'Nippy' 15, 132, 134, 172
  PB 120, 121, 123, 138
  PE 132
  steam 85, 86, 94
  'Sturdy' 138
  'Trusty' 133

Tilts and tilt vans 30, 40, 41, 43, 44, 46, 103, 104, 114, 120, 124
Timber/pole carriages/wagons 34, 36, 37, 50, 61, 72, 153, 155, 156, 157, 161, 164, 170
Trailers 16, 144, 149
Tranship stations 12
Trojan vehicles 131, 132
Twist, A. (Horse Superintendent) 76
Tyres, metal 58
  solid/pneumatic 116, 121, 122, 123, 130

Uxbridge 58

Van-guards 78, 81, 128, 136-37
Victoria & Albert Docks 73, 94, 113, 151

Wallis & Steevens steam tractors 87
Water cart 45
Wednesbury 58, 84
West Bromwich 66, 162
West Midland Railway 7
Westbourne Park (Alfred Road) depot 11, 75, 91, 114, 131
Westbury 73
Western National bus company 13
Western Welsh bus company 13
Weston-Super-Mare 58, 74
Weymouth 154
Wheels, construction of 58
  bearings 60-61
  see also 'Artillery' wheels, Muir-Hill wheels
Willis, Charles (lorry driver) 95
Witney 112
Wiveliscombe 82
Wolseley vehicles 30, 95, 96, 99, 105
Wolverhampton 12, 66, 79, 87, 139, 142
Worcester.................... 12, 14, 66, 83, 140, 152
World War I, effects of 10, 17, 66, 81, 99, 101, 106, 111
  ex-army vehicles 10
World War II, effects of 16, 83, 132, 135, 138

Yorkshire Steam Motor Co 86, 87
Younghusband, J. T. & Son (contractor) 18, 29, 66, 84

'Zonal' C&D scheme 16, 138